WINNING A...PPEAL

FOURTH EDITION

WINNING AN APPEAL

FOURTH EDITION

A short, readable, step-by-step explanation of how to prepare and present your case effectively.

With sample briefs.

MYRON MOSKOVITZ
Professor of Law
Golden Gate University

LCCN: 2007929472

ISBN: 1-4224-1175-3

NOTE TO USERS

To ensure that you are using the latest materials available in this area, please be sure to periodically check the LexisNexis Law School web site for downloadable updates and supplements at www.lexisnexis.com/ lawschool

Editorial Offices
744 Broad Street, Newark, NJ 07102 (973) 820-2000
201 Mission St., San Francisco, CA 94105-1831 (415) 908-3200
701 East Water Street, Charlottesville, VA 22902-7587 (804) 972-7600
www.lexis.com

PREFACE

I've had quite a bit of experience with the appellate process. I served as law clerk to a Justice of the California Supreme Court, where I saw hundreds of appellate briefs and watched many oral arguments — and how the judges reacted to them. Most of these were in proper *form*, but not many had much effect on how the judges decided the case. They just weren't particularly persuasive. Still, it would have been hard for me to articulate just what was wrong with them, in any general way. I knew what was missing from a particular brief or argument, but I knew of no general principles that might help appellate counsel in all cases.

I've handled quite a few appeals myself, with some measure of success. Why do I win? Like most lawyers, I've attributed my victories to innate brilliance. Could there be some general, unarticulated principles I was following without knowing it? It never occurred to me.

Then something happened that forced some introspection: I was assigned to teach Appellate Advocacy. Teaching the *form* of an appeal was no problem, but how could I teach students the *substance*, if that depended solely on native talents that by their very nature cannot be taught? At most, I might go over particular briefs and oral arguments, criticize them, and hope that my students would somehow get a "feeling" as to how to do it. I assumed that there were few, if any, general principles I could teach on how to win.

Gradually, I learned how wrong I was.

As I read and re-read student briefs, lawyers' briefs, and my own briefs, and as I watched oral arguments, the principles slowly emerged. I was surprised that so many of them involved no brilliant insights, but mere common sense — flavored with a healthy dose of experience. Once students learned these principles, the quality of their work improved enormously.

This book recounts what I have learned.

The text of the book explains the principles. Like a good brief, it is (I hope) concise — you can read the entire text in a couple of hours or so. In the back of the book are three sample briefs *applying* the principles. And before each brief is a description of the thinking *behind* the brief.

Many thanks to Diana D. Sam, Esq. (an excellent appellate lawyer), Professor Peter J. Honigsberg (University of San Francisco), and Professor Randall Aiman-Smith (Hastings) for their helpful comments.

Myron Moskovitz

TABLE OF CONTENTS

Chapter 1

THE KEY TO WINNING

§ 1.1 THE PURPOSE OF THIS BOOK

This book is meant to give you some ideas that will help you win in an appellate court, whether you represent the appellant or the respondent. These ideas cannot guarantee victory — nor can anything you do — because there are too many key factors beyond your control, such as the record on appeal and the attitudes of the judges assigned to your case. But proper application of certain techniques can substantially increase your chance of success, and permit you to do the best job in the least amount of time.

The appellate court is seen as foreign territory by most lawyers, who view it as an arena for quiet, scholarly debate far from the rough-and-tumble, think-on-your-feet type of practice common in the trial courts. Because of this perception (largely correct), lawyers are often uncomfortable writing briefs and arguing before appellate courts, and frequently their primary concern is simply to get through the ordeal without looking foolish. They will look at other briefs or at the court rules to see that their briefs are in the "proper form," and then just do their best to present a respectable argument.

This book is intended for the lawyer who wants to get *beyond* that point, the lawyer whose chief concern is *victory* for the client. This book is not about the *form* of an appeal; it is about the *substance* of an appeal.

Examples of many of the brief-writing techniques discussed appear in the sample briefs at the end of this book. Before each brief is an explanation of the strategic thinking that lie behind how each brief was written.

§ 1.2 HOW TO *WIN* AN APPEAL

"I'm right on the law, so I'm sure to win my appeal." This is "The Great Myth." Young lawyers don't know better; experienced lawyers should know better. But every appellate lawyer falls for this myth at one time or another.

Appellate judges are just as human as the jurors and judge who nailed your client in the trial court. If there was something that annoyed the lower court about your case or your client, it will probably bother the higher court too. Appellate court judges are not automatons who mindlessly look up the law and mechanically apply it to your case. They want to "do justice." If the established law gets in the way, "justice" will usually prevail. If the judge believes that your client sexually molested and killed a child, you will have a tough time getting a reversal just because the police violated his *Miranda* rights — no matter how clear the law seems to be.[1] The court's opinion might twist the facts, ignore the cases, or come right out and change the law, but one way or another, a court that *wants* you to lose will probably rule against you.

This is the key to winning an appeal: convince the appellate judges that ruling against your client would be *unjust*.

It's really that simple. Appellate court judges want to do the right thing. Indeed, they *pride* themselves on their sense of justice. As they see it, doing justice is their business.

Of course, it's not really that simple. A lot goes into "justice." Judges want to do justice for the parties, but sometimes that wish is trumped by their obligation to defer to another branch of government (such as a legislature) that has values different from those of the judges. And because the court is writing precedent, the judges will want to adopt a rule achieves justice for *other* people that will be affected by this precedent.

If you, the appellate lawyer, have this eye for justice, you'll go a long way. You will have a better chance of finding injustice in the appellate record and presenting it forcefully. It's amazing how successful a lawyer with this sense of justice can be, even with writing and oral skills that are not the best.

But writing, organization, and oral skills matter too. So this book will include many pointers in these areas. They support — but never supplant — the need to focus on the key: a sense of justice.

§ 1.3 SOME EXAMPLES OF "JUSTICE"

Each appeal poses its own unique challenge to find "injustice" and how to work it into your brief and oral argument. These examples are meant to give you a feel for how to look for it.

Example #1: A jury found that a used car dealer — your client on appeal — defrauded a customer. You have some viable legal arguments for reversal, but fear that the appellate judges will be biased against a used car dealer. Consider putting this bias *out front*, not by accusing the judges of bias, but by suggesting that the *jurors* might have been biased — even if the record contains no evidence of bias that supports a legal argument for reversal on this ground. Turn this bias to your favor, arguing that courts must be careful to ensure that rules of law are applied fairly to such a

---

[1] It can happen, however — at least temporarily. *See* Brewer v. Williams, 430 U.S. 387 (1977), where the Supreme Court reversed just such a conviction — over some outraged dissents. But "justice" eventually prevailed: the Court later invoked the "inevitable discovery" doctrine to uphold the conviction anyway. *See* Nix v. Williams, 467 U.S. 431 (1984).

"despised" member of our society. *See* Sample Brief #1, in the Appendix to this Book.

Example #2: A jury convicted your client of some drug crime. He has no prior record, but the law of your state nevertheless calls for a very lengthy "mandatory minimum" sentence. There is no point in challenging this harsh sentencing law directly, because courts have already rejected attacks on its constitutionality. But you have some viable arguments that the trial judge erred in admitting certain evidence or in giving certain jury instructions. On the law, these arguments are respectable, but not particularly compelling. Consider mentioning the mandatory minimum sentence frequently, whenever you make an argument about the evidentiary rulings or the jury instructions. Say, in effect, that the appellate judges should be especially vigilant on these issues when the *consequences* to the defendant seem so unfair — even if not illegal.

Example #3: Your client is a firefighter's union. State law prohibits firefighters and police officers from striking, but requires cities to negotiate with them — with a few exceptions. A city refused to negotiate, and the trial court held that one of the exemptions applied. You face a conservative appellate bench that is unsympathetic to unions. Conservative judges might be anti-union, but they are probably pro-police and pro-firefighter, so focus on *that* aspect of your case. Stress that while most government employees have the right to strike to protect their interests, only firefighters and police officers are denied this right, and these are the public servants most likely to put their lives and limbs on the line to protect the rest of us. Therefore, the statutory exceptions should be narrowly construed.

Example #4: You represent a city that enacted an ordinance limiting residential rent increases. Landlords claim that rent control is price control, barred by the federal antitrust law. On appeal to a conservative federal court not likely to be enamored of rent control, focus on federalism: federal law should not be construed limit the authority of local communities. While your adversaries cry "Socialism!," respond with "States' rights!" (It worked. *See* Fisher v. City of Berkeley, 475 U.S. 260 (1986)).

Chapter 2

AN OVERVIEW

§ 2.1 HOW APPELLATE COURTS DIFFER FROM TRIAL COURTS

Appellate courts differ from trial courts in several ways that directly affect how a lawyer should handle an appeal.

First, the appellate court has more time: time to read the record and the lawyers' briefs, and even time to do independent research. Not only do the judges themselves have more time to explore each point of law than trial court judges do, but appellate court judges have law clerks to help them perform these functions.

Second, the appellate court has a much greater interest in properly arriving at *and explaining* its notion of a "correct" decision than a trial court judge does. The appellate court will publish many or all of its decisions, which serve as precedent throughout the jurisdiction (and sometimes beyond it). These decisions will be read by thousands of lawyers, and the judge wants to be seen by them as an erudite scholar. While trial court judges often try to avoid explaining their decisions (fearing that this increases the risk of reversal), the appellate court judge takes pride in explanations. He has been selected to be an appellate court judge because he is more scholarly than other judges — at least he thinks so — and he wants to let the world know it.

These two differences have a major effect on how the lawyer should prepare his case in the appellate court. While in the trial court it may be safe to avoid mentioning arguments *adverse* to your position — in the hope that neither your opponent nor the judge will think of them — this may be fatal in the appellate court. Even if neither you nor your opponent mentions a good point in briefs or at oral argument, a judge or his law clerk may think of it, and you will never have had the opportunity to rebut it. Similarly, lawyers arguing in the trial court often rely on cases and statutes that are fairly easy to distinguish, in the hope that both their opponent and the judge will be too hurried to pick up on these distinctions — or simply not have the ability to see them. This tactic will seldom work in the appellate court. Usually it will backfire, making your case look weaker and you less credible.

The appellate court judge has a responsibility (and an audience) well beyond your case, client, and self, and she is not about to let your mistakes (or those of your opponent) mess up the law or her reputation. Ironically, because of this independent attitude on the part of the judge, it often happens that a lawyer does a poor job in the appeal and yet the decision comes out in his or her favor. This lawyer has nothing he can take pride in, because his efforts did not influence the court. The court simply ignored his brief and oral argument, did its own research and analysis, and wrote an opinion that bore no resemblance to the lawyer's brief, but which fortuitously arrived at the same result.

The techniques discussed in this book may help you influence the court so that the victory may truly be yours.

And finally, while the trial judge and jury seek justice between the parties, the appellate court has a larger constituency: the community or industry affected by its ruling. If you ask the court to adopt a new rule on punitive damages in order to achieve justice for your client, the court will consider whether your proposal is fair to *other* defendants. You must address this issue persuasively in order to win.

§ 2.2 SOME BASIC PRINCIPLES FOR INFLUENCING AN APPELLATE COURT

[A] You Are There to Win

Your frame of mind throughout all your work on the appeal should be: *I am doing this particular piece of work in order to help win the case.* Keeping your focus on winning will help you *omit* from your brief unimportant statements that detract from the impact of your best arguments and facts.

[B] Pay Attention to Everything

Virtually everything you do in an appeal might have some influence on the court. Don't think that only the Argument part of your brief counts. Your Statement of Facts is often more important. Indeed, particular words in your Statement of Facts can have some effect. An emotional conclusion can influence the court. Pay attention to every detail, and use every opportunity to present yourself and your case in a favorable light.

[C] Try to Make the Judge's Job Easier

If you want your brief to influence the judge, make her enjoy reading it.

While an appellate court judge's job may seem glamorous from the outside, it can be quite tedious to read hundreds of briefs that are dull, shallow, or sloppy. Even if such briefs contain good arguments buried in them somewhere, the judge is likely to be half-asleep by the time she gets to them or to be predisposed to reject them because she is annoyed by what came before.

Tell an interesting story, be concise, and be well organized. By checking to see that all of your citations are accurate, you can make it easy for the judge to find things.

You can make sure that your brief is filed with the clerk, but you can never be sure that the judge will *read* your whole brief carefully if she is in no mood to do so. A major part of your job is to create that mood.

[D] Be Credible, Be Reliable

A judge is more likely to accept your arguments if he accepts *you*. Whether he accepts you depends in large part on whether he thinks you are merely some sharp lawyer who is trying to slip something by him or, instead, someone who recognizes the difficult parts of the case and is trying to help the judge write a good opinion — in your client's favor, of course. If you want the judge to trust you, never misstate a fact in the record, never cite a case for a proposition for which it doesn't really stand, and never make arguments that fly in the face of common sense.

At times, it is even useful to tell the court arguments *against* your position — and then rebut those arguments. It may seem paradoxical, but the most effective appellate advocate is often the lawyer who appears to be the least one-sided in his presentation.

The need for credibility and reliability also explains why a good appellate lawyer should seldom (if ever) face any ethical problems: any tactic that might possibly be unethical will be tactically unwise; it will hurt the lawyer's effectiveness even if it turns out to be "legal."

If you have a "smoking gun" against you, the worst thing you can do is pretend it isn't there. It won't go away. You might get lucky and get a panel of judges who stick strictly to the law, but don't bank on it. It is better to bring up the issue yourself and confront it head on. At a minimum, this will force the judges to consciously realize any conflict between their emotions and their duty to uphold the law. And occasionally you might even *turn* the loaded gun to your advantage, by showing that these emotional factors led to an unfair trial.

[E] Think Creatively

There are actually very few court rules that *require* you to do things a certain way. If you get a creative idea of presenting your case that might help you win, look for a rule that forbids this. If you don't find such a rule, do it! You don't need a rule *permitting* you to do something novel.

Chapter 3

PREPARE YOUR WORKING OUTLINE

Your first task in representing the appellant will be preparation of a Working Outline. Later, you will modify this into the Outline of Argument, which will appear at the outset of your brief.

Your Working Outline — which the court will never see — is in many ways the most important paper you will prepare during the appeal. Careful preparation of this Outline will structure your analysis of each issue, organize the issues in the most presentable form, and — if done diligently — can end up saving you an enormous amount of time. An extra hour of work on your Outline can save you four or five hours later on — reorganizing the brief or repairing faulty reasoning.

§ 3.1 READ THE TRANSCRIPTS

To prepare your Working Outline, thoroughly review the record that has been filed in the appellate court — even if you were the trial lawyer and think you remember everything. This record will include the pleadings, motions, and other documents filed in the trial court, bound together in a book often called the *clerk's transcript* (if prepared by the trial court clerk) or *appendix* (if prepared by the lawyers). The record will also include transcripts of the trial or other hearings, usually called the *reporter's transcript*. Make sure that the copies of the transcripts that you use have the same page numbers as the transcripts filed in the appellate court, because in your brief you will need to refer the court to certain pages.

Read the clerk's transcript first. It will give you some background to help you understand the reporter's transcript more quickly.

If the clerk's transcript is long, first get an *overview* of the case by finding and reading some document that summarizes this case. This might be a trial brief, a motion for new trial, or a memorandum decision.

While going through these transcripts, do two things: (1) list the issues you see that may give rise to arguments for reversal, and (2) make your own working *index* of each transcript. Sometimes these transcripts will already include indexes prepared by the clerk or reporter, but these will be of limited use to you. What you need are indexes that tell *you* where there are key rulings and useful bits of testimony.

To make your index, note the page number of the transcript on which you find key rulings and significant evidence. Next to the page number, write a brief summary of the ruling or evidence.

You will use these indexes not only in preparation of your Working Outline, but also in working on all parts of the brief (especially the Statement of Facts) and even during oral argument. Writing indexes now may slow down your review of the transcripts a bit and may seem like a chore, but the time spent on this will be paid back many fold during your work on the appeal — especially if the transcripts are long.

§ 3.2 SPOT THE ISSUES

To spot the legal issues that may lead to reversal, you should get some assistance from documents in the clerk's transcript, such as motions and memoranda of points and authorities. When reading the transcripts, be alert for issues involving the admissibility of evidence and the correctness of jury instructions. These issues frequently arise during a trial.

Quite often, an issue will stand out clearly, because trial counsel argued the issue extensively. But just because an issue was not argued extensively at trial does not necessarily mean it should be ignored on appeal. Trial counsel may have dealt with the issue cursorily because he did not know the law or because he felt the issue was not important in affecting the outcome of the trial. Your objective is a different one — to win the appeal — and the issue might be more useful for this purpose.

You may have to do some *legal research* to help you spot the issues, especially if you are not very familiar with the area of law involved in the case.

Make sure that each issue was properly raised below and was thereby preserved for appeal (or is automatically preserved). If there is any doubt about this, then this is *another* issue that should be included in your Working Outline.

§ 3.3 WHAT ISSUES TO INCLUDE

Upon your first review of the transcripts, include all possible issues in your list — even ones you are not too sure about. Be overinclusive.

Later, after further reflection and legal research, drop the issues that turn out to be very weak, i.e., those that no reasonable judge is likely to accept. Inclusion of weak issues can give your brief an aura of desperation, and it may lead the judge to question your judgment.

After dropping all "unreasonable" issues, should you keep *all* "reasonable" issues?

On the one hand, marginal issues might divert the judge's attention from some much stronger issues you have. Also, if you list nine or ten grounds for reversal in your brief, some judges might find it inherently incredible that a trial judge would commit that many reversible errors, and your credibility may suffer from this. On the other hand, keep in mind that it is very difficult to predict what issues a judge will tend to favor. Many an appellate lawyer has been surprised to win a case on what he felt was a minor issue.

If you are faced with such a dilemma, consider a compromise: leave the minor issues in, but treat them in a way that lets the judges know that you think they are of lesser importance. Keep the discussion of these issues especially short and — if this will not break up the logical sequence of your argument — put these issues toward the end of your brief. This strategy is especially appropriate for issues that you know the court must reject because of rulings of higher courts, but which you wish to preserve if the appeal goes higher.

It is often helpful to present your issues to a colleague to get her reaction and prediction concerning how a judge might react. But do not select a colleague who is so sympathetic with your side that he or she is convinced by every issue you raise.

§ 3.4 BUILD THE OUTLINE

Once you have read the transcripts and made a list of the issues, it is time to start building your Working Outline.

The strategy for building the Outline is very similar to what an architect does when designing a house. First the architect designs the shell: how many stories, how many rooms, how large each room is and where it goes. Then he designs the shape of each room, hall, closet, etc. Then he goes into further detail, specifying where each fixture goes and giving exact locations for electrical outlets, railings, and the like. When he is done, he turns his blueprint over to the builder to carry out the design.

You build your Outline the same way. First design *the shell*: the three or four major issues. *Within* each major issue may be two or more *submajor* issues. And within each submajor issue may be some *minor* issues. *Try to refine each major issue into as many submajor and minor issues as you can.* This will enable you to see any gaps, errors, or duplications in your analysis before you waste time making these mistakes in your brief. Also, in preparing your Outline, you can do the needed analytical thinking *before* you start writing the brief, so you can devote most of your time and mental energy in writing the brief to good writing. Thus, you the analyzer will turn the detailed Outline over to you the writer, just as the architect turns the detailed blueprint over to the builder. If the Outline is good enough, you will then simply be transforming it from a cold summary into persuasive prose.

You cannot put together such a complete Outline at one sitting. After reading the transcripts, you may be able to list the major issues and maybe a few submajor issues. Then you will begin your legal research, perhaps discover you were wrong about one of the submajor issues, and have to rethink it. More research will uncover more submajor issues and the minor ones, and more thinking and research will show you that some minor issues are in the wrong place in the Outline, and others deserve more emphasis than you originally thought. Slowly, you shape the Outline into something that is logical, which minimizes overlap and duplication, and which sets up a concise, persuasive brief.

Framing the issues and arranging them in a proper order requires some careful thought. Several principles should generally be observed: (1) *focus on trial court error*, not on abstract issues of law; (2) as much as possible, make sure that each *major* issue is *a separate ground for reversal* that stands on its own feet, i.e., is not dependent on your winning another major issue; and (3) state as many viable *alternative* grounds supporting each issue as you can.

§ 3.5 AN EXAMPLE

Let's apply these principles to an example. You read the transcripts in a criminal case where appellant was convicted of armed robbery. The record shows that Mr. X told the police information concerning appellant's alleged involvement in the robbery. Based on this, the police forced their way into appellant's home, arrested him (without a warrant), searched him and found a gun in his pocket, then asked him if that was the gun used in the robbery — to which he replied "Yes." The trial court denied motions to suppress evidence of the gun and the "Yes."

Your legal research turns up several legal issues, i.e., several ways in which the police may have violated appellant's constitutional rights: (1) the arrest may have been invalid because the police had insufficient "probable cause" to believe appellant was the robber; (2) they may have had insufficient "exigent circumstances" to justify their failure to get an arrest warrant; and (3) they failed to advise him of his *Miranda* rights before asking him about the gun.

How should these issues be organized into a Working Outline for your brief? There are several possibilities.

First, simply arrange them as legal issues:

    I.   No "probable cause" to arrest.

    II. No "exigent circumstances" justifying failure to get warrant.

    III. No *Miranda* warning.

This arrangement would not be a good one, for it ignores the first principle: focus on trial court error. Appellate courts reverse because of specific erroneous trial court rulings, not abstract issues of law. The trial court arguably committed *two* errors: it denied the motion to suppress the gun; and it denied the motion to suppress the "Yes." So your major issues become:

    I.   Denial of motion to suppress gun was error.

    II. Denial of motion to suppress "Yes" was error.

The three "legal issues" you found enter the outline as *submajor* issues under the two major ones. Thus,

    I.   Denial of motion to suppress gun was error, as gun was fruit of illegal arrest, for either of two separate reasons.

        A. Arrest was illegal because no probable cause.

        B. Arrest was illegal because no arrest warrant and no exigent circumstances.

    II. Denial of motion to suppress "Yes" was error, as "Yes" was obtained in violation of *Miranda*.

This is much better than the first Outline. Note that the first major issue carefully shows that you have two alternative grounds for winning this issue. The second issue doesn't do this — but it should. It should read:

    II. Denial of motion to suppress "Yes" was error on either of two grounds.

        A "Yes" was product of *Miranda* violation.

        B. "Yes" was fruit of illegal arrest of appellant (for reasons set out in issue I).

By adding B, you have *doubled* your chance of winning issue II. Usually, it is wise to set out alternative grounds so long as they are reasonable. More than two grounds is even better. Even though *you* find a certain ground very persuasive, you can never be sure the appellate court will agree. Use backup arguments whenever you can.

In framing issues, it often helps to take the applicable *rule of substantive law* and *break it up into its constituent elements*. For example, your legal research on the above case may tell you that an arrest through forcible entry into a home is valid only if the police have both (1) "probable cause," and (2) an arrest warrant or "exigent circumstances." These two elements of the law defining "validity of arrest in home" thus give you your two issues under submajor issue A — assuming, of course, that the record lends itself to a respectable argument on each of these issues. (If, for example, the police clearly had probable cause, then you would drop the "no probable cause" argument.)

This same process can be used in framing issues *within* the submajor issues. Your legal research might show that "probable cause" may come from an underworld informant only if (1) he is shown to be "credible," and (2) it is shown that he obtained the information in this case in a reliable way.

If the record supports an argument that both of these were absent, then this portion of your outline might read:

    I.   Denial of motion to suppress gun was reversible error.

        A. It was error because gun was fruit of illegal arrest, for two separate reasons.

            1. Arrest illegal because no probable cause, for two separate reasons.

                a. Underworld informant was not shown to be credible.

                b. No evidence that informant obtained information in a reliable way.

You will find that this system of using the rule of substantive law as your starting point, then breaking it up into its components, almost always works as a sensible way to arrange an outline.

§ 3.6 SHOW REVERSIBLE ERROR

So, are we now done with the above example? *No.* There is *a fatal omission* in our outline. We could win all the points in our outline and still lose the appeal!

We have shown that the trial court committed two errors, but in virtually all jurisdictions, this is not enough to get a reversal. The law requires you to show "reversible" (or "prejudicial") error.

In many cases, the fact that the error (if it was error) was prejudicial is so obvious that this issue need not be discussed. But where evidence has been improperly admitted (as in the above case), you must show that if the fact-finder had not heard that evidence, there is a good chance that the verdict would have been different.

Thus our *final* Outline should read:

    I.   Denial of motion to suppress gun was reversible error.

        A. It was error because gun was fruit of illegal arrest, for either of two separate reasons.

            1. Arrest was illegal because no probable cause.

            2. Arrest was illegal because no warrant and no exigent circumstances.

        B. Error was "prejudicial" because jury might not have convicted on remaining evidence.

    II. Denial of motion to suppress "Yes" was reversible error.

        A. It was error on either of two grounds.

1. Product of *Miranda* violation.

2. Fruit of illegal arrest.

B. Error was prejudicial because jury might not have convicted on remaining evidence.

III. Even if each error was not separately prejudicial, the combined effect of the two errors was prejudicial.

Why is this Outline preferable to simply adding a new III to our previous outline, saying "III. Above errors are reversible"? Because this Outline makes it clear that we are arguing that each of the two errors was *independently* reversible. We should avoid having only an issue III that argues that the combined effect of the two errors was prejudicial, for if we argue this but fail to convince the court that *both* rulings were in error, we will lose the appeal. If possible, avoid framing an argument in a way that allows you to win only if the court also accepts another argument.

The lesson to be learned from this discussion of "reversible" error is this: to properly prepare your working outline, you must educate yourself regarding *the rules of appellate review* in your jurisdiction.

Chapter 4

THE BRIEF

§ 4.1 IMPORTANCE OF THE BRIEF

In trial court practice, it is common for a lawyer to submit a rather sketchy memorandum of law supporting a motion, expecting to make his most powerful arguments orally at the hearing on the motion. "I'm good on my feet, so I'll save my best stuff for oral argument."

While one may debate whether this is an effective technique in the trial court, you may be sure that it is *not* an effective way to practice law in an appellate court.

Because of the way most appellate courts operate, the brief is much more important than oral argument in affecting the outcome of the case. Oral argument normally does not take place until months after all of the briefs are filed. By this time, law clerks (and sometimes one or more judges) have read all the briefs, performed legal research, and written extensive memoranda on the case — often including a recommendation for disposition. Sometimes even a draft opinion has been written. Since all of this occurs before oral argument, the minds of one or more of the judges may well be made up before oral argument even begins. If you want to influence the court, write a good brief, and don't hold anything back — any scheme to "sandbag" will probably backfire.

Be sure to comply with the court's rules regarding the form of the brief — type of paper, colored covers, length, use of footnotes, form of citations, etc. These rules will not be discussed in this book, which is about substance, not form.

§ 4.2 THE OUTLINE OF ARGUMENT

The Outline of Argument (or "Table of Contents" or "Index of Argument") that will appear at the outset of your brief will be very similar to your Working Outline. Its basic structure should be identical.

There are some differences, however. Since your Working Outline is for your private use, there is no need to pay close attention to its exact wording. But your Outline of Argument will be seen by the court — in fact it will normally be the first part of your brief the court will see — so how it is worded is very important.

[A] Objectives of the Outline of Argument

There are several things you might accomplish by writing a good Outline of Argument.

First, you give the court *a quick overview* of your arguments and how they fit together (e.g., which of your arguments are alternative grounds for reversal).

Second, you can put a judge (or law clerk) in a mood to read your whole brief carefully if you start out by showing that you write clearly, organize concepts carefully, and respect the court's rules of appellate review.

Third, you may occasionally be able to *word* a part of your outline in such a way that it has *a persuasive impact by itself* on that particular issue.

Usually, your Outline of Argument should not be as long as your Working Outline. The Working Outline should be as detailed as possible, to the point that it tells you pretty much what you are going to say in every paragraph of your brief. Putting this much detail in your Outline of Argument would destroy its effectiveness in giving the judge a quick overview of your case. As a rule, it is sufficient to include major issues, submajor issues, and the next level down. Occasionally, however, you will want to go further down the scale, where this would include subissues that require lengthy discussion by themselves.

[B] Careful Wording is Important

To make it easy for the judge to see what actions of the trial court you are challenging, word major issues in terms of *trial court error*, not in terms of abstract issues of law. Instead of writing "I. Contributory negligence is no defense to an intentional tort," write, "I. The trial court erred by instructing the jury that contributory negligence is a defense to battery, an intentional tort."

Word all issues in a way that shows that you understand the rules of appellate review and are prepared to argue your case within them. Suppose a jury found your client negligent, and you write "I. The trial court erred in entering judgment against appellant, because appellant was not negligent." Such wording is a common mistake. It gives the appellate judge the impression that you are about to commit what he considers the cardinal sin: trying to "reargue the facts" in the appellate court. The correct way to present this issue is to write "I. The trial court erred by entering judgment on the verdict, because there was *no substantial evidence* that appellant was negligent." This crucial change shows that you are prepared to show that *respondent's* evidence *failed* to prove that your client was negligent, rather than arguing that *your* evidence (which the jury apparently did not believe) showed that he was not negligent. Because this conforms to the applicable rule of appellate review, the judge will know right away that he is reading the brief of a lawyer who knows what he is doing.

For clarity and persuasiveness, each heading and subheading should usually be a *complete sentence*.

[C] Including Facts

Should the issues be worded to include facts? Sometimes, if you can include *all* the relevant facts and still keep the statement of the issue fairly short (not more than two or three lines). In appealing a negligence case, for example, you might write "A. There was no substantial evidence supporting the verdict, because the evidence showed only that appellant did not exceed the speed limit, the weather was clear, and he had drunk only two beers in the hour before the accident." The problem with a statement of this sort is that it will often omit some fact that is somewhat damaging (e.g., the accident occurred at night, or appellant knew his brakes didn't always work well). Once the judge discovers this — your opponent will point it out — your credibility may drop. If you protect against this by including the negative facts, you reduce the persuasive impact your statement might have had, and you make your statement of the issue much too long and cumbersome to serve its main purpose: to give the judge an overview of your arguments.

Occasionally, you can make your statement of the issue both persuasive and honest by including a single fact, where you are prepared to show that such a single fact was determinative in the trial court, e.g., "A. The mere fact that appellant did not turn on his headlights at 6 p.m. on July 2 did not constitute substantial evidence of negligence."

Even where you cannot use such a "single fact" heading, put a "summarizing fact" in your heading for clarity. For example, instead of writing "The Arrest Was Illegal," write "Officer Smith Had No Probable Cause To Arrest Appellant Because The Victim Told The Officer That The Robber Wore A Red Shirt, While Appellant Wore A Blue Shirt."

[D] Which Issue Comes First?

Suppose you have four main issues. Which one should you put first? It is best to arrange them *chronologically*, unless there is good reason to do it some other way. Going back to our criminal case, it would be best to put the gun issue before the "Yes" issue, because this will minimize (though not eliminate) the need for repetition in the argument part of your brief. The police arrested appellant before they interrogated him, so deal with the arrest issue first. When you argue the interrogation issues, if there is a need to refer to some part of your arrest discussion, simply refer back to it, and the judge has already read it. If, instead, you were to discuss interrogation before arrest, you would have to either refer the judge ahead to your arrest discussion — which makes for very awkward reading — or include some discussion of the arrest in the interrogation discussion, which makes this part of your brief long, and does not obviate the need for some repeat discussion of the arrest in the arrest section of your argument.

The "good reason" for departing from this general principle of chronological order might come up where one of your arguments makes a stronger "injustice" claim than the others. Some attorneys fear that if the judge is not taken with the first argument, he might assume your appeal is weak and pay less attention to the balance of the brief. There may be some truth to this, but it is often hard to predict which of your arguments will be most impressive, and mixing up the chronological order of your issues can lead to a cumbersome brief.

Of course, where your major issues are not factually interdependent, there is no reason not to put your best argument first, and you should do so.

[E] Do Not Subdivide an Issue into One Subissue

The *purpose* of subdividing issues is to break them up into shorter sections that are easier for the judge to digest. If you have only one subheading, then you are not subdividing, and your subheading serves no purpose and might confuse the judge.

Here is a mistake commonly made when subdividing issues:

I. Denial of the motion to suppress the gun was reversible error, as the gun was found as a result of an invalid arrest.

A. The arrest was invalid because there was no probable cause to arrest appellant.

II. Denial of the motion to suppress appellant's statement was error.

Subissue A makes no sense. If you write a single subheading and have no others, then your subheading should be *incorporated into* the main heading. Thus the above example should be changed to read as follows: "I. Denial of the motion to suppress the gun was error, because the gun was found as the result of an arrest that was invalid because it was not based on probable cause." If probable cause is the only issue here, then this heading will have *no* subheadings under it.

Similarly, if you have only one issue to raise in your appeal, do not label it "I," because an "I" without a "II" makes no sense. Simply state your heading without any number or letter preceding it.

[F] Follow Your Headings

The text beneath a heading should reflect the heading. If your heading or subheading says "An Arrest Without Probable Cause Is Invalid," this is a statement of law only, and the text beneath it should discuss only the law. It should contain *no application* of the law to the facts of your case.

If you *want* that section of your brief to include a discussion of the facts of your case, then change your heading to show that you will do this. Thus the above heading should be changed to "The Arrest of Appellant Was Invalid Because There Was No Probable Cause to Believe a Crime Was Committed."

§ 4.3 THE STATEMENT OF FACTS

[A] Importance of the Statement of Facts

The Statement of Facts is often the most important part of the brief, because any feeling of "injustice" usually flows (or fails to flow) directly from the facts of the case. Most judges will have their minds pretty well made up right after they know the facts.

The reason for this lies in the nature of the appellate judge's job. The appellate judge has a surprising amount of freedom to decide the case as he likes. True, there will be an occasional case where he has no choice: he is controlled by a decision of a higher court or a statute, and application of that case or statute to these facts leads to only one result — even if the judge does not like this result. But this situation does not occur often. If a judge *wants* to reach a particular result, he can usually manage to do so and still look "respectable." He can distinguish cases, overrule or "disapprove" cases, twist the facts a bit, and sometimes even overlook cases or facts. And that's just what he will do, to achieve "justice" — as he sees it.

Therefore, to influence the court to rule in your favor, you really have two jobs of persuasion: (1) to convince the court that it *may* write an opinion in your favor, without looking foolish; and (2) to make the court *want* to rule in your favor. In the majority of cases, fulfilling the first requirement is not enough, because in the majority of cases, the court may — if it wishes — write an opinion in favor of either side without looking foolish! In these cases, if you cannot fulfill the second requirement, you will lose. If the facts are so unattractive for your side that fulfilling the second requirement is hopeless, then your only chance is to convince the court that it *must* rule your way — i.e., that under the law, it cannot write an opinion against you without looking foolish. This is pretty hard to do. Don't depend on it.

This explains the importance of the Statement of Facts: it can have a great impact in influencing the judge to *want* to decide the case your way.

The Statement of Facts is especially important for the appellant. In most jurisdictions, only a small minority of appeals are successful. To have a decent chance of success, the appellant must "touch the judge's heart" fairly early in the brief — in the Statement of Facts.

[B] When to Write the Statement of Facts

Generally, the best time to write the Statement of Facts is right *after you have written your Working Outline*. Don't try to write it before you write your Working Outline, because in order to decide which facts are relevant and helpful, you must know the *legal* issues you intend to argue.

Try to complete your Working Outline soon after you've read the record, so you can write the Statement of Facts while the record is still fresh in your mind.

Write at least a first draft of the Statement of Facts before you write the Argument portion of your brief. This will force you to become very familiar with the facts before you write your Argument, and this will enable you to *weave key facts into* your Argument, which will strengthen your Argument considerably.

As you do more intensive legal research and thinking while writing your Argument, you might realize that a fact is more or less important than you thought it was when you wrote your Statement of Facts. When this happens, simply go back and change your Statement of Facts.

[C] What Facts to Include

The Statement of Facts should include both procedural facts and substantive facts.

The *procedural* facts are usually stated first, sometimes in a separate section called "Statement of the Case" or simply "Procedural Facts." This should include all the facts about the procedural history of the case that will be helpful to the appellate court in deciding this appeal.

Do not clutter up this part of your brief with irrelevant procedural facts. If, for example, you are appealing after a jury verdict against your client in a negligence case, and your only claim is that there was no substantial evidence to support the verdict, state when the complaint was filed, generally what it was about, generally what the answer pleaded, when the case went to trial, and the verdict. There is no need to discuss rulings on demurrers, discovery motions, and the like.

You should, however, also include procedural facts that — while not directly relevant to the appeal — may tend to make your client look a little better, your opponent look a little worse, or the trial court somewhat biased or incompetent. If demurrers to your opponent's complaints were sustained four times before he got it right, this should be mentioned, as it just might make the appellate judge a little bit skeptical when he reads your opponent's brief.

In your Statement of the *Case*, you should indicate the name of each party to the appeal and the position (appellant, respondent, etc.) he or she occupies.

The *substantive* facts — often called "Statement of Facts" (as opposed to "Statement of the Case") — should include (1) all the facts that the appellate judge needs to know to understand the case (e.g., background facts), (2) all facts that support your arguments, (3) all facts that make your client look a bit more worthy of sympathy or your opponent look a bit worse, and (4) all facts that significantly hurt you (including all facts that support the judgment) that your opponent or the court are likely to discover.

You may not include facts that are not in the record, unless you establish that they may be judicially noticed. If evidence of a helpful fact is in some document that was in the trial court file but is not in the record before the appellate court, file a "motion to augment the record" to include that document.

[D] Tell a Good Story

The judge is just starting to read your brief, and you want her to enjoy it. If she has to plod through a dense Statement of Facts, she may well dread coming to your Argument, and she might just skim over it. Try to make your Statement of Facts as readable as possible.

Almost invariably, the best story is told chronologically — even if it was not presented chronologically at trial. If this requires you to skip around the record and take bits of

evidence from various parts of the transcripts, so be it. A Statement of Facts that simply summarizes the testimony of each witness, without regard to the chronology of the events, usually does not flow well.

Sometimes, however, when you intend to argue that the verdict is not supported by substantial evidence, summarizing the testimony from each witness is the best way to show the appellate court that you are not hiding potentially harmful evidence.

Keep the Statement of Facts concise. Do not clutter it up with facts that serve no purpose. Do not include *specific dates* of events unless they matter.

Don't frustrate the judge by leaving unanswered questions, even if the answers are irrelevant to the appeal. If you decide to include the fact that "the police searched appellant's car before they arrested him," a normally curious judge will wonder what, if anything, the police found in the car. Tell him briefly what the record says about this.

When writing the Statement of Facts, remember: the judge knows *nothing* about this case. Reread your Statement to make sure that you haven't unconsciously made any assumptions that the judge knows the case the way you do.

[E] Dividing Your Statement of Facts into Sections

If your Statement of Facts is going to be long — more than five pages or so — dividing it into sections might make it a bit more readable. Thus, your first heading might be "The Arrest and Subsequent Interrogation." Sometimes, dividing the Statement of Facts into sections relating to each *element* of a tort, breach of contract, etc., can help set up your argument (e.g., "Duty," "Breach of Duty," "Proximate Cause," etc.).

Divide your Statement of Facts into sections when you are raising issues involving both "out-of-court" and "in-court" facts. Here, your first heading might be "Facts Regarding the Search" (out-of-court), and your second heading might be "Facts Regarding Appellant's Challenge to Juror No. 5 For Cause" (in-court). Another way to handle this situation is put a separate statement of the relevant facts at the beginning of each major section of the brief.

If your Statement of Facts is especially long, consider including a brief one-paragraph introduction that summarizes the facts, e.g., "This case involves an arrest based on an informant's tip that appellant was selling heroin at his apartment." This will help the judge follow your Statement of Facts.

[F] Watch Your Language

To make sure that the judge follows your story, assume that the judge does not know the argot and practices used by the witnesses. Doctors, police officers, and other people in particular occupations often do things and use language that other people (including many appellate judges) do not understand. It is easy to forget this, especially if you are accustomed to dealing with such witnesses in your practice. If a doctor testified that "the plaintiff suffered a contusion to the cartilage of the tibia," explain this in layman's language (e.g., "the plaintiff bruised his knee").

Avoid using the same words used by a witness where those words are unclear or ungrammatical. If Officer Boyd testified "I would of grabbed the perp if he run," do not write "Officer Boyd would of grabbed the perp if he run." Write, "Officer Boyd would have grabbed the defendant if he had tried to run away." If you fear that such a clean-up may sacrifice accuracy on some point of fact, then *quote* the witness, so the judge will not think that *you* don't know proper grammar and word usage.

Use the *names* of the people involved in your Statement of Facts. Constant reference to "appellant," "respondent," "intervenors," and "real parties in interest" makes for difficult reading. The judge may forget who is who and have to go back to the title page to check it out. Use of names also tends to "humanize" the case and make the Statement of Facts more interesting.

If the facts are unusually complicated, involving many people, and your Statement of Facts must be somewhat long, consider beginning your Statement of Facts with a short "Cast of Characters." For example:

Smith — the appellant, plaintiff at trial

Jones — Smith's landlord

Brown — Smith's real estate broker

etc.

[G] Be Honest, and Follow the Rules

Be absolutely scrupulous in your Statement of Facts. If you just once say that such-and-such happened, and the record does not show this, your credibility may be so damaged that the judge will put little faith in anything you say thereafter. Even if you don't think your opponent will "catch" you, some sharp law clerk might. If you feel you must "stretch" the meaning of a certain piece of testimony, then say that this testimony "may be construed to mean . . . ," or simply quote the testimony, if it is not too long.

After *each* statement you make, cite the exact page of the record that supports your statement. This is usually required by the court's rules, but even if it isn't, do it. By doing so, you demonstrate your credibility, and you also make the judge's job a lot easier. He can go straight to that portion of the record if he wants to see for himself what the testimony was.

Perform this task of citation carefully. For especially important facts, cite *line numbers* as well as page numbers (e.g., "Reporter's Transcript, page 236, line 12 through page 237, line 6" — usually abbreviated as "R.T. 236:12-237:6"). Include a citation at the *end of every sentence* (and sometimes in the middle of a compound sentence), not merely at the end of a paragraph. Doing this carefully is not as much work as it may seem, as you must look up these pages anyway when you write your Statement of Facts. These careful citations will also give you easy references when you need to look up facts while writing your Argument.

If evidence supporting a certain fact appears more than one place in the record, normally only one citation is necessary. Multiple citations should be included, however, where the fact is central to your appeal or where the testimony at each citation is not quite as clear as you would like it to be.

[H] Show Respect for the Rules of Appellate Review

If you are arguing that there was no substantial evidence supporting *a verdict* against your client, you must assume that all disputed issues of fact were resolved *against* your client. So if you include in your Statement of Facts testimony by your client that was contradicted by other evidence, be sure to include that other evidence.

If, on the other hand, you are appealing after *a nonsuit or directed verdict* was entered against your client, the rule of appellate review is just the opposite: it is assumed that all of your evidence was true. Here, you can freely use all of your evidence in your Statement of Facts.

If you plan to argue that some error was *prejudicial* (e.g., where the trial court erroneously refused to admit some evidence), you should include in your Statement of Facts evidence on *both* sides of an issue, to show that — but for the error — the verdict might have been different.

[I] Where to Get the Facts

You may not assume that any statement appearing *somewhere* in the record qualifies for inclusion in the Statement of Facts. If you claim that there was no substantial evidence supporting the verdict, you may use any evidence that was *admitted at trial*, but you may *not* use allegations of the complaint or answer. If you are claiming that a demurrer to the complaint was improperly sustained, you may then include facts alleged in the complaint. If you claim that summary judgment was improperly granted, get your facts from the affidavits filed for and against the motion for summary judgment.

Unless counsel made a concession or entered into a stipulation, you may not use a statement *by counsel* (orally or in some memorandum of law) as authority for a substantive fact. Facts come from witnesses, not lawyers.

[J] How to Persuade in Your Statement of Facts

By custom, the Statement of Facts is not supposed to be overtly argumentative. It is meant to be similar to the opening statement at trial: merely state the facts and leave the argument for later. Nevertheless, there are ways to be somewhat persuasive in your Statement of Facts without being overtly argumentative.

You may include certain facts that are not technically relevant to the issue on appeal. If, in our earlier example involving an arguably illegal arrest, one of the police officers used a racial insult while arresting the appellant, mentioning this fact may influence the judge against the respondent, however slightly. If you are appealing a search or speedy trial issue, consider including any facts that suggest that your client might not be guilty, even if these facts will not be used in your Argument.

Careful use of certain *adjectives* can add to the impact of certain facts. If you feel that the record is very thin in showing facts supporting probable cause to arrest, you might say that, "The *only* facts indicating that appellant might be the robber were . . . ."

Short *quotations* from the record can sometimes have a more powerful impact than your paraphrasing. If the arresting officer testified, "He didn't seem to match the description given by the informant," this is much stronger than any paraphrase, even if you use almost exactly the same words. The judge expects the lawyer to "puff," but not to change the witness's own words.

The *absence* of evidence on a certain point is itself a fact! Thus, it is appropriate for you to say that "There is *no evidence in the record* that the clothing worn by appellant at the time of arrest matched that of the robber — as described by the victim — in any way."

You may briefly *summarize* a lengthy recitation of facts for emphasis: "Thus, when Officer Jones arrested appellant, he knew only that . . . ."

You may try to deflate the negative effect of certain facts by adding ameliorative facts. For example, "While there was evidence that the coat appellant wore was the same color as that worn by the robber, there was no evidence that it was dirty, as reported by the victim." This may diminish the impact of the matching colors, if left to respondent to bring out.

§ 4.4 LEGAL RESEARCH

This section will not discuss specific treatises, computer research services, legal research tools, and how to use them. The focus here will be more on what to look for than how to find it.

You have already done some legal research in order to prepare your working outline. Now, before you write your Argument, you will need to do even more intensive legal research, to make sure that your Argument approaches "perfection."

[A] The Importance of Good Research Techniques

Do legal research for two reasons.

First, find cases and statutes that enable or "compel" the court to write a respectable opinion in your favor. Judges like to write opinions that cite precedent (the prior acts of legislatures and courts) to support their conclusions, so it looks like they are merely following the law rather than making it. So give it to them.

Second, and more important, find writings that could influence the court to *want* to go your way. Find well-written cases, articles, and treatises that demonstrate the *justice* of the rule you want the court to adopt. If they are written by well-known, well-respected judges or scholars, all the better.

Even sloppy research techniques will eventually uncover these things, if you have an unlimited amount of time to rummage around through an entire field of law. But no lawyer has this much time to spend on legal research on a single case. Usually, your time will be governed by: (1) your client's pocketbook (if you represent a private client); or (2) your caseload (if you're working for a government agency).

Since the *time* available for research is somewhat fixed, the *quality* of your research product will depend largely on the *speed* at which you do your research. So good research techniques will make you more efficient and thereby improve your brief.

Another important factor affecting your speed is experience. The more research you do, the more proficient you will become.

Legal research can be one of the most time-consuming tasks in preparing an appellate brief, so it is important to use this time as efficiently as you can.

[B] Getting Ready

Unless you prefer to work on a computer, get a loose-leaf binder and fill it with blank, lined paper. Put your *Working Outline* in the front of the binder. With tabs or dividers, divide your binder into enough sections to cover every major and submajor issue in your working outline. On each tab or divider, indicate which issue is in that section.

Now, you are ready to start research on the first major issue. If, while researching this, you come across something affecting another issue, simply make a note of it in the appropriate section of your binder.

While some attorneys prefer to use note cards on which to write up their research, the above system keeps everything together and is well designed for speed — not beauty.

[C] The Most Effective Way to Find Helpful Cases

Generally, legal research occurs on two levels.

The first level is simply a matter of educating yourself in the area of law you are dealing with in your brief. If you are not familiar with the general rules regarding probable cause for arrest, find a treatise (or recent case) that discusses these rules in your jurisdiction. If the area of law is so specialized that you are not familiar with treatises on the subject, ask a law librarian to recommend one. This level of research is fairly straightforward and should not take too much time.

The next level is the time-consuming one. Here, you are looking for specific authorities to support specific arguments you want to make. This can take an enormous amount of time. If you do this poorly, it is likely that you will run out of time, will not find helpful authorities, and will either present a weak argument or be forced to drop certain points.

When working on this level, the most important principle to remember is to have a good idea of what you are looking for. Don't just meander around the reporters. *Conjure up in your mind what type of case would help you the most — and then go look for it.*

Let's assume that you plan to argue that the police lacked probable cause to arrest your client. An informant gave the police certain information that the police used to arrest appellant, and you want to argue that this was insufficient to constitute probable cause. What kinds of cases would support your argument?

Instead of running off and reading dozens of cases on probable cause, first sit down and *imagine* the *ideal* case that would help your position. This would probably be a case with facts similar to yours, but where (1) the police had a *stronger* case for probable cause, and (2) the trial court found the arrest valid, but (3) the appellate court held that there was not sufficient cause and *reversed*. If the appellate court reversed *there* — you will argue — *a fortiori* it should reverse *your* case, where the prosecution's showing was even weaker.

This is your *ideal* case. Now go find it. Unless you are very lucky, however, you won't find the *ideal* case, because it probably doesn't exist. But you might find something very close to it. You might find a case that arose in a different factual setting, but where, one could argue, it seems that the police did have a "stronger" case for probable cause, and yet the appellate court reversed.

As long as you keep this mental fix on what you are looking for, your research will proceed much faster. If you have available 50 cases on probable cause from your jurisdiction, you can skim and quickly discard every case in which a trial court finding of probable cause was affirmed or a trial court finding of no probable cause was reversed. All you want are cases where a trial court finding of probable cause was reversed. Within this smaller group (maybe 15 or 20 of the 50 cases), you will look for cases where you sense that the showing of probable cause was as strong or stronger than it was in your case. You will be surprised how fast you can do this — especially compared to how long it would have taken you to actually read all 50 cases. This speed comes from focusing on what you want to find.

[D] Think Defensively When Selecting Cases

You are looking for cases that will support points you are making. When you find a likely candidate, take a moment to consider how your opponent (or an unfriendly judge) might try to dispose of the case. Can it be argued that the holding you rely on is "mere dicta"? Is it arguable that the case is distinguishable on its facts from your case? Is the case poorly reasoned or unclear? If the case is vulnerable to any of these potential attempts to undercut it, your best solution is simple: *Don't use it* (unless you are unable to find a case which is *less* vulnerable).

Thinking defensively can save you a lot of time and trouble later on, and it will put your opponent in a more difficult position. He will be forced to reach for tenuous arguments if he wishes to attack your authorities, and this should weaken his whole presentation.

Similarly, when seeking authority to support a point, do not select a case that you will have to distinguish yourself. Suppose you claim that an arrest was invalid because the police had no probable cause to believe that Appellant committed a crime. You seek cases imposing a high standard of probable cause. Usually, it is *not* a good idea to select as primary authority a case that holds that there *was* probable cause in that case — even if that case contains language that helps you. If you do use that case, your opponent will probably argue that the language is dicta or that the language should not be read as strongly as you desire, because the court found no probable cause. You might then have a good "yes, but . . ." response, but why select a case that invites such trouble in the first place? You are better off using a case that found *no* probable cause.

[E] How to Read a Case

Suppose your research turns up 30 cases that might be relevant to the issue you are researching. If you were to read each case from beginning to end and then write a short summary (facts, issues, holdings, etc.) of each case, this would take you many hours. There must be a quicker way, and there is.

Here, as always, speed depends largely on knowing what you are looking for. First read any synopsis that appears at the outset of the case. This is not complete and cannot be relied on for all purposes, but it will tell you generally what the case is about and whether the appellate court affirmed or reversed. This might be enough to enable you to discard 50% of the cases you find! In the previous example, if the synopsis tells you that the appellate court affirmed a trial court finding of probable cause, there is no need to read any further. (If, however, the case is strong authority against your position, consider anticipating your opponent's use of the case by attacking it (by distinguishing it, etc.) in your own brief.)

When you decide not to use such a case, there is also no need to spend any time writing up a summary of it. Do, however, make a note in your binder indicating the name and citation of the case and that you have read it. If you fail to do this, you will find yourself picking this same case off the shelf time and again as other research leads you to it.

Suppose the synopsis tells you that you should not immediately discard the case, that it might be useful. Keep reading. Write a short note to yourself about how and where the case can be used in your Argument. (If, however, you find yourself inspired to write a draft of what you will say about the case in your Argument, go ahead and do it *now*. It might sound spontaneous, and it might save you some time later on.) You might note key facts, holdings, and useful language you might want to quote. Do not take the time needed to make an *elaborate* note. It is only a note to yourself. Do not expect to rely on this note when you write about the case in your Argument. Then, it will be quicker to look at the whole case itself. It will also be safer, since you will have the exact language of the court before you and will be less likely to make a mistake in anything you say about the case. In fact, if when you first read the case you decide you will definitely use it, it usually saves time to print the case immediately and put it in the back of your binder. This print might also be handy at oral argument.

If you decide to use a case because you like what it says on a certain issue, be sure to read (or at least skim) the balance of the case. Because the case involves some facts somewhat similar to yours, it often happens that other parts of the court's opinion discuss issues relevant to other issues in your Argument. You may find that discussion useful. On the other hand, you may find such discussion potentially *damaging* to other issues in your Argument. If so, you may wish to reconsider your decision to use this case anywhere in your Argument.

[F] Find Recent Cases from Certain Courts

If your case is pending before a certain panel of a certain court, that panel will probably be most influenced by cases from the following courts, in descending order of importance (roughly):

1. That panel,

2. The supreme court of that jurisdiction,

3. Other panels of your court,

4. Other appellate courts in your jurisdiction,

5. The United States Supreme Court,

6. Federal courts of appeal,

7. Well-respected high courts of certain other states,

8. Federal district courts,

9. Other courts in other states.

It may seem surprising to see the United States Supreme Court so far down the list. Most judges are rather parochial, however, and they usually feel more comfortable using cases from their own jurisdiction. They assume that relevant U.S. Supreme Court holdings have already been incorporated into their local cases. Where this is not so — as where the U.S. Supreme Court has rendered a relevant *recent* decision — that decision will assume greater importance, of course.

This list may be a useful guide in helping you decide how to spend your limited research time most effectively. In other words, don't bother looking for cases from other states unless you have first exhausted your own state and still have time for more research.

Similarly, the court will be most impressed by *recent* cases. Old cases might be based in part on statutes since repealed, doctrines since over-ruled or modified, or values that have since changed. So check out the newer cases first, and if you still have research time left, then look at the old cases.

When should you consider your research done? A fair rule of thumb is, when you have some persuasive authority supporting every point you make in your Argument. If you *cannot* find good authority for a certain point, you might wish to reconsider whether to include the point or how much weight to give it.

§ 4.5 THE ARGUMENT

[A] When to Write the Argument

The Argument is usually the most important part of your brief, and also the most time consuming.

To determine when you should begin writing the Argument, start with the date you must send your brief to the printer, and then count backwards in time. Estimate how long it will take you to write the Argument, and then *add on several days* to allow your draft to "simmer" in your mind, for reread-ing, and for editing.

This last part is extremely important. Do not plan to turn in your brief immediately after you finish writing the Argument. After you finish writing, put the brief aside for a day or two, then reread it. You will invariably see some way of improving it. You will see better ways of expressing something, new examples or arguments, and even errors that could embarrass you. Make these changes, set the brief aside for another day or two, and read it again. After a final editing, turn it in.

If you omit this simmering-rereading-reediting process, you will end up with a product that is not your best — and you will probably kick yourself when you read the brief after it is submitted to the court.

So, if you must send the brief to the printer on Wednesday, March 30, and you estimate (liberally) that it will take you seven days to write the Argument and conclusion, add four or five days for the simmering process, and assume you will start writing your Argument no later than March 15, unless you plan to work weekends.

Generally, it is not a good idea to start writing your Argument until you have "formulated" it by refining your Working Outline and finding authority for each point in it.

But if you get a great idea earlier that inspires you to dash off a terrific paragraph or two, go to it. You can always change it later.

[B] Read It as You Write It

As you write your Argument, switch back and forth in your mind between two roles. One role is the advocate who is *writing* strong prose and presenting the best points, in an effort to persuade. The other role is the judge or law clerk who will be *reading* your argument.

Do not overlook or underrate this second role. As you write, ask yourself such questions as:

- Would this sentence be clear to a judge who cannot read my mind?

- Would this presentation of the facts be clear to someone who is not as familiar with the facts in this case as I am?

- If I were a judge who was skeptical about my case, would I see some hole in my Argument that must be plugged to be convincing?

- Would I see the relevance of the cases I reply on, without having to go read those cases?

- Would I get the impression that the Argument is so one-sided that I must read the other side's brief to find out what is really going on?

Once you are able to be your own best critic, the quality of your briefs will improve enormously.

[C] Getting Started

For many people, this can be the most difficult part of writing anything. "Writer's block" is a curse that afflicts lawyers as well as novelists. There are, however, some readily available means of overcoming it when writing the Argument.

The key is to break up the Argument into smaller, more manageable parts, so you are not facing the awesome task of creating a 40-page Argument, but only the simpler task of writing a three or four page *section* of the Argument.

You have already done much of this breaking up by putting together your Working Outline. The more detailed your Working Outline is, the smaller each section will be, and the easier it will be to write each section. Beyond this, it is often possible to break the sections themselves into smaller parts by using a general formula for the structure of each section.

[D] Structure of Each Section

The following formula generally works to create a readable structure for each major section of the Argument:

- First, state briefly what the trial court did and very briefly (in no more than a sentence or two) a summary of your objection to it.

- Then state the law.

- Finally, apply the law to the facts.

The first part of this formula is usually very short, simply informing the court of the alleged error you are attacking and how. For example,

The trial court denied the motion to suppress the gun, impliedly rejecting appellant's argument that the arrest was illegal because the police had no probable cause to believe that appellant had committed a crime. This was error, because the record fails to show that the police had any information establishing the credibility of the informant.

The second part, the law, should include not just the relevant rule, but also a short statement of the *reason behind* the rule. This shows why the rule is a just one, and might get the judge to apply the rule with gusto. Judges do not like to see themselves as clerks, mechanically applying rules to facts. Inspire the judge to see the justice of your position.

If the rule of law includes a term that is somewhat vague — how much cause is "probable" cause? — you might need to explain how a few cases *applied* the term to certain facts, in order to infuse the term with some meaning.

If the rule of law is *in dispute*, or if either party is proposing a *new* rule, then this part may be lengthy, and it should probably be made into a separate subsection. Here, be sure to use some of the techniques discussed *infra* regarding how to persuade the judge to *want* to adopt the rule you propose.

The third part is often the most difficult and the most important. Here you must carefully *apply* the rule of law to the facts of your case that relate to this section of your Argument. *Go over all of the key facts.* Repeat them and analyze them, with correct citations to the transcript after each fact. You can't assume that the judges remember all of them from your Statement of Facts, so repeat the facts that help you. Do not assume that the judges will forget or overlook the facts that hurt you; state them and find a way to explain them.

Cases can be useful in this third part. If the police had some information that the informant was credible, you might state this information, and then present a case in which the police had similar information and yet the court held that it was insufficient.

Make sure that the text of each section agrees with the heading of that section.

[E] How Much Law Should You Explain?

How much should you assume the judges know about the area of law involved in your case? It depends on how often they deal with it.

If you have a criminal appeal involving the validity of a search, you can usually assume that the judges are familiar with at least the basic rules of law in this area, as appellate judges deal with such issues fairly often. For you to discuss the history of the exclusionary rule could be mildly insulting, as well as a waste of your time (and the judge's).

The particular, narrow issue in your case, however, should be discussed in detail. So, if your particular search issue involves the requirement that an underworld informant be proved credible before the police may base a search or arrest on his information, you should explain the rules on this question. Do not assume that the judges are intimately familiar with so narrow an issue. *You* know about it, because you have been working closely with it. But the judges probably haven't.

Sometimes you should explain the basic rules and cases for a whole broad area of law, where it is unlikely that the judges get many cases in this area. For example, state court judges seldom see cases involving antitrust or copyright issues. If your case involves such an issue, you should explain some of the basic rules in these broad areas before going into the narrow issues involved in your case.

In short, do not pitch your argument so low that you insult the judge's intelligence, nor so high that the judge cannot follow your argument.

It is usually helpful (and sometimes required by court rules) to tell the court what *standard of appellate review* applies to this case. Should the court look for substantial evidence? Abuse of discretion? Clear and convincing error? If the issue is purely one of law and no deference is to be given to the trial court (e.g., a general demurrer was sustained), Appellant should point this out.

[F] Explain Why the Rule is Just

The appellate judge does not see herself as a mechanic. She does not enjoy mindlessly applying a rule to a set of facts, and she does not appreciate a brief that tells her "Here is the rule. Simply apply the words of the rule as I tell you to, and reverse the trial court." You must convince her to *want* to decide the case your way.

Behind every rule is a reason. There are always some cases and treatises that explain why the rule is what it is. Find a good explanation and include it in your brief. If you can't find one, use your own words. This does not have to be very long — even a sentence or two can be very effective in motivating the judge to see the justice underlying the rule and — most important — why it would be unjust to decide the appeal against your client.

After you state the rule and explain the reason behind the rule, apply *the reason* to your facts.

Here is an example:

> The trial court erred by overruling Appellant's hearsay objection to the testimony of Officer Brown that "Ms. Smith told me that [Appellant] had run the red light."

> A noted authority wrote that "In order to encourage witnesses to put forth their best efforts and to expose inaccuracies that might be present, the Anglo-American tradition evolved three conditions under which witnesses are ordinarily required to testify: oath, personal presence at the trial, and cross-examination. The rule against hearsay is designed to insure compliance with these ideal conditions." McCormick, *Evidence*, § 245.

> Ms. Smith met none of these conditions — she took no oath, was not present at trial, and could not be cross-examined. Therefore, she was not encouraged to put forth her best efforts to tell the full true

story to the jury, and Appellant was deprived of the right to expose any inaccuracies in her story by cross-examining her. Admission of Officer Brown's hearsay testimony was error.

[G] Using Cases

Lawyers often feel that they must load up their briefs with lots of cases in order to look impressive. The result can be an unreadable mess.

Following certain principles can make your use of cases more effective.

Never cite a case without a purpose, and make that purpose clear in the text surrounding the citation. Consider this example:

> Officer Peters' arrest of appellant Cole was without probable cause. *People v. Smith*, 52 N.Y.2d 444, 450-451 (1981).

The citation to *People v. Smith* might be called a "floating" citation. It just floats in the brief. It has no persuasive value, because it gives the judge no idea of what it stands for or why it is there. From the way the above statement is written, it would appear that *People v. Smith* held that Officer Peters' arrest of appellant Cole was without probable cause! As *Smith* was decided many years before Peters arrested Cole, and Cole was not a party to the *Smith* appeal, this interpretation of the above statement is obviously wrong. But what is the right interpretation? Perhaps the attorney who wrote the statement meant that one of the rulings in *Smith*, if applied to the facts of Peters' arrest of Cole, would invalidate the arrest. If so, he should have said so precisely. Thus,

> In *People v. Smith*, 52 N.Y.2d 444, 450-451 (1981), the court held that Smith's arrest was invalid because the police may not base a decision to search or arrest solely on information from an underworld informant unless they have reason to believe he is credible. As Officer Peters had no reason to believe that Mr. Fink was credible, the arrest of appellant Cole was also invalid.

One way to briefly indicate why you are citing a case is to summarize its holding or facts in parentheses right after the cite. For example, "*See* People v. Smith, 52 N.Y.2d 444, 450-451 (1981) (arrest without probable cause is invalid)."

Similarly, do not *string-cite* without a purpose, and that purpose should be apparent from the brief. A brief that cites ten cases for an undisputed point of law simply looks cluttered, not impressive, and this clutter tends to interfere with the chain of thought you are trying to get the judge to follow. If the point of law you are stating is not disputed, it is enough to cite one or two cases, preferably from the highest court in your jurisdiction. Where, however, the point of law is not clearly established, or the point is disputed by your opponent, a string-cite may help persuade the court that there is substantial authority in support of your position.

When you string-cite, cite the strongest cases first. These may be the only cases in the string that the judge reads. (Citation manuals say to list cases in reverse chronological order. Don't do it. Your job is to win, not to "look proper.")

Use cases from your own jurisdiction in preference to out-of-state cases wherever you can, and use recent cases in preference to older cases.

Cite concurring and dissenting opinions only rarely, and only for a very good reason. Such use implies that the established law is contrary to what you are proposing. If, however, you concede that you are urging a change in the present rule, concurring and dissenting opinions show that there is at least some judicial sentiment on your side.

If you intend to rely heavily on a certain case, briefly summarize the facts of the case that are relevant to the holding you are using. This will assure the judge that you are not merely pulling language from the case out of context.

[H] Secondary Sources

During your research, in your effort to find supporting case law, you will probably use secondary sources — digests, legal encyclopedias, and the like.

In general, it is *not* a good idea to *cite* such a source in your brief as the chief or only authority supporting a certain point. These sources state only abstract propositions of law, without factual underpinnings, and they may not fully or accurately reflect the cases they purport to distill. Most judges would prefer to see the case itself, rather than a second-hand report of it. Also, these digests might include cases *against* your position.

It might sometimes be helpful, however, to include a secondary source as an *additional* cite, placed *after* your supporting case citations. This might show the judge that the case you rely on is not an aberration, but is consistent with the general pattern of case law on this topic.

There are times, of course, when a prominent secondary source serves as a *primary* source of authority on a certain point. While treatises such as Williston on Contracts and Wigmore on Evidence are good repositories of case law, they also include statements of the "preferred view" of a very prominent expert — Williston or Wigmore — on certain points. These are persuasive in themselves, and cites to them (and quotes from them) can be very helpful. The same is true of law review articles, especially those by people well-known in their fields.

In addition, in some jurisdictions, certain treatises on *procedure* are so respected by judges that they might occasionally be cited alone on an undisputed procedural point. Examples are Moore's federal practice treatise and Witkin's treatise on California Procedure.

[I] Be Reliable

Never cite a case for a proposition for which it does not stand. If you want to stretch a holding a bit, do so openly, telling the judge what the court did and how you justify the stretching. Your credibility is at stake here, and if the judge feels that one of your cites or statements about a case is deceptive, he may give little credence to anything you say thereafter.

[J] Make the Judge's Job as Easy as Possible

Be sure that your citations are accurate, so the judge who wants to look up a case will find it where you say it is. Give "point-cites," indicating the page (or pages) of the case that discusses the point you are making. For example, "An arrest is invalid if it is not based on probable cause. *People v. Jones*, 87 Ill. 2d 97, 102 (1967)." If the *Jones* case is 30 pages long, why force the judge to search through all 30 pages to find the point you are making, when it can be found on page 102 and you know it?

[K] Use Quotations — But Sparingly

Quotes can be effective. They use the exact language of a source more authoritative than you: a court or treatise. The language itself may be very persuasive.

The persuasive impact of quotes can be diluted, however, if quotes are used too often, so don't use them where they do not really add much to your point or where the point is undisputed.

Do not make your quotes too long. Quotations force the judge to adjust to a different writing style and then revert to reading yours. This is disturbing to some judges and tends to disrupt the flow of your argument. A quote should almost never exceed twenty lines. If a longer quote is so juicy that you cannot bring yourself to cut it down, then at least *italicize* key parts of it so the judge can focus on those if she so chooses. Also, consider putting part of the quote in a footnote, where the judge can choose to ignore it and simply continue reading the text.

[L] Use Proper Form of Citations

When citing or quoting cases, statutes, regulations, or other authorities, be sure to use the proper form of citation. This takes very little work on your part, and it makes you look more professional.

Ask the appellate court clerk if there is a particular style manual used by the court. If no single manual is used by your jurisdiction, follow a manual which is used nationally, such as the "Bluebook," officially called *The Bluebook: A Uniform System of Citation* (Columbia Law Review Ass'n et al. eds.).

It is usually safe to use the form used by the judges themselves in their published opinions.

[M] Complete All Thoughts

Do not assume that the judge will make connections that you make in your mind but fail to put down on paper. The judge might do this; then again, she might not. She should not have to work for the connections. It is *your* job to make everything crystal clear, to make the judge's job as easy and enjoyable as possible.

When you are using a case as precedent, discuss the case and then say how it *connects* to your case, even if this seems somewhat obvious to you. For example,

> In *Green v. Brown*, 93 Pa. 145, 152 (1971), the court held that contributory negligence is no defense to an intentional tort. Therefore, in the case at bench, appellant's alleged failure to signal was no justification for respondent's intentionally forcing him off the road.

Similarly, when you are distinguishing a case, do not rest on a mere recitation of the aspect of the case which you believe distinguishes it. Do not say,

> *Black v. Blue*, 83 N.J. 92 (1958), relied on by respondent, is distinguishable because there the dangerous conditions in the building had been caused by the tenant's child.

To complete the connection, you must add one more sentence:

> In the case at bench, however, the dangerous condition was not caused by the tenant or anyone related to or connected with her in any way.

When the appeal appears to turn on which rule of law is adopted, you might spend much of your Argument discussing which rule of law is best, as a matter of policy and precedent. When you are done with this, however, do not forget to show the judge how the rule of law you support *applies* to the facts of your case, in order to clearly sustain your burden of showing reversible error.

Remember this rule of thumb: It is usually best to *spell out the relevance of every point* you make, large or small. It is better to "state the obvious" than risk having the impact of your arguments missed by some judge who does not see the connection — for whatever reason.

[N] Use Alternative Arguments Wherever Possible

This point was made earlier, in discussing how to prepare your Outline. But it also applies *within* sections of your Argument anywhere it might help.

For example, there might be more than one way to deal with a case raised by your opponent. The case may be from another jurisdiction. It may have been wrongly decided, ignoring principles that your jurisdiction deems important. And it might also be distinguished on its facts. If the case is potentially damaging to you, use *all* of these arguments if they are reasonable.

When using alternative arguments, make it clear to the judge that they are alternatives. For example, say "Even if *Thomas* were correctly decided, it is nevertheless distinguishable from our case."

When making alternative arguments, put your strongest argument first, so you get the judge on your side as soon as possible. If you save your strongest argument for the end, the judge may become skeptical of your case before he gets to it.

[O] Make the Court Want to Decide the Case Your Way

A good discussion of the case law can assure the court that there is sufficient precedent to *permit* it to decide the case in your favor without looking foolish. But something more is usually needed in order to win the case: you must convince the court to *want* to decide it your way. While the case law can sometimes help in this effort, generally two other devices are best for this purpose: policy arguments and the facts.

Here is a useful test for assessing whether you have written a persuasive brief: If you cover up all discussion of cases in your brief, the remainder — the facts and policy discussions — should still convince most people to rule in your favor.

Policy arguments help persuade the judge to adopt a *new* rule of law. Describe how the rule will operate *generally* (not just to your case) and why this is fair, good for society, and furthers basic policies recognized by the Constitution or the legislature.

Suppose you want to persuade an appellate court to overrule prior cases holding that a residential landlord has no common law duty to provide habitable premises, and to adopt a new "implied warranty of habitability" and allow tenants to sue landlords for breaching this warranty. Show the court that the old cases arose at a time when most rented dwellings were incidental to rented farms, which the occupant could repair as well as the landlord, and at that time legislatures made no requirements that landlords make repairs. Today, however, most rented dwellings are in cities, and tenants are less able than landlords to provide for repairs to modern plumbing, electrical wiring, and the like. Also, today's legislatures have recognized this by empowering cities to enact housing codes and enforce them against owners. (It worked. *See* Green v. Superior Court, 10 Cal. 3d 616 (1974).)

If you have more than one respectable policy argument, put the best one first, and emphasize it. Don't let it get buried in the middle of a paragraph.

Policy arguments also help convince the judge to *apply* a settled rule of law to your case in a favorable way. Suppose you represent an elderly widow who knew nothing about financial matters, but entrusted her life savings to an investment company that deceived her about the return she would receive. The trial court ruled that the statute of limitations had run on her lawsuit. Applying the rule that the statute begins to run when a "reasonable investor should know" of the fraud, the trial court held that your client "should have known" that defendants lied from the beginning — as soon as she received her first check showing a lower return. Argue that the policy of laws against fraud is to give the most protection to unsophisticated investors. While a more experienced investor might have "smelled a rat" when he got that first check, it is unreasonable to expect your client (and the thousands of elderly widows like her!) to have such awareness.

[P] Use the Facts

Even though you have fully stated the facts in your Statement of Facts, the judge — who is not as familiar with the case as you are — will probably not remember them all or realize the significance you want to attach to them. So *retell* some of the story in your Argument. Then stress and repeat the key facts which help you. While it is important to be concise, this is one place where repetition is appropriate. If you have some good facts, burn them into the judge's mind. Be sure to give a proper citation to the record whenever you refer to a fact in your Argument.

If your key facts appear in one or two short documents that were introduced at trial or in a few pages of the reporter's transcript, consider *attaching* copies of these as *appendixes to your brief.* True, the judge could find these anyway by looking through the record, but he might not be in a mood to take that trouble. If he already has them in his hands while he is reading your brief, he is more likely to read them. Attaching them as appendixes also makes them (and the facts they contain) stand out from the rest of the record, and this might emphasize their importance in the judge's mind.

Where you have both good facts and good policy arguments, use them both, of course. But often you will not have both. One may be a bit weak, so you must do an especially good job on the other. If the police might have violated *Miranda* while obtaining a confession from a vicious killer (your client), you might be better off skimming over the particular facts of your case and, instead, emphasizing the importance of compliance with *Miranda* as a means of ensuring protection of the Fifth Amendment rights of citizens generally. If, on the other hand, you rely on a rule of law that is not fully accepted in your jurisdiction but you have sympathetic facts, stress the facts. If you know that the court you are facing will not be receptive to your proposal to extend the *Miranda* rule in some way, you might focus more attention on the fact that, in this case, the alleged violation of *Miranda* might have resulted in a false confession made to protect a relative.

[Q] Relate Your Case to the Judge's Experiences and Values

Use examples or analogies to which the judge can relate personally wherever possible. If you are challenging the right of the police to stop your client at random on the street and ask permission to look in his duffel bag (where they found stolen goods), discuss how the court might resolve the case if the police had stopped a lawyer or judge and asked to look in his briefcase. If your case involves real property or stocks, explore how the principle you are urging might affect the average homeowner or stockholder. Most judges have purchased a home or a few shares of stock at one time or another.

Show how certain values the judges are likely to have affect the case. If you are challenging a summary judgment entered against your client, your careful analysis of the intricacies of summary judgment law might be correct, but quite boring. If, in addition, you stress that summary judgment effectively denied your client the right to a jury trial, you might touch an emotional chord that moves the judge in your direction. If you are representing the respondent and trying to support the summary judgment, you might mention the ever-increasing caseload of the trial courts and the utility of summary judgment in cutting out useless jury trials.

[R] Explain How a Proposed Rule Will Affect Society

If either side is urging the court to adopt a new rule or an extension of an old rule, the judges may be very concerned about how the proposal might affect matters out in "the real world." If you are the one making the proposal, show how it will improve the situation and how it will not cause other problems. If you are opposing the proposal, do just the opposite.

For example, if you are proposing or opposing a new rule regarding the procedures that an administrative agency must follow, explain how the rule would operate. Would it speed up agency decisions? Would it cost the state more money? Would it result in more lawsuits ("court congestion") challenging agency decisions? Would it make the bureaucracy more responsive to the public?

Suppose a party is urging the court to adopt or extend a rule imposing additional liability on landlords who fail to obey building codes. Would this cause rents to be increased? Would it result in better public safety? Would it cause units to be removed from the housing market?

Give your own reasoned speculation on these questions, if that is all you have. It is better, however, if you can cite some authority backing up your speculation. Cases and statutes will seldom be useful here. Instead, look for law review articles and non-legal literature. A brief using such materials is sometimes called a "Brandeis brief," and the court will usually take judicial notice of these materials even if they were not introduced at trial. If you cite particularly impressive studies or reports which might be difficult for the judge to obtain, put copies of these in an appendix to your brief.

If you propose a new rule, it is usually best to *minimize* how novel it is or how much it will change anything in society. Most judges are rather conservative. If something is to be changed, they would prefer a small change to a big one.

[S] The Appellant Must Answer the Trial Court

The first place the appellate judge will look for a justification for what the trial court did is any place the trial court said why it did so. If the trial court judge wrote an opinion or memorandum of decision, answer it. If the reporter's transcript contains a brief oral statement by the trial court revealing its reasons, answer it. Do not get so wrapped up in the opposing party that you forget that, in a sense, your true opponent is the trial court.

[T] Anticipate (and Rebut) Rebuttal Arguments

Many lawyers will instinctively disagree with this advice. Why anticipate an argument that your opponent might never make? Don't you run the risk that the court will be impressed by the argument? Yes, you do, but it is usually worth the risk.

In the trial court, anticipating your opponent's argument might not be worth the risk. A trial judge is usually under time pressure and is less likely to dwell on a case and see a legal argument that could have been made, but wasn't. Even if he sees it, why should he do the lawyer's work and raise the argument?

The situation in the appellate court is quite different. The judges (and their law clerks) have more time to devote to each case, are quite used to reviewing points of law, and want to write opinions that look good. If the opinion is based on an argument that is logically defective or overlooks some statute or policy, the legal community will hold the judge responsible for this — and he knows it. He cannot pass the buck to weak appellate counsel. (As to *certain types* of arguments, in certain types of cases, he may rely on a rule that bars consideration on appeal of an objection or argument not raised in the trial court. This often arises where a party has failed to object to the introduction of certain evidence. Here, the appellate lawyer need not anticipate the argument, because it may *not be made* for the first time on appeal.)

Therefore, if you fail to raise an argument against you that might have been made, you run the very substantial risk that a judge or law clerk will see the argument, never hear the rebuttal to it you might have made, and rule against you on that issue. By failing to raise the argument, you effectively *forfeit* your right to participate in its resolution.

A good job of anticipation was done by the Respondent in *People v. Lovett*, 82 Cal. App. 3d 527 (1978), where defendant was convicted of possession of heroin. On appeal, his attorney complained that during a lunch recess at his preliminary hearing, the heroin disappeared. But his argument on this point was poor.

> Although defendant, understandably, tries to make as much as possible of all this, it is not quite clear what he is driving at. The main thrust of his argument seems to be that the loss of heroin deprived the conviction of any evidentiary basis. That claim has no merit whatever. The seizure of the heroin was testified to by Officer Flanders [and a police chemist testified that the material was in fact heroin]. The real problem, as the Attorney General realizes, is *People v. Hitch*, 12 Cal. 3d 641 at pages 652-654 (1974). [*People v. Lovett, supra*, 82 Cal. App. 3d at 533.]

The court went on to accept the Attorney General's argument that *Hitch* did not require reversal here. Had the Attorney General not raised and rebutted the *Hitch* argument, the court might have seen it and — unaware of a potential rebuttal — upheld it.

There are times, however, when you probably should *not* raise the argument: (1) when it is not likely that a judge or law clerk will be aware of the argument (perhaps because only someone with the knowledge of a specialist in an obscure area of the law would know of it), and (2) you can think of no effective rebuttal to it. (This advice might have to be modified if you are aware of a *case* or *statute* (rather than merely an argument) that is directly contrary to your position. The ABA Code of Professional Responsibility, Ethical Consideration 7-23, provides: "Where a lawyer knows of legal authority in the controlling jurisdiction directly adverse to the position of his client, he should inform the tribunal of its existence unless his adversary has done so; but, having made such disclosure, he may challenge its soundness in whole or in part."

Note that *both* of the above conditions should be present, before you decide to ignore the argument. If you have a good reply to an esoteric argument, make it, although you should not devote a lot of space to it. Even if it is unlikely that the court would have seen the argument, your candor may impress the court and make the rest of your brief seem more credible.

What if the converse is true, i.e., there is a good argument against your position that the court is likely to see, but you can think of no good reply to it? Then you had better think a little harder. If you can't come up with a decent reply, you will probably lose that issue. Ignoring the problem won't make it go away. Keep thinking until you come up with an answer, or consider dropping that issue.

If there is a single "fatal flaw" that afflicts most lawyers on appeal, it is that they fail to meet the tough argument that is made (or could be made) against their position. By ignoring it, they hope the court won't see it or be affected by it. Almost invariably, the court sees that this is the turning point in the case. It often decides the case on this issue with no input on it from the losing attorney.

At this point, you may be thinking "All right. Maybe I should deal with arguments against my position. But why do so in my Appellant's Opening Brief? Wouldn't it be better to wait to see if my opponent raises the issue in his Respondent's Brief? If he does, then I can answer it in my Reply Brief."

There are advantages to this. It gives you more time to think (or procrastinate) about the issue, and if respondent does make the argument, it allows you to respond to it as it is made by respondent, rather than as you guess it might be made.

There are, however, advantages to anticipating the point in your Opening Brief.

First, it shows that you are confident in your case — so confident that you are not afraid of any argument the other side *might* come up with.

Second, it enhances your credibility, by showing that you are not trying to hide anything or duck important issues. This helps present you as a fair person who is trying to help the judge come to the correct decision. This makes your whole brief look more convincing.

Third, it makes your brief more complete. A judge or law clerk sometimes uses a brief as an aid in research, memo-drafting, or opinion-drafting. If all of the relevant facts, arguments, and authorities are in your brief, she may have no need to use your opponent's brief for this purpose. If she frequently looks at your brief but reads your opponent's brief only once, your relative opportunity to persuade her is enhanced. Try to envision your brief as something that can help the judge *throughout* her work on the case, and design it so she will find it useful.

Finally, anticipating your opponent's argument can take the steam out of it. If you fail to anticipate the point, the judge will read it for the first time in the Respondent's Brief. She may be impressed with it, and it will fix in her mind. You then might have an uphill battle trying to convince her in your Reply Brief that the argument is wrong.

If, instead, you raise and rebut the argument in your Opening Brief, you can deflate the argument as soon as you state it, before it becomes implanted. When the judge later sees the argument again in the Respondent's Brief, she might well think "I've seen this argument already and I know the answer to it," and just skim over that part of the brief.

[U] Be Moderate, Be Reasonable, Be Courteous

To maintain your credibility, do not make arguments or statements that appear to fly in the face of common sense or the plain language of a statute or case, unless you back them up with strong policy arguments, legislative history, or something equally persuasive.

It often helps to *concede* a point graciously and even gratuitously, especially if you don't need it.

Your use of language — especially adjectives — can have a significant effect on how reasonable the judge thinks you are. Do not overstate or exaggerate points in your favor. Be honest about how much weight should be attributed to them. Sometimes, understatement can be very effective.

The most overused word in most briefs is "clear," as in "It is clear that Officer Jones lacked probable cause to arrest appellant." Upon reading this statement, many judges would think "Here's another attorney trying to show by bombast what he can't show with the facts." A judge once commented, "How come the answers to difficult questions are always 'clear' to the lawyers and never 'clear' to me?" It is better to show with facts from the record that the officer lacked probable cause, and perhaps summarize with something like "No reported case has upheld a finding of probable cause under similar facts." Use the word "clear" only when the point is very "clear," and then show why.

Authorities can be useful to show the reasonableness of your position. Cases, statutes, law review articles, and other publications can show that you did not just pull a wild idea out of thin air, but that it is supported by respectable people. Where possible, show how moderate your position is by citing people who might be expected to be on the other side. For example, if representing a defendant in a personal injury case, cite a decision from a court known to be "pro-plaintiff." If representing the prosecution in a confession case, cite a noted civil libertarian.

Use moderate language when attacking your opponent's arguments. Do not say that his arguments are "ludicrous" (even if they are), say that they are "questionable," or that they "appear to be in error." If your opponent's argument is incomprehensible, call it "a bit difficult to follow." Many judges place a high value on professional courtesy, and they can become quite annoyed at an attorney who appears to be wantonly patronizing or demeaning to opposing counsel. For this reason, almost never attack opposing counsel himself, even when he deserves it.

Sometimes you need to show some type of bad faith or negligence on your opponent's part, to sustain a default judgment or punitive damages, or to obtain attorneys' fees on the ground that an action is frivolous. When doing this: (1) focus on the opposing party rather than his attorney as much as possible; and (2) state the facts strongly, but go easy on the adjectives and commentary. If your point is good, the facts will speak for themselves.

Be careful when criticizing the lower court. Such criticism is often necessary, since you are appealing from that court's judgment. But be very moderate in the language you use, and make it clear that you are attacking a particular decision rather than the general competence of the judge. Judges are a protective breed, and appellate judges often resent attacks on their "lower" brethren. Appellate judges might know more about certain trial court judges than you do. If the trial judge is not too bright, the appellate judge probably knows this without your telling him. Sometimes it might even be advisable to compliment some aspect of what the trial judge did. For example, "While the trial court showed great compassion toward respondent and his plight, it abused its discretion by setting aside respondent's default for the third time."

[V] Develop a Theme

Even though the major issues in your Outline of Argument are separate reasons for reversal, it is sometimes possible to develop a theme that runs through two or more of them. Working this theme into your argument where appropriate can add to the persuasive impact of your brief.

For example, suppose the jury awarded large punitive damages against your client — but not so large as to be reversible under the applicable law. You have respectable arguments that, on three occasions, the trial judge erred in admitting certain evidence. In each of these three sections of your Argument, mention that this evidence probably contributed to the high punitive damage award.

[W] Writing Style

This is not the place to discuss grammar, punctuation, and style. There are some excellent books on writing style, including legal writing, and it might be a good idea to consult them occasionally. *See, e.g.*, ELLIOT BISKIND, LEGAL WRITING SIMPLIFIED (1971); FRANK E. COOPER, EFFECTIVE LEGAL WRITING (1953); DAVID MELLINKOFF, LEGAL WRITING: SENSE AND NONSENSE (1982); SIDNEY PARHAM, FUNDAMENTALS OF LEGAL WRITING (1967); WILLIAM STRUNK, JR. & E.B. WHITE, THE ELEMENTS OF STYLE (4th ed. 1999); HENRY WEIHOFEN, LEGAL WRITING STYLE (1978); RICHARD C. WYDICK, PLAIN ENGLISH FOR LAWYERS (5th ed. 2005).

[X] Be Concise

One point deserves emphasis, however: keep your brief as concise as possible.

"Concise" is not the same as "short." A lengthy brief can be concise if the author comes to each point quickly, writes clearly, and omits all "fluff." On the other hand, a fifteen page brief can seem interminably long if it is unclear, boring, and never gets to the heart of the case.

You have little control over the attitude or mood of your judge. He may be bored, sleepy, or impatient. He may think he knows all about this area of the law, having little interest in what some young lawyer wants to tell him. Indeed, his experience with briefs may have led him to expect so little that he sees brief-reading as a chore to be done as quickly as possible. If he begins to read your brief and it strikes him as somewhat difficult to follow, he might feel that it is not worth his time or mental energy to follow your analysis. If he is interrupted by a phone call, he may not want to take the time to go back and retrace your complicated train of thought.

The judge who reads your brief may have none of these attitudes. Then again, he might have all of them. Since you want his vote, you had better write your brief so it is easy for him to read. By doing so, you will not lose the judge who has none of these attitudes. In fact, she will appreciate your efforts to make her job a little easier.

Keep it concise, and keep it simple. Most sentences should be fairly short. Compound sentences should be the exception, not the rule. Each paragraph should be short, seldom more than three or four sentences. Each section of your brief should be fairly short, not exceeding five or six pages. If it is longer, find a way to break it up into logical subsections, each with a sub-heading that guides the judge.

[Y] Write a Two-Page Brief

If you consistently have trouble keeping your briefs concise, here is an exercise you might try: write a Two-Page Brief. Assume that, after the judge reads your Statement of Facts, he will read only your Two-Page Brief, and you must convince him now or never. You get only two pages, so you'd better state your best arguments in as few words as possible. After a bit of practice forcing yourself to pare things down this way, your briefs should improve. (The Two-Page Brief might serve as a pretty good Summary of Argument, discussed below.)

[Z] Guide the Judge as You Go Along

Remind him where you've been and where you are going, so he can clearly see how the point you are now making *connects* to your chain of analysis. This is particularly important if you find it necessary to include a lengthy discussion of case law on a certain point. Don't immerse the judge in such a detailed discussion of cases that he loses sight of how it affects this appeal. Tell him at regular intervals.

Maintain a flow of continuity in the judge's mind. Each new paragraph should begin with an implied or express reference to the idea discussed in the prior paragraph. Remember, you may be writing your brief one piece at a time, but the judge is reading it straight through. Make it easy for him to follow your chain of thought.

[AA] Keep Your Language Reasonably Simple

Do not use a big word or phrase where a small one will do. Do not use two or three words where one will do. Do not use obscure words where familiar words will do. You may impress the judge with your vocabulary, but he may not want to take the time to run to the dictionary, and your meaning may thereby be lost on him. Avoid formal legal words used in wills and contracts, such as "whereas" and "heretofore."

Do not use many *pronouns* in a lengthy sentence or paragraph. If the judge must retrace his reading in order to divine who "he" is and what "it" is, he might lose the chain of logic you want him to follow — and he might also find the brief too tiresome to bother with.

Don't use slang; it looks undignified. Don't use words or expressions known only by people who work in a certain field (such as law enforcement). One or more of your judges may have been a civil lawyer who will not know what you mean when you say "Officer Peters suspected that appellant was involved in a 211, so he ran a make with DMV on appellant's vehicle to see if it was hot." If you quote testimony that uses such language, translate it for the judge.

You are not writing the Great American Novel. The subtle ambiguities that make great novels have no place in a brief, where the judge is not reading for pleasure but to get a job done as quickly as possible. Help him by being clear.

[BB] Write for Two Audiences

In most appellate courts, the bulk of the work on a given case will be assigned to one judge — the "primary" judge. This judge and her law clerks will be responsible for preparing a memorandum or draft opinion for the other judges, and usually this will be prepared before the oral argument.

For this audience, you want your brief to be very complete. Ideally, this judge should be able to find out everything she wants to know about the case from your brief alone. This includes all relevant citations to the record, all relevant cases and statutes, and arguments that could be made against your position and your responses.

Think of your brief as this judge's "constant companion." If the judge frequently reads parts of your brief to find authorities that help her prepare the in-court memorandum, she will frequently read your arguments too. By helping this judge perform her job, you might multiply the number of opportunities you have to persuade the judge.

In addition, if you are helpful to this judge, she is more likely to trust you, and she will be more likely to accept your arguments.

Keep in mind that this "primary" judge is usually the most important judge hearing your case. Her memorandum and views on the case are much more likely to have an impact on the other judges than anything you submit. In fact, if the other judges are pressed for time, they are more likely to read that judge's memorandum than your brief. Therefore, it is important that you do whatever you can to get this judge on your side. You don't know which judge it will be, and you don't know what arguments are most likely to appeal to her. You do know, however, that she has a big job to do, and a brief that is complete will help her do it and might be read by her more than once.

The other "secondary" judges need something slightly different. They want to read the main facts, the main issues, the main arguments, and the main cases and statutes and little else. They want the brief short and sweet, so it won't take too much time to read. They would prefer not to wade through the detail and tangential information that is helpful to the memorandum judge.

You might be able to address the needs of *both* of these audiences in one brief, by using footnotes.

[CC] Footnotes

Footnotes can be very useful to help make the *text* of your brief concise.

Your main arguments should flow smoothly through the text of your brief, so the judge can easily follow your chain of analysis. Interruptions to discuss incidental points should be kept to a minimum, in frequency and in length, but sometimes it may be helpful to discuss some incidental point. You may wish to distinguish some out-of-state cases mentioned by your opponent (after having dealt with his major, in-state cases in your text). You may wish to add some additional citations. You may wish to deal with an unclear aspect of the record, or to rebut a potential argument against you that might occur to the judge, but is answered by a single citation.

None of these things may be important enough to insert in the middle of your text, because the price you will pay for such insertion is an interruption in the flow of your main argument. Nevertheless, omission of this discussion might also cost you something. The answer to this dilemma is the footnote. The information will be there for the judge who wants to be complete (e.g., the judge responsible for the in-court memorandum), but the judge who is in a hurry or who just wants to get the main argument (e.g., another judge) can ignore the footnotes if he chooses.

Some people (particularly trial court judges) say that they dislike footnotes. "Too distracting" is one criticism. Footnotes can be distracting, but they are not nearly so distracting as including the same information in the text of your brief, where it intrudes directly into your main argument. Others say "If it is important enough to appear in your brief, it is important enough to put in the text." True in some situations, but not all. Some topics are important enough to warrant discussion, but not important enough to warrant interrupting your main argument.

[DD] How Long Should Your Brief Be?

Keep this rule of thumb in mind: your brief should be as short as you can make it, while saying everything you consider worthwhile. This should help keep your brief concise.

Do not, however, keep it short at the cost of either clarity or the completeness of your arguments. If you must spell something out, do so.

Many judges will tell you that brevity is the most important quality in a brief. They say this for two reasons: (1) most briefs are poorly written, and the shorter they are, the less poor writing the judge must read; and (2) judges simply have too many cases and too much to read.

As for the first reason, your brief is going to be different. It will be a joy to read and helpful to the judge. As for the second reason, the court's case-load is not your responsibility. Your client has retained you to win the case, not to ease the judge's burden. Don't gratuitously annoy him with useless verbiage, but don't omit useful information or arguments merely to please the judge.

§ 4.6 THE CONCLUSION

The Conclusion is usually used to summarize the arguments, adding: "For the above-stated reasons, the judgment should be reversed." This sometimes wastes an opportunity to do a bit more.

First, the Conclusion can be used to briefly summarize what the judge has read in your brief, so he leaves your brief with a reminder of all of your arguments, not just your final one.

Second, you can use your Conclusion to add some broad perspective on the case that might not be quite so appropriate in the middle of your brief. For examples, see the Conclusions in the sample briefs at the end of this book.

Finally, your Conclusion should specify the relief you want (reversal for new trial, for new sentencing, for dismissal, etc.).

§ 4.7 SUMMARY OF ARGUMENT

Right after your Statement of Facts, give the judge a brief summary of what your Argument will be.

A summary may be of little help if your argument is very short, but your Argument is long, it will give the judge an overview of your position while the facts are fresh in his mind. This will help him follow your Argument, which he is about to read.

Don't put your Summary of Argument *before* the Statement of Facts unless the court's rules require this. It will have more persuasive impact after the judge knows what happened.

The Summary also gives you another opportunity to persuade, so insert a very brief statement of your best points in your Summary of Argument. This is why you should not write your Summary until *after* you have written your Argument, as only then will you know your best points.

To write a good, persuasive Summary of Argument, put yourself in the following frame of mind: Assume that the judge will not read beyond this point in your brief — he will read *only* your Statement of Facts and your Summary of Argument, so you must convince him *now or never*. (This might not be far from the truth. Many judges will quickly come to a tentative decision about the case early in the brief, even if they do end up reading your whole brief.)

Present your Summary in simple prose, and keep it short, no longer than a page or two.

Where local custom or court rules require a "statement of issues," this can also serve as a vehicle for such a summary, although it is a bit more awkward. These issues can be framed simply by turning your carefully worded Outline of Issues into questions.

Thus, suppose you decided to word your first issue in your Outline as "I. The trial court erred in entering judgment on the verdict, because there was no substantial evidence showing that appellant was negligent." The first item in your "statement of issues" might read "Was there substantial evidence showing that Appellant was negligent?" Occasionally, insertion of facts in the statement of issues may add to their persuasive impact, but keep it short.

§ 4.8 EDITING

You have finished your Conclusion, so now you simply sign your name and file the brief. Right? Wrong! You have one more very important task: editing your brief.

After you've finished writing, let your brief "simmer" in your mind for a day or two, then reread it to see if any of the arguments can be improved.

There are, however, some additional, more mundane editing chores to be done.

Make sure that all parts of your brief *fit together*. Reread your Statement of Facts. When you wrote your Argument, you may have realized that certain facts were more (or less) important than you originally thought. Adjust your Statement of Facts to mesh with the Argument. If you rearranged the structure of your Argument, readjust your Outline of Argument to fit it, making sure that the final Outline remains logical and readable.

Next, take out any particularly harsh language you used against your opponent or the trial court. Such language can alienate an appellate judge who treasures "professional courtesy" and the image of her fellow judges. If you have strong feelings about your opponent or the lower court, it is all right (perhaps even healthy) to release them in your first draft — so long as you later reexamine and edit what you wrote when you are in a calmer mood.

Bring your research up to date. It may have been several weeks since you did your research. In that time, there may have been rehearings (or hearings in higher courts) granted in cases you cited. New cases may have come down (or new statutes enacted) that may affect your case. If your brief is long and time is a problem, at least check your major points and cases.

Check all *numbers*. If the judge wants to see *People v. Johnson*, which you cited as 47 N.Y.S.2d 230, she will be annoyed when she opens volume 47 to page 230 and does not see *People v. Johnson*. The same is true of transcript pages. Note that while you can catch most misspellings simply by reading your brief, you cannot catch mistakes in numbers this way; you must check your manuscript or, preferably, the original sources.

Wherever possible, make your brief more concise. Cut out repetition (unless you intended it) and delete unnecessary words.

Carefully check the grammar, spelling, and punctuation of your entire brief. Errors in this area can spoil the effect of a beautifully written brief. The judge may so focus on these errors that she is distracted from your artful persuasion. If errors appear early in your brief, the judge might quickly decide that this lawyer is a slob who takes little professional pride in his work, and therefore what he has to say probably isn't worth much.

Finally, make sure that your brief *flows*. Check transitions from one paragraph to the next and one section to the next. You wrote the brief in pieces, but the judge will read it as one complete message. Make it easy for her to follow from one part to the next.

§ 4.9   GET FEEDBACK

Ask another lawyer to read your brief — *before* you file it. This person should tell you of any spots where the brief is not clear, readable, and sensible. She should also tell you of any fairly obvious arguments against your position that you should rebut.

This person need not be an expert in the field of law covered by the brief. You should have held any discussions you needed with such an expert at an earlier time. Now you are more concerned about how the brief will look to the judge, who is probably not a specialist in this field of law.

When your colleague criticizes your work, don't be defensive. It is natural to feel proud of your work. But even if your response is "right," your brief might lack effectiveness. If your colleague does not find your brief clear or persuasive on some point, a judge might well have the same reaction. So listen — don't just try to talk her out of her criticism.

It might also be helpful to get some intelligent lay feedback. An intelligent lay person should be able to follow most of your brief. If there are spots he or she does not understand, read these spots over carefully. Were they not understood because they require some prior legal knowledge, or because you did not write clearly enough? When in doubt, assume it is the latter and fix it up.

You have spent many hours preparing your brief, so don't waste them by turning in a sloppy end-product. To many people who read it — judges, law clerks, and other lawyers — your brief represents the best job you can do as a lawyer. You should be proud of it, and careful editing is essential if it is to present you at your best.

§ 4.10 RESPONDENT'S BRIEF

There are very few court rules you must follow in preparing a Respondent's Brief. Your focus should be on constructing a document that will help you win. Much of the advice given above regarding the Appellant's Opening Brief also applies to the Respondent's Brief. You will have a better chance of winning if the judge reads and enjoys your brief, so be concise. You will have a better chance of convincing the judge if you are credible, so keep your citations and statements about cases reliable and your arguments reasonable. And focus on the *justice* of your position wherever you can.

There are, however, a few things to note specifically about the Respondent's Brief.

[A] The Statement of Facts

Write your own Statement of Facts. Do not simply refer to Appellant's Statement of Facts. You should tell the story in a light that makes your side of the case look best, emphasizing certain facts, adding explanatory facts to facts that hurt you, and using adjectives that help you.

Usually, certain *presumptions* help the respondent. If appellant is challenging a jury verdict, respondent is allowed to presume that the jury resolved all disputed issues of fact in his favor, and all facts that may reasonably be *inferred* from the evidence may be invoked by respondent. Use these rules to include evidence and inferences that help you, and you may properly ignore those that don't.

The rule is just the opposite if appellant claim that a nonsuit should not have been entered against him, or that the trial court failed to give a requested jury instruction on a certain issue, or that summary judgment should not have been granted against appellant.

If appellant's Statement of Facts violates these rules, point this out at the outset of your Statement of Facts. For example, "Appellant has neglected to mention the fact that . . .," or "Appellant relies on testimony which was impliedly rejected by the jury, in that . . . ." There is no need to call your opponent's action fraudulent or deceptive. Simply state the error, and the judge can draw his own conclusion as to the motives or abilities of your opponent.

[B] The Outline of Argument

If the Appellant's Outline of Argument presents the issues in a logical way that suits your own arguments, follow it. This makes the judge's job a bit easier. He can put the two briefs side by side and compare the opposing arguments on each issue. Of course, you should reword the headings to help your case.

However, there is no requirement that you follow the Appellant's Outline, and you should not do so if this will make your brief less logical or readable. Where this is the case, write your own Outline. In your Argument, indicate at the beginning of each section to which of appellant's arguments you are responding.

There is one issue often not raised by the appellant for which respondent should be especially alert: whether the claimed error was *prejudicial*. More judgments are affirmed on the ground of "harmless error" than on any other ground.

[C] The Argument

In each section of your Argument, begin by briefly stating the appellant's argument to which you are responding. To help the judge, identify the page of Appellant's Opening Brief on which that argument begins. Then, briefly (in one sentence) summarize your response. The remainder of your section will be an elaboration of this response.

Use the presumptions in favor of a respondent on factual matters, but don't assume that you can sit back and rest your case on them. Even where all inferences and factual disputes are given to the respondent, appellate courts sometimes find that respondent failed to prove all elements of a cause of action or defense. Show the court specific facts (with correct citations to the record) that fulfill each element of your case.

If the law provides that the trial court has *discretion* in the matter on which it ruled, be sure to point this out. Don't rest on this, however, as appellate courts sometimes hold that such discretion has been abused.

Use any statement the trial court gave for its action. This statement might appear in a written memorandum of decision or opinion, or sometimes in any findings of fact or conclusions of law. Where there is no written statement of reasons, look in the reporter's transcript for some oral statement the judge might have made from the bench.

If you can support the trial court's ruling with any reasons it did *not* give, do so. In most cases, the appellate court will affirm the trial court's *ruling* if it is correct on any ground, even if the *reason* given by the trial court was incorrect. (The incorrect reason might be deemed "harmless error.")

Rebut all of appellant's respectable points, and deal with all of his important authorities. These issues and authorities are probably the guts of the appeal. Your failure to deal with them will not make the judge overlook them — it will simply tell her that you have no decent response. If you have trouble thinking of a good response, think a little harder. You *must* address those issues.

As for the appellant's minor or obviously silly points or cases, don't rebut them all, or your brief will simply look cluttered. You lose nothing by ignoring these items, for it is very unlikely that anything will turn on them. Do, however, pick out a couple of these points or cases and explain why they are illogical, not supported by the record, or inapposite. This may induce the judge to wonder about your opponent's reliability on his major points.

Rebut all good arguments that appellant *could* have made, or that he might make against your arguments in his Reply Brief. Remember, in most jurisdictions the Respondent's Brief is the *only* brief respondent has a right to file. The appellant gets the last word, and you will get no chance to respond to his Reply Brief — except at oral argument, which may be too late. The appellant might be "sandbagging" — saving his strongest point for the Reply Brief, knowing that you cannot then file a written response.

But even if you think your opponent is not sharp enough to do this, the *judges* (or their law clerks) might think of a counter-argument to your brief. Time and again, a good lawyer submits a weak Respondent's Brief because he refuses to "give the court ideas' by going beyond the specific arguments in the Appellant's Opening Brief. He then loses the appeal because the court saw a way to improve the appellant's argument and did so. If the appellant has done a poor job, but you can see a way in which his argument *could* be made more powerfully, you should consider raising the issue and dealing with it. If you don't, you may effectively forfeit your right to respond to that argument.

§ 4.11 APPELLANT'S REPLY BRIEF

The Reply Brief should contain your answers to the best arguments in Respondent's Brief. Your Outline of Argument should reflect this limited response. Don't bother with all her minor points, though it might be helpful to point out one or two of her more inexcusable mistakes, thereby calling into question her reliability on her better arguments.

Do not write another Statement of Facts for your Reply Brief. If respondent has misstated any facts or violated any presumptions, point this out in the Argument section of your Reply Brief.

The Reply Brief should be short. Do not use it to repeat at length what you said in your Opening Brief. Such repetition is unnecessary, as usually the judge will not read any of the briefs until all are filed, and then he will usually read all three at one sitting. Do, however, briefly interweave key points made in your Opening Brief (especially facts) into your Reply Brief.

Your Conclusion should restate, very briefly, your main arguments, so that will be the last thing the judge sees before he puts down the three briefs.

Chapter 5

ORAL ARGUMENT

§ 5.1 THE PURPOSE OF ORAL ARGUMENT

Many lawyers are very uncomfortable at oral argument. They face not one but several imposing figures in black robes high up on the bench. Some of these figures may look rather stern, especially the presiding or chief judge, who wants to move his calendar along. From watching a few previous arguments, the lawyer may have gotten the impression that one or more of the judges is bored, nasty, or doesn't think much of the attorney's arguments.

This perception might well be correct. Many judges have a rather low opinion of oral argument. They see it as a ritual that must be endured so the public can see them occasionally and the attorneys can feel that they have had an opportunity to have the judges listen to them. Seldom do the lawyers willingly deal with the truly difficult issues on which the case turns. At most, many judges believe, oral argument gives the judge the chance to think about and to crystallize her views of the case. But rarely does a lawyer influence her conclusion.

Of course, once a lawyer perceives that judges think little of oral argument, she sees little reason to put much effort into preparing or performing an oral argument, and does a poor job. This simply reinforces the judge's impression that oral arguments are not useful, and so the cycle continues.

A major reason for the inadequacy of many oral arguments is the failure of lawyers to conceive of a *purpose* to oral argument, and to structure their preparation and performance around that purpose. Having no clear purpose in mind, many lawyers are happy if they get through oral argument without being embarrassed by difficult questions.

Why orally argue your case? Usually, it is not required. In fact, many courts encourage a waiver of oral argument, sometimes with letters sent to all counsel. The "carrot" offered for waiver is a faster decision, as oral argument need not be calendared in the case. Unless you can think of some way oral argument might increase your chance of winning the case, you might as well waive it, take the carrot, and save your client some attorney's fees, unless your opponent refuses to waive. (There is some risk, however, that the court will view a waiver by the appellant as an indication that he believes that the appeal has little chance of success.)

Let's examine how oral argument might help you win the case, keeping in mind that, presumably, you've already said everything you have to say, *in your brief.*

Some judges relate better to the spoken word than the written word. For some, the spoken word helps them put together thoughts which were not fully formed after reading the briefs. Such judges may be influenced by an oral argument that does no more than sum up the main arguments in your brief.

There is, however, a way in which oral argument can be even more helpful to your chance of winning the case: to enable you to deal with any problems the court has with any of your arguments.

You have spent many, many hours writing the brief in this case. While doing so, you have been addressing a nonresponsive audience — you do not know what the judges will think of your arguments (or your opponent's), what objections they may have, what new problems they might see. You hope that you have anticipated much of this in your brief; that is, in large part, what makes a good brief. But you are not perfect and you have no crystal ball. Each judge is an individual whose reactions to a particular problem cannot always be accurately and completely predicted, even by those who know him well. It can be quite distressing to write a good brief and later receive a decision against you which is based on reasons to which you had a good response, but did not put in your brief because you did not know quite how the judges would see the case. Wouldn't it be nice if you could *talk* to the judges for a few minutes, find out their views, and respond to them, all before they vote and write their decision? (In many courts, the judges meet, discuss the case, and take a tentative vote immediately after oral argument. Thus, oral argument occurs at a critical moment.) Oral argument gives you one brief chance to do just that!

Seen in this light, your oral argument will take on quite a different look. Instead of a speech, it will be more like an informal discussion. Instead of dreading questions (which interrupt the smooth flow of your speech), you will welcome them as revelations of the judges' problems with your case and as opportunities for you to respond to the issues the judges think the case turns on, and thereby save your case. Coincidentally, this approach will also please the judges, as you will be showing a sincere interest in *their* concerns, not just delivering your prepared speech on *your* concerns.

Let's examine how your might prepare for an oral argument of this nature.

§ 5.2 YOUR FRAME OF MIND

Most appellate courts do not set a case for oral argument until they have read the briefs, considered the merits, and *drafted an opinion* — or a memorandum that can easily be converted into an opinion. This might have been prepared by only one of the judges (or her law clerks), but the other judges usually defer to that judge.

Having gone to this much work on the case, these judges have pretty well made up their minds — *before* the oral argument even begins! They are no longer neutral and open minded.

When you arrive in court for your oral argument, this is probably *their* frame of mind. You can't tell, of course, *which way* their draft opinion decides the case. There are two possibilities: it's in your favor, or against you.

If it's in your favor, you will probably win — no matter what happens at oral argument. Rarely does an oral argument change the judges' minds.

If it's against you, you will probably lose. But you do have a chance, and you'd might as well take it.

So at the outset of oral argument, *your* frame of mind should be: "They read my briefs, they read the cases, but I've probably lost. *This is my one chance to turn them around.* I can't do it by just repeating what I said in writing, so I'd better do something *very different.*"

If you are wrong and the draft opinion is in your favor, terrific — starting with this "probably lost" frame of mind will do no harm. But if you are right, you still have a small chance to win. Take it.

§ 5.3 DEVELOP A THEME

With this frame of mind, develop a theme. A theme is important for the brief, but it is crucial for the oral argument. The theme goes to the guts of the case, and it is meant to hit the judges in the gut. It should be more emotional than intellectual. It's about justice, not legal technicalities.

Your theme might be "the right to jury trial," where summary judgment was granted against your client. It might be "the right to present the whole story to the jury", where your client was barred from introducing certain evidence. It might be "the rights of citizens to know what their government is doing," where you claim that an environmental impact report was inadequate. It might be "time after time in this case, the police ignored the Constitution," where you charge that the police committed both 4th and 5th Amendment violations in searching and interrogating your client.

Weave your theme into all of your separate legal arguments. Start your oral argument with the theme, and mention it in response to judges' questions whenever you can.

Your theme might not change the mind of the judge who wrote the draft opinion, because he is already "committed" to his work. But there are more judges on the court. Your goal is to hit at least one of them in the gut. After the argument, the judges will probably confer, and you want that one judge to say to the opinion-writing judge, "Hey, I've got second thoughts on this case. Maybe we should reconsider. . . ." If you can accomplish that, you've done a great job at oral argument.

§ 5.4 PREPARATION

Develop a theme to deliver when the judges are silent. But it is likely that most or all of your oral argument time will be taken up by the judges' questions. Get ready for them.

When you see a good lawyer handle questions adeptly, it may appear that he is simply thinking well on his feet, but usually this is misleading. He has spent several hours on preparation, anticipating those questions and formulating answers.

A good rule of thumb is: prepare to the point that you feel that no reasonable question will surprise you.

[A] Know the Record

The judges often think they know the *law* better than the lawyers do, but they expect each lawyer to know the *record* in the case. Do not memorize the record, but have it with you at oral argument, and have it marked, tabbed, or indexed in such a way that you can quickly find anything the court is likely to ask for.

If a question arises as to Officer Peters' key testimony, don't expect to remember what he said and don't guess at it. Simply turn to the relevant page of the transcript and read it to the court. If done smoothly, the court will appreciate your preparation and professionalism. If, instead, you spend several moments fumbling through the record — "Just another minute, your honor; it's in here somewhere" — the judges will become bored and irritated at this waste of their valuable time. A precious portion of your limited oral argument time is also being wasted.

Try to anticipate which parts of the record you are most likely to be asked about, and have those at your fingertips. Index the balance of the record, so if a question arises concerning some part of the record you didn't expect to come up, it will at least be accessible. The index of the transcripts you prepared earlier (when developing your Working Outline) can be very useful here.

[B] Know the Cases

The judges might ask you about some of the major cases relied upon by you or your opponent, especially the facts. Indeed, after a lawyer invokes a case during oral argument, the next question he will often hear is "And what were the facts of that case, counsel?" This judge is trying to see if you are stretching the language of the case beyond its true holding, or if there were some facts that justified the holding but which are absent or different here. Therefore, you must not only be prepared to recite the relevant facts of the cases you cite, but also to explain why each case is not distinguishable from the present case.

By the same token, you should be familiar with the facts of the major cases your opponent cites, and be prepared to distinguish them, so that if a judge shows an interest in any of these cases, you have a persuasive response.

If you can remember the facts of the cases, fine. But don't take any chances. Bring a copy of each major case with you, and have key parts of each underlined or otherwise marked so you can turn to the relevant parts quickly and smoothly. Even if you remember the facts of a case, a judge (or opposing counsel) might remember them differently. If you have a copy of the case there, you can simply read the relevant part to the court to clear up any misconceptions.

If there are one or two *very* important cases on which your case turns, and it is likely that the facts or language of these cases will come up, don't bring a copy of these cases; bring the volumes of the official reports in which these cases appear! When you are asked about one of these cases, reach for the book, hold it so the court can see it, and read from the relevant part. This leaves no doubt that you are relying on the real thing, not your memory or your notes.

Be sure to Shepardize the main cases and check for statutory changes before you argue. There is often a substantial delay (several months or more) between the time briefs are filed and oral argument is held. A lot can happen in this time. During this period, read over advance sheets and keep an eye open for anything new that might affect your case. If something new does come up, inform the court by letter and mention it at oral argument. Consider doing this even where the new authority is adverse to your position (and somehow deal with this new authority). The court may appreciate your candor, and they might have found the authority anyway. But do not take up valuable oral argument time with *minor* new cases. You are there to win, not to educate with trivia.

[C] Anticipate Questions

Sit down and write a list of every potential weakness in your case. List every reasonable argument your opponent made. List every reasonable argument your opponent *could* have made.

"Reasonable" means an argument that might seem persuasive to someone of normal intelligence. The fact that you find an argument unreasonable does not necessarily mean that some judge would also find it unreasonable. You are an advocate for one side, and you may have persuaded yourself that your side is right. Detach yourself from this attitude and imagine how someone not so involved in the case might see it. In fact, to be safe, try to imagine how someone who has prejudices *against* your position might see it, and what arguments he would come up with. You might ask a friend, spouse, or another lawyer to read your brief and your opponent's brief and ask them what weaknesses they see in your case.

When you finish writing your list of weaknesses, think of an answer to each one. If you can, think of more than one answer to each one.

Here is one useful time-saving device. When you read your opponents' brief and see a new argument, think of one or more responses to it and make a note of this right away. Later, when preparing for oral argument, you will find these notes quite useful.

Be especially prepared for *procedural* questions, such as "But was there an objection to that evidence at trial, counsel?" You are probably most interested in the substantive questions of law in the case, but often the judges will seek a way to duck those issues by holding that they were not properly raised or preserved for appeal. Be ready for this.

When you go in to argue your appeal, you should know every potential argument against you — and your answer to it — so well that you feel that you are ready for just about any question and nothing will surprise you. This feeling of self-assurance will improve the quality of your whole argument, as well as ensure that your answers to the questions are the best answers you can give.

[D] Prepare a Short Recitation of the Facts

Often the judges will want the appellant's counsel to recite the facts of the case at the outset of the argument. Sometimes, you will wish to recite the facts without waiting to be asked. Either way, you should have a short recitation prepared in advance. Unlike the give-and-take argument you hope to elicit for the bulk of your argument time, the recitation of the facts is more like a short speech, and you should write down a list of those facts you want to include.

The basic principles for preparing a recitation of the facts are the same as those for writing the Statement of Facts. Tell a good story (chronologically), stress the facts that help you, and deflate those which hurt you, while obeying the rules regarding the appellate court's review of the facts.

There is, however, a key difference between your recitation of the facts and the Statement of Facts in your brief: you must be much more selective in your oral recitation. Your time for oral argument is *very short*, and you want to spend as much of it as possible answering the judge's questions. You don't want to spend eight or ten minutes of a thirty minute argument reciting the facts. Therefore, select the *key* facts that relate to the issues you intend to argue. Do not include unimportant details. If you can do so without breaking up your story, omit facts relating to issues you do not intend to argue (i.e., the issues on which the case is less likely to be decided).

In other words, keep your recitation of the facts as short and sweet as you can.

[E] Prepare a Speech Outline

The outline of your oral argument, or Speech Outline, should be very different from the Outline of Argument in your brief. It should be much shorter. If the judges do ask questions, your allotted time will pass very quickly. So select only two or three major issues for your outline. You cannot reasonably expect to get through more.

[F] What to Include in Your Speech Outline

Select the issues on which the case is most likely to turn. This may include the strongest arguments against you as well as the strongest ones in your favor. Often, for example, it is essential that you address your opponent's argument that the alleged error was "harmless error."

Select the issues that tie into *your theme*. The theme is your main instrument for turning around judges who have already written a draft opinion against you.

Arrange your two or three issues in order of importance, i.e., how important you think it is for you to address them in oral argument. It is possible — if the questioning is especially active — that you may spend most or all of your allotted time on the *first issue*! Keeping your issues in the same chronological order as how they arise in the facts is only a minor goal in arranging the order of the issues. It is more important to cover the most important issues.

Usually, your argument on each issue should not include much discussion of cases. Case law *enables* a judge to rule in your favor, but seldom is it a key factor in making him *want* to rule in your favor. If the judge wants to rule in your favor, he can find cases in your brief to support his ruling.

If relevant new cases have been decided after your brief was filed, do not waste oral argument time so informing the court, unless one of the cases is *very* relevant. Simply send the court a letter regarding these cases, before oral argument if possible.

You have a much better chance of influencing the court if you mention the best *policy* arguments you made in your brief. Show how certain fundamental values likely to be held by the judges will be affected by a proposed rule. Explain how a proposed rule might operate in the "real world," i.e., how it might affect the day-to-day practices of courts, administrative agencies, businesses, police officers, etc. These arguments should fit into your theme. They can be especially effective with judges who are not familiar with the inner workings of a certain industry or activity.

If you can, include in your Speech Outline examples and analysis involving lawyers or judges and common experiences that judges are likely to have had. If your case involves an issue of real property law, think of an example involving renting a law office, buying a home, or investing in a small apartment house. If your case involves the police stopping a car, discuss how a judge or lawyer might react in a similar situation. (Do not, however, ask the judges directly, "How would you feel if you were stopped?" Some judges might be offended by such questioning.) When you do this, you will often be amazed at how the judges light up. After hearing a calendar full of many dull soliloquies on case law, most judges will be delighted to hear and discuss something down-to-earth, which invariably reminds them of things that have happened to them.

If there are a few key *facts* that help your case, work them into your Speech Outline, even if you already included them in your recitation of facts.

When you have selected the policy arguments, examples, facts, and analogies you wish to include in your Speech Outline, *list the best ones first*. This ensures that, if your time for argument gets short, you will have given the court your best arguments.

[G] Prepare a Conclusion

The final image the court has of you should be a strong one, so prepare a strong Conclusion. It should be very short, no more than three or four sentences. It should include only two items: (1) what you want (affirmance, reversal for new trial, reversal for dismissal, etc.), and (2) a brief reminder of your strongest one or two arguments. This is what you want ringing in the judges' ears when they meet after oral argument to discuss and vote on the case.

[H] Preparing Respondent's Speech Outline

If you are representing the Respondent, you should also prepare a Speech Outline, following the above principles.

As Respondent, however, you will have the advantage of seeing the judges' reactions to Appellant's argument before you argue, and this should affect your decisions as to what points to emphasize. To keep your presentation smooth, these points should be *worked into* your Speech Outline *just before you get up to argue*.

[I] Rehearse

If you have time and someone to help you, a rehearsal (or "moot court") can improve your oral argument.

One way to rehearse is to stand in front of a mirror or friend and give a speech. This has a limited value. While it can make your delivery flow more smoothly, it can also lead to the argument you actually give to be less spontaneous and lively. Worse than that, this type of rehearsal prepares you for the wrong type of activity. It prepares you to give a speech, and it gets you used to the idea that you are there to deliver and complete a speech. It does not prepare you for the give-and-take of the questioning you hope to elicit from the judges.

A better way to rehearse is to have a friend review the briefs and your list of tough questions and then make you defend your case. Your friend should ask easy questions, hard questions, and even "off-the-wall" questions to expose you to thinking on your feet. Your friend should also quiz you on the record and the cases.

Rehearse on your feet. Stand at a podium, with your papers at hand, and have your friend sit at a desk in front of you.

Hold your rehearsal at least two or three days before the oral argument. If the rehearsal discloses any areas in which you need further preparation, this should allow you enough time before the argument in which to do it.

If you can arrange it, have your rehearsal taped — preferably video-taped — and then review the tape. This can tell you whether you have any nervous or distracting habits, such as saying "um" or "you know" frequently, tapping your pen, looking at the ceiling, or leaning on the podium.

After a good rehearsal, you should be ready for just about anything.

[J] Scout the Court

If you have the time, sit in on a few arguments heard by the court which will hear your case. You may be able to tell whether the court is eager to ask questions, or quiet and not very responsive. This could affect how you structure or present your argument. If the court is quiet, speak slowly, pause, and somehow encourage the judges to let you know what they are thinking.

Watch each judge, and get some idea of what he or she responds to during argument. Note if the judges show that they like or dislike certain mannerisms or styles of attorneys presenting their arguments. Note how formal the court expects the attorneys to act.

Check where you are supposed to sit and lay out your papers, whether the presiding judge warns counsel before time runs out, where the clock is —

and where the bathroom is! You don't want to worry about such things on the day you argue.

[K] Find Out How Much the Court Prepares for Oral Argument

There is one more reason to scout the court: to discover how much the court usually knows about a case before it hears oral argument. You don't want to spend the first five minutes of your argument explaining the facts of your case if the court is already quite familiar with the facts. Nor do you want to waste additional time explaining elementary rules that the court already knows from reading the briefs.

On the other hand, if you incorrectly assume that the court knows the facts and issues in the case, you might argue for ten or fifteen minutes only to have a judge lean over the bench and say, "Counsel, just what is this case all about?" You have just wasted half your time and probably annoyed the judges.

So find out what to expect, and then tailor your approach to the court's level of preparation. If you don't have time to scout the court yourself, call some attorneys who have argued before it and ask them what to expect.

Some presiding judges have a practice of reciting a litany along the following lines, at the outset of each argument: "Counsel, the Court has carefully read all the briefs and is familiar with the facts and issues in the case, so please limit your oral argument to anything new." This can paralyze a novice attorney who comes to discuss the very "facts and issues" that the judge just said he does not want to hear. But watch how the other attorneys handle this. They might not take it seriously. Often, a presiding judge will make such a statement merely in an effort to hurry along his calendar. But once the argument begins, it may turn out that one or more of the judges is *not* as intimately familiar with the case as the presiding judge suggested. The best course of action might be to politely ignore the presiding judge's litany. Do not be bullied into waiving or truncating your argument, if your argument might win the case for you.

[L] Get Some Sleep

Get a good night's sleep the night before you argue. You need to be as alert as you can be when you must listen to a judge's question, understand it, and respond quickly with the best answer you can give. (I once made the mistake of taking a "red-eye special," leaving from San Francisco at midnight, to Washington, D.C., to appear in the Supreme Court the next day. If you must travel far, do it at least a day before you argue.)

[M] What to Do with Your Client

Think carefully before you invite your client to oral argument.

Sometimes, when you see a lawyer argue a case, you will see one of the judges looking around the audience. He might be playing a little game called "Guess which one is the client." He knows the client is there, because the lawyer is spending a good portion of his argument praising the client and berating the opposition and the trial court. This is not an effective argument, but this is what many clients like to hear.

Even the best attorneys can succumb to this temptation to please the client. Deal with it ahead of time. If you'd like your client to attend (or your client insists on attending), tell him what to expect — and what *not* to expect: a soliloquy on what a good guy he is and what a bum the other guy is. Your goal at oral argument is victory, not massaging your client's ego.

§ 5.5 WHAT TO DO AT ORAL ARGUMENT

This is your chance to *engage* the judges. The worst thing you can do is *read* a speech to them. The next worst is to *memorize* a speech to them. The best approach is to *talk* to them — face-to-face and heart-to-heart — about why a gut sense of justice requires a ruling for your client.

Initiate a conversation. Instead of acting like an accomplished orator, using histrionic gestures, florid phrases, and the like, use normal language in a normal tone of voice. Instead of writing out a speech to read or memorize, write only an *outline* of what you plan to cover and simply glance at it from time to time. This relaxed attitude will make it much easier for reticent judges to participate in a discussion with you.

[A] Your Opening Lines

First greet the judges and tell them who you are and whom you represent. "Good morning, your honors. I am Alex Paul and I represent the appellant, Damian Jay."

Next — if you represent the appellant — ask to reserve rebuttal time. "I would like to reserve five minutes for rebuttal." If you fail to ask for this, it might not be offered to you. The importance of rebuttal is discussed below.

Next, state some facts. How many facts depends on the court's level of preparation (which you have determined by scouting the court). If the court is usually not very familiar with the facts of the cases it hears, give *Fact Recitation Number 1*. This is your prepared recitation of selected facts that tells the judges enough to permit them to understand the case. (Do not *read* your recitation to the court. Glance down at it when you need to — then look up and *talk* to the judges.)

If the court usually is familiar with the facts, give *Fact Recitation Number 2*. This is a very brief statement of just a few key facts. Its purpose is merely to refresh the court's recollection about the case and ease the mental transition the judges must make from the case they heard right before yours. You might begin Number 2 by saying "As the court may recall, this case involves. . . ."

If you are not sure whether the court is familiar with the facts, ask whether the court would like a recitation of the facts. If the answer is yes, deliver Fact Recitation Number 1. If the answer is no, deliver Fact Recitation Number 2.

If you believe the court will be familiar with the facts, deliver Number 2, but have Number 1 available. It sometimes happens that the judges are usually familiar with the facts, but for some reason are not in this case. As soon as this becomes apparent, deliver Number 1.

Next, give a *brief outline* of what you intend to cover. "My brief discusses five reasons for reversal. I plan to argue only two of them, and submit the others on the brief — unless the court has any questions about them. The two I will argue are as follows. First, the gun should have been suppressed, as it was found due to an arrest made without probable cause. Second, appellant's admission that he was at the scene of the robbery should have been suppressed, as this was obtained in violation of his *Miranda* rights."

Now pause. Give the judges a chance to break in with "I do have some questions about your second point, counsel," or some other indication of their concerns.

[B] Answering Questions

Your speech outline is a guide for you to fall back on if no questions from the judges are forthcoming, or if their questioning becomes momentarily exhausted. Generally, that is the only purpose of your speech outline. It is not something that you must get through at the cost of answering the judges' questions.

The important points in your Speech Outline — especially your *theme* — should be *worked into your answers* to judges' questions, wherever appropriate.

Your frame of mind should be very flexible. You should be willing to depart from your Speech Outline at any time — even in the middle of a point you are making — to answer a judge's question. It does not matter that the question is dealt with somewhere else on your Outline. Answer it as soon as it is asked. Don't say "I already answered that" or "As I said before." If the judge had understood what you said before and found it persuasive, he wouldn't be asking the question now. He is indicating what bothers him about the case, so take advantage of this opportunity to address his concern.

Similarly, never answer a question with "I'll get to that point in just a minute, your Honor." This would tell the judge that you care more about your speech than her concerns. Her question lets you know what she thinks is the heart of the case, so why not go straight to that heart, instead of wasting some of your precious time on something else?

A more difficult problem arises when one judge interrupts a discussion you are having with another judge. If Judge #2's question relates to the discussion, integrate your answer into your discussion with Judge #1, so you are speaking to both judges. If, however, Judge #2's question is unrelated to the discussion, you must decide whether to answer it then or put if off. If you have more to say to Judge #1, you risk losing the opportunity to persuade him if you turn to Judge #2's question. In this case, it might be wise to tell Judge #2 — as politely as you can — that you will answer his question just as soon as you finish answering Judge #1. If you must do this, don't forget to answer that question when you are done with Judge #1.

Remember, this is your case and you are there to win. Making the judges like you usually helps you to win. But sometimes you must risk some dislike in order to maintain control of your objective: to persuade a *majority* of the judges to rule your way.

A similar problem arises when one judge starts to dominate the discussion with questions on some tangential point that he finds intellectually interesting but which is not important to the resolution of the appeal. Find a way to return the discussion to the relevant issues. Do this as politely as possible. Your oral argument time is very limited, and you can't afford to waste it entertaining a judge. You are there to win, not to play.

Pay particular attention to questions from "swing" judges. If you have a 3-judge panel and you know that one judge is probably sympathetic to your position and another is probably against you, give particular attention to the third judge — the swing vote. Spend a bit more time on her questions and her concerns. Don't ignore the other two, however. By giving good answers to hostile questions from the judge who is against you, you may be answering some of the concerns of the swing judge. By amplifying upon friendly comments or questions from the judge who is on your side, you also might impress the swing judge. This might also accomplish one more thing to help you win: you give your friendly judge ammunition to use in any conference among the judges that will occur after oral argument.

[C] Listen Carefully

When a judge asks you a question, listen very carefully to his *whole* question before you decide how to answer it. During your preparation for oral argument, you made guesses about what questions are likely to be asked. The first few words of the judge's question may give you the impression that he is asking a certain question you expected, when in fact he means to ask something slightly (or very) different. If you spend time answering questions that were not asked and fail to answer questions that were, you waste your time, annoy the judges, and fail to deal with their concerns about the case. So listen carefully to the whole question.

Sometimes a judge's question is awkwardly phrased or simply unclear. Try to figure out what meaning he has attached to it. If you can't, politely ask him to restate it — perhaps by blaming yourself for your "inability to understand the question." This may seem difficult, but it is better than spending time answering a question that was not asked.

Be alert for the question *behind* the question. Sometimes a question is clearly worded, but it is not the real question on the judge's mind. If you are arguing that there was no probable cause to arrest Appellant, a judge might ask, "But how much is needed in order to constitute probable cause?" This sounds like it calls for an answer generally stating the law, but it also suggests that the judge is not convinced that there was inadequate cause *here*. If so, your general statement of the law, in response to his purported question, is not likely to change his mind. Go further and explain why the facts known to the police officer in *your* case were not sufficient to constitute probable cause to arrest.

Questions are windows to the judge's mind, but sometimes the windows are a bit smudged.

Do not assume that every question from the bench is hostile to your position. Sometimes a judge who is friendly to your position will ask a rhetorical question *through* you (not *to* you) to another judge whom he is trying to convince. Listen very carefully to detect if this is the case. If so, amplify the "question" if you can. If you have nothing to add, simply express your agreement.

[D] Tone

Your tone should be serious and aggressive, but reasonable. Do not exaggerate or use unduly strong adjectives (such as "clear," or "outrageous"). Be honest: don't overstate the record or an authority.

Never talk down to a judge. Because you have been working on this case for some time (and you might even specialize in this area of the law), you might know much more about the subject than some of the judges. You might even be smarter than some of the judges. Nevertheless, you must deal with each of their questions and comments respectfully and reasonably. Do not show surprise if a very elementary question is asked. Just take it in stride and answer it.

On the other hand, don't be intimidated by the judges. Many appellate judges are former trial attorneys, and some take particular delight in "cross-examining" a hapless young lawyer into a corner. Listen carefully to the judge's question and — pausing to think if you need to — give the best answer you can. Never let the judge's *tone* dictate your answer. If he says, "Counsel, of course you would concede that . . .," make no such concession unless (1) it is unreasonable to do so, and (2) it doesn't cost you your case. Usually, any concession you make should have been well thought out ahead of time. If fact, if you can *volunteer* your concession before being asked to do so, this will show that you are reasonable and in control of your case. This can also save time that otherwise might be spent on an unimportant point.

If you have any doubt as to whether it is wise to concede a point, *don't concede it.* Just say that you are not prepared to concede it, or submit the point "on the brief."

The most important thing to keep in mind when a judge tries to intimidate you is that you are there to win the case, not to please the judge. If you must argue with the judge, do so as respectfully and courteously as you can, but do argue with him. Sometimes a judge will argue just to test a position he agrees with, or just to have some fun. If he is arguing because he believes what he is saying, he will probably respect you for defending your position. But even if he might be offended by your refusal to accept what he says, you must take that chance and argue your case. Remember, he is not the only judge on the panel. If you back down in front of him or concede a point, you may lose the votes of the other judges.

If a judge presses you with tough questions, do not bluff, evade, or squirm — physically, verbally, or intellectually. Look him in the eye and state the best answer you have. If he doesn't accept it, do not behave as if you have lost the point. Don't feel that you have to think of another (usually weak) response on the spot, and don't wriggle away to another issue — as in "Well, even if that evidence shouldn't have been admitted, the error was not prejudicial." If you want to move to another issue, do it because you want to, not because you are forced to.

The point is this: do not look weak in front of the court. If *you* seem weak, your *case* seems weak, and you risk losing the votes of the judges whose minds were not made up before the argument began. If your point really *is* weak, you should not be raising it at oral argument.

[E] Beware the Straw Man

"Counsel, suppose the facts were slightly different, in the following respect. . . . Would the rule you propose still apply?"

When you hear this, watch out. The judge might be setting you up with a "straw man": an easy target for a rebuttal that will blow down not only the straw man (the application of the rule to the hypothetical facts he suggested), but your whole proposal with it.

Sometimes you must accept the straw man and deal with it. The rule you propose clearly does encompass the judge's facts, and you would appear unreasonable if you did not concede this. If so, you must be prepared to show that application of the rule to those facts does not lead to absurd or unfair results. The court will not wish to adopt a rule which will be a poor one to use in other cases. Often, however, you can reasonably avoid dealing with the straw man. "Your honor, the rule I propose need not encompass that situation, for the following reason."

It is very difficult to decide on your feet how to approach the straw man. Think of a few potential straw men during your preparation for oral argument and plan how to handle them.

[F] Use Your Strong Points

To field "straw men" and other tricky or unexpected questions, it helps to have a quick mind. But it is difficult to train your mind to become any quicker than it is, and even the quickest cannot always respond to every question directly.

You will find that you can respond to most questions simply by repeating some variation of one of your strongest points — or, even better, your theme.

If you are appealing from a summary judgment granted against you, your strongest point might be that there was a triable issue of fact on some issue, because one of your affidavits would support a jury verdict for you on that issue. If a judge asks you some unexpected question on the law of negligence and you are unable to think of a direct answer to it, try to think of a way to respond by referring to your key affidavit.

Make a list of your strong points — no more than three or four — and have it in front of you at the podium. When you have trouble thinking of an answer to question, glance at the list and select the most responsive point. Usually, your answer will be persuasive as well as responsive, as it will keep the discussion focused on the points that give you the best chance at victory.

[G] Focus on the Judges — Not Your Opponent

To many lawyers, opposing counsel is seen as the enemy, to be opposed, rebutted, and embarrassed on every minor point at every opportunity. This attitude will cause you to misdirect your attention and your energy. You are at oral argument to convince the judges, not your opponent. So focus on the judges. Watch them and listen to them, and try to discern what bothers them.

Do not feel compelled to respond to every point your opponent wrote in his brief or argued at oral argument, or else you will find yourself wasting valuable oral argument time on points that did not impress the judges anyway.

§ 5.6 RESPONDENT'S ARGUMENT

As respondent, you have a big advantage in going second, because you can first watch the judges while your opponent is arguing. You can see how the judges react to the appellant's arguments and to the case generally. Then, when it is your turn to argue, you already have some idea about where to focus your time and effort. If the judges brushed off or ignored certain arguments made by appellant, you need not waste much time with those. If one or more judges seemed impressed by other arguments made by appellant — or if the judges raised issues not initiated by the appellant — go directly to those issues, thereby getting maximum benefit from your limited oral argument time. Thus, you may obtain some very valuable last-minute knowledge not available to the appellant.

Don't waste this knowledge, but use it. Even though you (like appellant) should have prepared a Speech Outline before oral argument began, you must be fully prepared to abandon part or all of the outline if this seems advisable from what you learn about the judges during appellant's argument. If you prepared to argue issues #1 and #2A, and you just heard the judges ask about nothing but #2B (or even #3), you might be foolish in sticking to your original, now obsolete plan. Do mention, of course, the strongest points in your Outline, even if these issues were not discussed during the appellant's argument.

You need not discuss the issues in the same order that Appellant discussed them. Your presentation will be much smoother if you instead follow the order set out in your Speech Outline (or those parts of it that remain pertinent after you've heard the judges' responses to Appellant's argument). Work the points you wish to emphasize (and your rebuttals to what Appellant just said) *into* your Speech Outline.

§ 5.7 APPELLANT'S REBUTTAL

As appellant, you have an opportunity to recoup some of respondent's advantage of watching the judges. If you reserved time for rebuttal, you can do *the same thing*: watch the judges during the opposing argument, and then tailor your response to the concerns expressed by the judges.

Often, you can learn even more than respondent, because many judges will not begin to "warm up" to the case and reveal their concerns until after they have been thinking about the case for twenty or thirty minutes. In other words, they might be quiet during your opening argument, and begin to speak during respondent's argument.

Reserve enough time for an adequate rebuttal — at least five minutes. In a thirty minute argument, even ten minutes might be appropriate for rebuttal. Subtract this from your allotted time, and ask the presiding judge to tell you when your opening time is up (or keep an eye on the clock).

Unless you are in the middle of an important exchange with a judge, end your opening argument on time. If you go over, you risk a deduction from your rebuttal time. Your rebuttal time is much less than the full argument time the respondent has after he has watched the judges, so preserve what little of it you have.

While respondent is arguing, keep your head up and your eyes on the judges. Do not look down at your notes or the record, and don't watch opposing counsel. Tell your co-counsel not to pass you notes unless it is extremely important. Take advantage of what you can learn about what the *judges* are thinking now.

Immediately before you get up to deliver your rebuttal, *use* what you have learned about the judges during your opening argument and respondent's argument to decide how you can best use your rebuttal time. Do not simply complete the "speech" you didn't have time to finish during your opening argument. Because of your just-acquired new knowledge about the judges, that "speech" is now obsolete.

In deciding how to frame your rebuttal, keep in mind the rule that rebuttal is not supposed to be used to raise new issues not discussed by the respondent. Some courts enforce this rule.

Since rebuttal time is very short, do not expect to be able to discuss more than two points. If the judges ask questions, you might not even get past your first point. So make sure that your first point is the most important point you must cover in order to win the case. You now have the maximum amount of knowledge about the judges' key concerns. Don't avoid the one tough issue and deal with an easier, unimportant issue just because you have a better answer to the easier issue, and don't just continue with your opening speech. This is your last chance to win the case, so give it your best shot.

§ 5.8 WHEN TO STOP

If it appears that you have won *a certain point*, stop arguing it. If you continue to give further reasons why your position is right, you waste time and you risk giving a judge an idea that could jeopardize your point.

If it appears that you have won *the appeal*, sit down. Further argument might open up a problem. Don't "fill up" your remaining time discussing minor issues. The court will appreciate your saving it some time.

Suppose you represent the respondent and you have just heard appellant's counsel deliver an unconvincing opening argument. If you are *sure* the court intends to rule in your favor, do not present your argument. Your argument could give a judge ideas against your case. Also, if you argue, your opponent will then be entitled to rebut your argument (if he has reserved rebuttal time). If you don't argue, there is nothing to rebut.

To make sure that you have won, however, you should stand up and ask the court if it has any questions for you, before you rest your case.

If you are arguing for either side and you do not think you have won, do not sit down before your time is up merely because the judges are giving you a hard time. It is frustrating fighting a brick wall, but that's what you're paid for. Keep arguing. You never know what might happen.

§ 5.9 MISCELLANEOUS TIPS

If you mention a case during your argument, do not interrupt the flow of your presentation by giving its official cite. Simply refer the court to the page of your brief on which the citation appears.

Occasionally, it can be helpful to use visual aids such as photographs and diagrams at oral argument. To avoid quarrels about the accuracy of any visual aid you prepare, use exhibits that were admitted into evidence in the trial court. Make sure that the trial court clerk has sent these exhibits to the appellate court and the appellate court clerk has the exhibit you want available for you to use at oral argument.

If you are asked a question about the record and don't know the answer, say so and request permission to supply an answer by letter within five days. Usually, this request will be granted.

Avoid confusing details. It is much harder to absorb information by ear than by eye. The judge can read your brief at his own pace, and can study or skim over details as he chooses. But an oral presentation cannot be so easily controlled. So leave out unimportant facts. Do not say "The accident occurred on March 21, 2003" unless the exact date is significant.

Quotations from the record or a case or statute can be very effective in appropriate circumstances, but they can also break your rapport with the court, since you must read the quotation. So keep the quotation very short, read it slowly, and don't use more than one or two quotations in your argument.

Jokes and quips can help establish rapport with the court, but they can also cause you trouble. What may seem funny or witty to you might be unfunny — or worse, offensive — to one of the judges. Jokes are especially risky if the case involves a very serious subject, such as a killing. Usually, a safe rule to follow is this: do not be the first one to crack a joke or quip. Wait until you are "invited" to do so by a *judge* attempting some witticism.

A similar problem can arise with metaphors and examples. If you call a police officer's monotone delivery of a *Miranda* warning "as meaningless as a recital of the Pledge of Allegiance [or the Lord's Prayer]," you risk offending one or more of the judges. Generally, avoid metaphors that raise any possibility of touching some patriotic or religious nerve, or contain any hint of racism, sexism, ageism (a sensitive subject for some older judges), or any other ism. It just isn't worth the risk. Think of some other metaphor.

§ 5.10 STYLE

On the appellate level, style is often overrated as a factor in affecting the outcome of the case. What you say is much more important than how you say it. The judges may admire the lawyer with an impressive vocabulary, bold voice, and commanding "presence," but they are no more likely to rule for him than for a quiet lawyer who calmly and carefully explains why his position is the correct one. Just be yourself, and follow some simple rules regarding effective communication to a small group of people.

Avoid doing anything that might distract the judges from listening to what you have to say. Don't wear loud clothes, wander away from the podium, tap your foot, or say "um" frequently. One prominent appellate lawyer has summed up this principle with what he calls the "pink tie" rule: "Don't wear a pink tie to court, not because it is tacky, but because instead of listening to you, the judge won't be able to keep his eyes off that damn pink tie!" MILLMAN, CRIMINAL APPELLATE PRACTICE MANUAL 415 (Cal. State Public Defender 2d ed. 1982). Former Supreme Court Justice Robert Jackson put it slightly differently: "You will not be stopped from arguing if you wear a race-track suit or sport a rainbow necktie. You will just create a first impression that you have strayed in at the wrong bar." Jackson, *Advocacy Before the Supreme Court*, 37 A.B.A. J. 801, 862 (1951).

Since you are trying to engage the judges in a dialogue rather than give a speech, be somewhat informal and conversational. Relax — but do not slouch or otherwise appear undignified.

Maintain eye contact with *all* the judges, not just the presiding judge or the judge who is asking most of the questions. Eye contact with a reticent judge can sometimes encourage her to say something that will reveal her concerns. Keep your head up, not down on your notes. Just glance at your notes from time to time.

Speak loudly enough for all the judges to hear you. One or more of the judges might be elderly and a bit hard of hearing. Speak slowly enough that the judges can easily follow your chain of logic. Pause periodically so they can ask questions without feeling that they are interrupting you.

Above all, *it is essential that you speak with conviction* (even if your client has many convictions!). If you don't believe in your case, why should anyone else? If you have doubts about whether your case should win, find a way to put them aside for thirty minutes. Act, if you have to. If the court gets the feeling that you are just doing your job and don't believe what you are saying, you are likely to lose the case.

§ 5.11 DEALING WITH ANXIETY

If you are anxious *before* you argue, don't worry about it. This is normal, and it need not interfere with your performance. Even the most experienced lawyers get pre-argument butterflies.

If you display anxiety *during* your argument, however, this may cause a number of problems. Your delivery might be weak, you might be inattentive to questions, and you might not be able to think of your best answers to them. Also, you might be tempted to end your anxiety by ending your argument before your time is up.

Anxiety is caused by fear, in this case a fear that you will perform poorly during the argument. Fear is overcome by confidence. There are several ways to gain this confidence.

[A] Get Experience

The more times you argue, the more you will realize that you can argue well, and the more confidence you will gain.

[B] Practice

Rehearsals can help give you the confidence that you can answer any question thrown at you.

[C] Prepare Well

When the first question is asked and you realize that you've already thought of a good answer, this tends to cure your anxiety better than anything else can. You then feel ready for anything, and you relax.

Concentrate on the issues and the judges — not yourself. If you immerse your mind in your objective — convincing the judges — you will tend to be less self-conscious and therefore less anxious about what everyone is thinking about you.

Chapter 6

PERSUADING AN APPELLATE COURT TO HEAR YOUR CASE

§ 6.1 THE PROBLEM

Attorneys often need relief from an appellate court where there is no *right* to appeal and the court need not accept the case for review on the merits. This is the situation when you petition for certiorari in the United States Supreme Court, petition for hearing in a state supreme court (where some intermediate appellate court has already heard the appeal-by-right), or petition for some extraordinary writ (such as mandamus, prohibition, or habeas corpus).

Two prominent features distinguish these situations from the ordinary appeal: The court has total, unbridled discretion as to whether it will accept the case for resolution on the merits; and it seldom gives any reason for refusing to accept it.

In most courts, the great majority of these petitions are quickly denied. Appellate courts are quite busy working on cases they *have* accepted (or must accept), and they must limit their caseloads. Sometimes the court sends a simple notice conveying the bad news: "Petition denied."

So how do you persuade a court to hear your case? This is a difficult question, and the answer will vary from court to court and time to time, depending upon the current interests of the judges and how busy they are when you file your petition.

Since courts seldom state reasons for denying petitions, there is no substantial body of law indicating *why* courts grant or deny such petitions. A few cases and court rules discuss this in general terms (e.g., "an important question of law"), but these give only limited guidance.

§ 6.2 THE BASIC PRINCIPLE

No matter when you file your petition or what court you file it in, there is one basic principle you might use as your guide: To induce a court to *hear* your case, persuading the court that you are right on the merits usually is *not enough*.

The attitude of most appellate courts may be summed up (rather crudely) as follows: "*So what* if you (and your client) were mistreated by the lower court? Given the volume of litigation these days, mistakes sometimes happen. If we took every one of these cases, we would have no time for our *real* job — clarifying the *law* for the guidance of a broader group of people than you and your client. You've had your day in court, so goodbye."[2]

Breaking through this wall is difficult, but it can be done. Appellate courts do grant petitions in certain cases, and those cases tend to have certain features.

Here are some things to look for in your case that might enhance the likelihood of getting a hearing. If your record permits, emphasize them in your petition.

§ 6.3 SHOW SERIOUS INJUSTICE BY THE LOWER COURT

Showing that you are right on the merits usually will not be enough to get you a hearing. If, however, the record permits you to go *beyond* merely "being right" to a showing of serious injustice, then stress this.

Procedural injustice is rarely enough. In a criminal case, the appellate court might not care much that your motion to suppress evidence was improperly denied, if the record shows that your client in fact committed the crime. But the record suggests that he might well be *innocent*, the court might be more inclined to grant a hearing. For *this* purpose, point to persuasive testimony for your client on the question of innocence.

Similarly, in a civil case, show (if you can) that the lower court did not merely misunderstand the law, but behaved arbitrarily or injudiciously. It might also help to stress that large amounts of money are involved (a large damage award, an injunction that can be obeyed only by spending a lot of money, etc.).

§ 6.4 SHOW CONFLICTS OR LACK OF CLARITY IN THE LAW

Appellate judges see as one of their main jobs resolving conflicts in decisions of lower courts, whether they be lower appellate courts or trial courts. Similarly, if lower court decisions are murky, appellate judges often want to clarify the rules. So emphasize such conflicts or lack of clarity when petitioning for a hearing.

When the conflicting lower court decisions are reported, you can guide the appellate court to them simply by giving correct citations. But sometimes

---

2 Or: "Your case is touching.
        Your tale is sad.
        But we're too busy.
        So it's too bad!"

you will be aware of decisions that are unreported, especially if they are trial court decisions. Find some way to bring these to the appellate court's attention. Consider attaching copies of these decisions to your petition. If a decision is not available, consider attaching an affidavit from a lawyer who handled the case, explaining what happened.

When you are arguing the *merits* of your case, you often to try to reconcile possibly conflicting decisions, i.e., to show that decisions that appear to be against you really are not. When petitioning for a hearing, however, your strategy should be different: Try to exacerbate rather than minimize any conflict in the cases.

§ 6.5 SHOW THAT THE LOWER COURT OPINION WILL CREATE A NEW, INCORRECT RULE OF LAW

If the lower court opinion is to be *published*, the effect of the decision may go well beyond your client to the general public. If the opinion states a new rule of law that is incorrect, the appellate court will probably want to get rid of that opinion.

So point this out when you can — *except* in one situation. In some jurisdictions, an appellate court (such as the California Supreme Court) has the authority to "depublish" lower appellate court decisions. The decision stands, but it will not appear in the published reports. This may help "the law," but it does your client no good at all. Avoid stressing that the opinion in your case is to be published if the court can resolve that problem simply by ordering "depublication."

§ 6.6 SHOW THAT AN ISSUE IN THE CASE IS IMPORTANT TO SOCIETY

Where possible, show that some institutions in society (hospitals, the police, school administrators, insurance companies, etc.) need guidance on some issue in your case. Unless court rules prohibit this, attach newspaper clippings, magazine articles, or other material that demonstrates the concerns of people working in or with these institutions.

If, for example, your case involves the legality of the detention of a student by a high school official, show the court (if you can) that educators have expressed concern about the paucity of legal guidance on school detentions. Ask affected organizations to send *amicus curiae* briefs or letters to the court explaining their concerns.

If your case contains an issue involving the validity of a certain contractual provision, find a way to show the court that the provision is commonly used in form contracts throughout the jurisdiction. If the validity of a local ordinance is at issue, show that other cities or counties have enacted similar ordinances.

§ 6.7 PIQUE THE COURT'S INTEREST

Even if the legal issues in your case are unlikely to be significant to anyone other than your client, there might be something fascinating about them.

Suppose, for example, that some aspect of your case resembles the famous "lifeboat" cases that most lawyers (and judges) read about in law school, where some stranded seamen dine on one of their brethren in order to survive. Such cases rarely occur, but many judges would just love to sink their intellectual teeth into one.

If part of your case involves baseball, movie stars, steamy sex, or another popular subject, emphasize it. The judge who reads your petition might want to tell his friends that he was one of the judges who decided "The Barry Bonds Case" or "The Case of the Horny Lawyer."

§ 6.8 FIND OUT ISSUES THE COURT CURRENTLY CARES ABOUT

If you know which panel of judges will review your petition, try to learn what issues the court cares about. Look over recent decisions by the court in the area of law involved in your case.

You might also discuss your case with some practitioner who is familiar with the court. He or she might suggest an approach that might catch the court's eye.

§ 6.9 SHOW IMMEDIACY — THAT THE ISSUE MUST BE RESOLVED NOW

Often appellate judges hope that a difficult issue will evaporate, so they will not have to decide it. If the trial court denied your pretrial motion to suppress evidence or motion for summary judgment, why should the appellate court hear your complaints now? You might win the case at trial, or the case might settle, and the court will be spared the burden of handling the case.

If your case includes such a weakness, deal with it in your petition. Here are some possible cures:

- The case will not settle, as it involves political or ideological differences, not just money.

- Given the trial court's pretrial ruling, a trial cannot save you, as it is inevitable that you will lose at trial. (For example, in a criminal case, the trial court denied your motion to suppress a confession.)

- By the time a trial or ordinary appeal occurs, the damage will have been done. (For example, the trial court denied a preliminary injunction to restrain injury to property or to restrain election campaign law violations.)

- This case presents a good *opportunity* for the court to clarify the law, as the facts of the case create a good vehicle for addressing the legal issues. If the case were to "wash out" at trial, the appellate court would be deprived of this opportunity.

§ 6.10 DRAFTING YOUR PETITION

Check the court's rules for what must be in the petition, whether it must be verified, etc. Make sure that the court receives copies of whatever parts of the lower court record it needs to pass on your petition.

Two points deserve special attention in drafting the petition.

First, if your case contains one or more of the attractive features discussed above, emphasize them. It does not matter that these features played only a minor role in the court below. It does not matter that your best chance for reversal on the merits lies with some other, more mundane issue. At this point, your main goal is to get your foot in the door. Once the court takes the case, you can then brief and argue the case to win the merits.

Second, put a *summary* of your petition at the very beginning. This should be short — no more than two or three pages. It should briefly summarize the key facts and state the features that might interest the court. Appellate court judges and law clerks do not want to spend a lot of time on these petitions. You have no assurance that they will read your petition carefully from beginning to end. They might just skim it or read the first few pages. Your summary at the outset will — you hope — catch their attention quickly and get them to treat your petition as worthy of serious consideration.

§ 6.11 DON'T FRET IF YOUR PETITION IS DENIED

If you follow these suggestions and still your petition is denied, don't blame yourself (or me). Following these suggestions will, at most, increase the likelihood of success from very low to fair-to-middling. You may do a great job, but your petition may be denied for reasons well beyond your control (such as the court's workload). So don't feel bad if this happens — you have lots of company.

Nevertheless, filing the petition may well be worth the effort. If you are one of the lucky few, you may salvage your client's case — and the result might be a landmark decision which emblazons your name in legal history!

THREE SAMPLE BRIEFS

Here are three briefs that were actually filed in real cases. Each arises in a different context. The first is an appellant's opening brief in a civil case. The second is an appellant's opening brief in a criminal case. And the third is a respondent's brief in a civil case.

These briefs satisfy the *form* requirements of the rules of court in the jurisdiction in which they were filed. Be sure to check the rules of your jurisdiction when preparing your brief. Some require citations to comply with the "Harvard Blue Book", and others have their own peculiar rules. Some require all briefs to be printed, and others allow typewritten briefs — if they are double-spaced.

Rules tell you the *form* of what you write, but they don't tell you *what* to write. That comes from a *concept* — the theory behind the brief. This might be a legal theory, an "emotional" theory, or some combination of the two. Before each of these three briefs is a description of "The Concept Behind This Brief."

Brief writing is problem solving. Your client has a general problem — he needs to persuade a court to reverse or affirm what another court did. Your job is to help him solve the problem. To do this, you first have to define more precisely what the *real* problem is. The "Concept Behind This Brief" explains how I defined the problem, and how I decided to try to solve it.

As you read these briefs, look for examples of tactics discussed in this book. Keep an eye out for: little facts that make my opponent look bad, selective use of *quotes* of actual language used in the record, the occasional use of *argument* in the Statement of Facts, the use of *italics* to highlight important language, the use of the *absence* of evidence, and policy arguments showing the horrible things that might happen if the court should make the unfortunate mistake of ruling against my client.

Sample Brief #1

AN APPELLANT'S OPENING BRIEF IN A CIVIL CASE

[A] THE CONCEPT BEHIND THIS BRIEF

This brief was filed in *Palmer v. Ted Stevens Honda, Inc.*

Ted Stevens was a dealer in new and used cars. Bill Palmer brought his red Ferrari to Don Alvard, one of Stevens' salesmen, and asked Alvard to sell it for him. Alvard agreed to do so, taking the car "on consignment". Alvard was to sell the car for at least $29,500, give that amount to Palmer, and keep any surplus as a commission.

Instead, Alvard reconsigned the car to another dealer, who sold the car — and then declared bankruptcy! When Palmer demanded $29,500 from Stevens, Stevens refused, saying he had never authorized Alvard to take cars on consignment. Palmer sued Stevens for the $29,500, plus punitive damages for fraud and other torts.

The jury awarded Palmer the $29,500 — plus $150,000 in punitive damages. Stevens then retained me to handle the appeal.

While reading over the trial court transcripts, I was, of course, looking for *legal* issues on which to base the appeal. But I was also looking for something else — something more important: the *real* issues. What had made the jury so angry with Stevens that they would whack him with a punitive damage award? Whatever it was, it might also anger the appellate judges. If that happened, they might find a way to slide around my legal arguments, no matter how solid they looked in the abstract. So rather than pretend the problem wasn't there and hope no one else would see it, I decided to find it myself. There might be a way to defuse it, or — better yet — to turn it to our advantage.

The jury felt that justice required them to hurt Ted Stevens, so I would have to find a way to convince the appellate judges that justice required them to reverse.

I found the real issues — or at least thought I did. From reading a cold transcript, it's not easy to capture the emotion of the courtroom and the silent reactions of the jurors. But reading between the lines, you can get some hint of the feelings pervading a trial.

Here, two things might well have angered the jurors. First, Stevens' trial lawyer seemed to be rather arrogant and obnoxious in the way he treated witnesses and argued various motions. Second, Stevens was a car dealer — an occupation that the public might see as having pretty low ethics. This was highlighted by one incident that caught my eye. Stevens' own testimony in the case was brief, and seemed on paper to be fairly straightforward. But one line stood out:

> THE COURT: Mr. Stevens, one of the jurors has asked that you remove your dark glasses.

> How any trial lawyer could allow his client to testify with dark glasses on is beyond me, but when that client is a car dealer, the situation is much worse. The lawyer's message to the jury seems clear: this guy is a such a sleazeball that we don't want you to see his eyes when he tells his tale.

So I decided to deal with these "real" issues in our brief. And I would go even further: not just to defuse these issues, but to *turn* them to our advantage. The brief would imply that — for exactly these "real" reasons — there was something unfair about the trial. Stevens had an unlikable trial lawyer, but it is unfair to hold this against the *party*. And society's prejudice against car dealers probably played a role in this case, and this is just as unfair as any other stereotyped prejudice.

This became my *theme* — not explicit, but implicit.

The brief raises these "real" issues, but very gently. I couldn't *prove* that these were the reasons for the verdict, I couldn't expect the appellate court to write an opinion reversing the verdict for those reasons. But if the brief could say just enough to make those notions credible, it might get the court to *want* to go our way. Then, if our *legal* arguments were decent, the court would have the "hooks" to give us what we wanted: a reversal.

I even used two newspaper articles as "appendices" to show how the public holds car dealers in low esteem. You rarely see such things in briefs, as the rules do not expressly *allow* them. But if the rules don't expressly prohibit them, why not give it a try?

Did this use of the "real issues" work? We'll never know for sure. The court reversed the judgment. *See* Palmer v. Ted Stevens Honda, Inc., 193 Cal. App. 3d 530, 238 Cal. Rptr. 363 (1987). The court bought most of my *legal* arguments, but it never said whether it was influenced by my discussion of the "real" issues. Courts seldom do. But I suspect these issues played a role.[3] My opponent wrote a pretty good brief on the legal issues, and the court could have written a presentable opinion accepting his arguments instead of mine. But the court ruled our way — maybe because it *wanted* to, not because it *had* to.

---

[3] I'm pretty sure my points about the conduct of Stevens' trial lawyer hit home, because they almost backfired! At oral argument, one confused judge glared at me and asked, "Did *you* represent the defendant at the trial?"

[B] WHAT TO WATCH FOR WHILE READING THIS BRIEF

You might get the most out of this section by reading it *after* you read — or at least skim — the brief. *Note*: To save space in this Book, the brief is single-spaced. Most court rules require double or one and a half line spacing.

[1] The Statement of the Case

A Statement of the Case is, by custom, a non-argumentative recitation of the key *procedural* facts that led to the appeal. It is usually pretty dry, offering few chances to be persuasive.

But why not take advantage of every such chance you get? You shouldn't overtly *argue* anything, but by arranging and phrasing these facts in a certain way, you can give them some persuasive effect. Sometimes, just by juxtaposing two facts together — "The trial judge did *this*, but then he did *this*!" — you can impart a "feeling of error." I want the judge who finishes reading my Statement of the Case to come away frowning, squirming, and thinking, "Something is wrong here. I'm not sure exactly what it is, but maybe the rest of this brief will tell me." This is what I tried to do here.

[2] The Statement of Facts

To write an effective Statement of Facts, you *first* must decide what *arguments* you plan to make in the Argument section of your brief. This is because the two are intertwined — each one supports the other and, in a sense, dictates how the other is written.

Here, just to make sure the judges get the point, I *tell* them about this interrelationship right up front, in a brief paragraph at the outset of the Statement of Facts. Because I plan to argue that the trial judge's evidentiary rulings were erroneous, it is essential to show that these rulings were *prejudicial*, i.e., that the case was so close that the jury might have gone the other way had these errors not been made. Therefore, I must summarize the evidence presented by *both* sides. (If I had made only my *first* argument — that there was no substantial evidence supporting Respondent's theories, I could *not* legitimately summarize *our* evidence, because *our* evidence was not the evidence that supported Respondent's theories.)

I then tell the story, the way *I* want it told. The witnesses did *not* testify in the order presented here, and each witness did *not* tell his or her story in the orderly fashion presented here. I read the transcripts, took notes, and then *rearranged* everything when writing this Statement of Facts — to accomplish the goals I wanted to accomplish. This is perfectly legitimate, so long I don't misrepresent anyone's testimony.

I try to be fair. I don't leave out any facts that hurt me, because I don't want my opponent blasting me in his Respondent's Brief by accusing me of being deceptive or not telling the whole story.

I summarize *Palmer's* testimony fairly, but include some things that weaken him a bit. Showing that he admitted illegally removing his smog equipment (in order to increase his gas mileage) makes him look somewhat sleazy.

My Argument will deal with a critical issue: whether there was in fact a "consignment" agreement. The Statement of Facts sets this up by *quoting* Palmer's exact testimony on this, because all by itself it tends to show that there was no such agreement. If I had merely paraphrased this, using my own words, the judge might think I was just "puffing."

After summarizing Palmer's testimony, the brief goes through every other witness for the Respondent. My strategy is to paint Alvord — not Stevens — as the bad guy. So wherever a witness said something that seems to get Stevens off the hook, I put it in.

Respondent called Stevens as a witness, questioning him about whether Stevens denied there was a "consignment." Stevens' denial was used to support Respondent's tort claim for "bad faith denial of existence of a contract." The Argument section of the brief will deal with this, but I try to *set up* my Argument *here*, by showing Stevens' exact testimony and the events surrounding it.

The Appellant's Evidence begins with a short introduction explaining what I will show. This is slightly argumentative, but it adds impact to the detailed recitation which follows.

I finish off with "There was no evidence that . . ." a couple of times. These can be very effective. The implication is that if there was no evidence of this, it didn't happen.

[3] The Summary of Argument

This section of the brief is not always required. Most lawyers do not bother with it. But it is one more opportunity to persuade. I keep it short — no more than a couple of pages — and use it to give the judge an overview of the longer Argument that follows, so he can read it more easily. In addition, I try to make this Summary persuasive, tying the Statement of Facts (which the judge just read) together with the *essence* of my legal argument.

[4] The Argument

It's nice to start out with some concession, so the judge will see right off the bat that you are reasonable, and not just another fire-breathing advocate who gives no quarter. So I begin by showing that I understand the rules on appeal: the substantial evidence rule requires affirmance of $11,359 of the judgment against my client. This doesn't give up that much — over $150,000 is at stake — and since I've decided that I have no chance of reversing the $11,359 anyway, why not *use* this "disadvantage" to my advantage?

The structure of each subsection of the Argument is pretty much the same. It usually begins with a short summary of the law, and then quickly gets into the facts — applying the legal principles to the facts of the case. Avoid long discussions of law with no application to the facts.

Whenever I refer to a fact, I always cite the page of the record that supports it — even though this was already done in the Statement of Facts. The judge might want to check up on me, and I don't want to force him to go back to the Statement of Facts to find the right citation.

Sometimes, where the subsection is unusually long, I start with a summary of my entire argument in the subsection, so the judge may follow the argument more easily.

[5] The Conclusion

Most Conclusions merely summarize the legal arguments. I try to go further, using the Conclusion as a persuasive tool, by hitting the justice issue head-on. I even attached an "Appendix", a newspaper clipping about a poll taken on the public's view of car salespeople. (As this was not in the record, I probably should have asked the Court to take judicial notice of it, instead of just attaching it.)

IN THE COURT OF APPEAL OF THE STATE OF CALIFORNIA
SIXTH APPELLATE DISTRICT

WILLIAM J.G. PALMER,

Plaintiff and Respondent

vs.

TED STEVENS HONDA, INC.

Defendant and Appellant

No. H001189

Santa Clara County
Superior Court
No. 542238

APPELLANT'S OPENING BRIEF

On Appeal from the Judgment of the Superior Court of the State of
California for the County of Santa Clara

Honorable Conrad L. Rushing, Judge

Myron Moskovitz
536 Mission St.
San Francisco, Calif. 94105
Phone: (415) 442-6646

E. Day Carman
Carman & Mansfield
111 West St. John St.
San Jose, Calif. 95113
Phone: (408) 993-8200

Attorneys for Appellant

TABLE OF CONTENTS

Page

TABLE OF AUTHORITIES

Page

Cases

Statutes

Other Authorities

STATEMENT OF THE CASE

A first amended complaint was filed in the court below by Respondent William Palmer against defendants Donald Alvard, Stevens Pontiac-GMC, Inc., United Pacific Insurance Co., and Appellant Ted Stevens Honda, Inc. CT (Clerk's Transcript) 413-426.

In it, Palmer alleged the following facts. Palmer entered into a consignment agreement with Don Alvard whereby Alvard — alleged to be acting as an employee of Appellant — would attempt to sell Palmer's Ferrari automobile for him. When the car was sold, Palmer would receive $29,500 from the proceeds, and the consignment fee would be any excess proceeds of the sale. Without Palmer's consent, Alvard reconsigned the car to Ferrari of Los Gatos, which then sold the car. Before Ferrari of Los Gatos could transfer the proceeds of the sale to Palmer, however, Ferrari of Los Gatos filed for bankruptcy. Palmer filed a claim in the bankruptcy action, and was paid $18,141 in settlement of that claim. He also sent demand letters for the full $29,500 to Alvard and Appellant. When they denied liability, he filed this action for fraudulent inducement, negligence, fraudulent concealment, breach of consignment agreement, conversion, bad faith denial of contract, and breach of implied covenant of good faith and fair dealing. Palmer prayed for general damages, attorneys' fees, and punitive damages of $100,000. CT 413-426.

A single answer was filed by all defendants. CT 548-551. In it, they denied several allegations of the complaint, and they alleged "that any consignment agreement entered into between the parties was entered solely on behalf of DON ALVORD, as an individual in no way authorized or ratified by TED STEVENS HONDA, INC. . . ." CT 549.

Before trial, Respondent moved to exclude any evidence which would prove his allegation that he recovered $18,141 from Ferrari of Los Gatos in the bankruptcy action, because of the "collateral source" rule. CT 572, RT (Reporter's Transcript) 17-19. Respondent conceded, however, that the $18,141 should be deducted as a "set-off" from any award which might be made by the jury against Appellant. RT 19. Appellant opposed the motion, but the trial court granted it, on the ground that evidence of the bankruptcy proceeding would confuse the jury. RT 30, 34-35. The court ruled, however, that the $18,141 would be deducted as a set-off before any judgment was entered. *Id.*

While the court ruled that no evidence of the *recovery* in bankruptcy could be introduced by Appellant, it nevertheless granted (over Appellant's opposition) Respondent's request to present evidence that Ferrari of Los Gatos *did in fact* file for bankruptcy and that is why Respondent lost the car and the proceeds of the sale. RT 60-62.

Also before trial, the court granted Respondent's request to present evidence to the jury regarding the attorneys' fees incurred by Respondent in prosecuting this lawsuit, because "the fact that plaintiff incurred attorney's fees may be evidence of the bad faith denial of the contract." RT 18.

Because of these rulings, Respondent was allowed to tell the jury, in his opening statement, that Ferrari of Los Gatos went bankrupt (RT 193) and state that Appellant had deprived Respondent of his car and proceeds "and gave him nothing" (RT 188). Respondent failed to mention the $18,141 recovery he received, and Appellant was allowed to say nothing about this in his opening statement.

Because of these rulings, Respondent was allowed to tell the jury in his opening statement that "it has taken over two and a half years of litigation, over $50,000 of attorney's fees, to bring this case to you." RT 188.

Evidence consistent with these rulings was introduced, jury instructions consistent with these rulings were given, and closing arguments consistent with these rulings were made.

By a vote of eleven to one, the jury returned a verdict for Respondent, awarding him $29,500 actual damages and $150,000 punitive damages, plus interest, against Appellant only. RT 784-785, CT 705-706.

Judgment was thereupon entered for Respondent against Appellant (only), in the amount of $11,358.53 ($29,500 minus $18,141.47), plus interest of $3,629.20, plus punitive damages of $150,000. CT 761-762.

Appellant filed a motion for new trial, claiming that (1) erroneous exclusion of evidence of Respondent's recovery of the $18,141 in the bankruptcy proceeding misled the jury into believing that actual damages were $29,500, and this might well have improperly influenced the jury to set punitive damages at $150,000 (about 5 times the $29,500); (2) the court had erroneously allowed Respondent to present evidence of attorneys' fees incurred in this lawsuit; (3) the court had erroneously allowed Respondent to present evidence that it had taken two and a half years to get the case to trial and that Appellant had lost several discovery motions during this period; (4) the jury's punitive damage award was excessive. RT 787-790; CT 730-731. This motion was denied in its entirety. CT 812.

Appellant then filed a notice of appeal to this Court. CT 799.

STATEMENT OF FACTS

In this appeal, Appellant contends that there is no substantial evidence in the record supporting Respondent's theories of fraud and bad faith, and therefore punitive damages should not have been awarded. In addition, Appellant contends that the trial court's key evidentiary rulings (indicated above) were erroneous and highly prejudicial to Appellant. To demonstrate such prejudice, it is necessary for us to summarize the evidence in favor of Appellant as well as the evidence in favor of Respondent.

Respondent's Evidence

The key witness for Respondent was Respondent *William Palmer*, who testified to the following facts.

In May of 1979, Palmer purchased a 1978 red Ferrari automobile from Ferrari of Los Gatos, paying $42,000 by check. RT 236-237, 291. Palmer instructed the dealer to remove the smog emission equipment which is required by law to be on the car (RT 289-290), because the car was "getting too hot" and because removal "would increase my mileage" (RT 294). Palmer knew that this was illegal. RT 295.

The salesman who sold the car to Palmer was Donald Alvard. RT 237. At Palmer's request, Ferrari of Los Gatos stored the car at the dealership for some time. RT 237. Later, when Ferrari asked Palmer to move the car, Palmer asked Alvard to store the car at Alvard's home, and Alvard agreed to do so. RT 240. Alvard stored the car for about 6 months. RT 303. In February of 1981, Palmer picked up the car from Alvard's house. RT 244.

In 1982, Palmer decided to sell the car. RT 246. Sometime in October of 1982, he phoned Alvard to see if he was interested in buying it, because Alvard had earlier expressed such an interest while he was storing the car. RT 246-247. Alvard said that he was not interested, but his new employer — Appellant Ted Stevens Honda, Inc. (hereafter called "Honda") — might be interested. RT 247. Alvard was now the used car manager at Honda. *Id.* Palmer had never heard of Stevens Honda, Stevens Pontiac, or any other Stevens dealership. RT 307.

On October 30 (RT 263-264), Palmer came to San Jose, phoned Alvard at his home, and arranged to meet him at the Ted Stevens Pontiac dealership on Blossom Hill Road. RT 248. When they met, Alvard said that he was used car sales manager for the "Stevens group" of companies. RT 251. Alvard drove the car, and — on behalf of the "Stevens group" — offered Palmer $24,500 for the car. RT 254. Palmer said that was not enough, and Alvard replied that he had called Ferrari of Los Gatos and was told that the wholesale value of a 1978 Ferrari was only $24,500, so he could not offer more. RT 254.

Alvard then suggested that Palmer leave the car with Honda for sale on consignment. RT 258-259. The terms of the consignment contract would be that Palmer would receive $29,500 from the sale, Honda would keep any excess proceeds from the sale, Honda would pay all advertising and selling costs, and Palmer would pay for any repairs needed for the car. RT 260. Alvard said that if he failed to sell the car at the Honda dealership in Los Gatos, he might move it to the Stevens dealership in San Rafael and try to sell it there. RT 261.

Palmer then gave Alvard the car, an ownership card, and proof of liability insurance. RT 261. Palmer kept the "title" (pink slip) to the car, however (RT 262), and he was unclear as to whether he had entered into a consignment agreement with Honda:

> Q. Did you ever ask Mr. Alvard for a consignment agreement, written agreement?
>
> A [Palmer]. No. As I said, when we talked about that agreement, we don't have a consignment agreement, we don't have an agreement, meaning "we" again is the plural, meaning Stevens. Then he made the comment, "Well, you have the title. As long as you have the title, we can't sell the car." [RT 262:16-22]

Alvard did not tell Palmer that consignment of the car to Honda was conditional on the car passing smog emission or safety inspection. RT 262-263. Palmer left the car at the Stevens Pontiac dealership. RT 263.

At that time, Palmer had a poor opinion of Ferrari of Los Gatos, because he had tried to sell the car to them and did not like the price they offered, and because of their "bad reputation." RT 295-296. There is no evidence, however, that Palmer told Alvard of any of this, and Palmer admitted that he did not instruct Alvard not to have any dealings with Ferrari of Los Gatos regarding his car. RT 297-299.

On November 3 or 4, Alvard phoned Palmer to tell him "that they could not sell the Ferrari as is, that the car did not have California smog emission equipment on it." RT 264:13-17. Alvard said that the smog equipment which Palmer had removed could be reinstalled, at a cost to Palmer of $800. RT 264. Palmer told him to go ahead and have it reinstalled. RT 265.

On December 21, Palmer phoned Alvard and told him that he had changed his mind about selling the car. RT 268.

On December 28, Alvard phoned Palmer, said that he had a buyer for the car, subject to arranging financing, and that Palmer should send him the "title" (pink slip). RT 271. Alvard said that the buyer did not want smog equipment on the car, so Palmer's equipment had not been reinstalled. RT 281-282. Palmer complied with Alvard's request that same day, sending the pink slip to Alvard (*id.*, RT 277-278), along with a check for $164 made out to Alvard (not to Honda), to pay for a safety inspection and repairs to the car (RT 281-281, 283).

Palmer received no money from Alvard, tried to phone him, and drew the conclusion that Alvard was avoiding his calls. RT 272.

On January 6, 1983, Alvard phoned Palmer from Alvard's home to tell Palmer that the car had been sold by Ferrari of Los Gatos. RT 273. Alvard said that he (Alvard) still had the pink slip. RT 274. To "protect myself," Palmer got the pink slip back from Alvard. *Id.* Nevertheless, the car was sold by Ferrari of Los Gatos. RT 275.

Palmer then phoned Mr. Burnett, the owner of Ferrari of Los Gatos, and Burnett acknowledged that Ferrari of Los Gatos owed Palmer the money from the sale. RT 373-374.

Over objection, Palmer was allowed to testify that he had incurred attorneys fees of about $56,000 in this lawsuit. RT 284-287.

Over objection, Palmer was also allowed to testify that there had been over 12 "law and motion matters in this lawsuit in an attempt to bring it to trial," that "We have had to battle, take depositions too, forever to get information," and that it had taken about two and a half years to get to trial. RT 287-289.

Respondent called *Mary Lou Dibbern*, Palmer's fiancée, as a witness. RT 217. She was with Palmer when he met with Alvard in October of 1982, and she recalled that Alvard said that he was taking the car on consignment for Ted Stevens, not for himself. RT 219-221.

Respondent called *Tony Schwager* as a witness. RT 420. Mr. Schwager ran the car repair shop which did a smog and safety check on Palmer's car, at Alvard's request. RT 422-423. When Alvard brought the car to Schwager, Alvard said that this was "his private deal." RT 428. Alvard said that once the car was "smogged" (i.e., the smog emission controls were reinstalled), Alvard would place the car "on Ted Stevens' lot." RT 431. Schwager billed Alvard — not Ted Stevens — $164 for his work on the car. RT 428-429.

Schwager saw Palmer's car in the repair lot at the Honda dealership in 1982. RT 421-422. However, he never saw Palmer's car in the area of the dealership where cars were offered for sale. RT 427.

Schwager testified that, after he received his subpoena to testify, Alvard asked him to testify that he had found a European and California exhaust system for the car, and this was not true. RT 424.

Respondent called *Frank Schonig* as a witness. RT 556. He testified that he was familiar with Palmer's car and, while driving by the Honda dealership, he had seen it in the area of the Honda lot where other cars were displayed for sale. RT 556-558, 560. He knew that the other cars were for sale because they had stickers on them. RT 571. He did not, however, see any stickers or others signs on Palmer's car which would indicate that it was for sale. RT 564. He also saw a car like Palmer's in the Honda showroom, but he was not positive that it was Palmer's car. RT 558.

Respondent called defendant *Donald Alvard* as a witness. RT 478. After he sold the car to Palmer, they became friends (RT 511), and Alvard later stored the car at his home for Palmer (RT 485). On October 30, 1982, when he discussed the possibility of consignment with Palmer, Alvard was hoping that Palmer would sign a consignment agreement with the Stevens group, rather than with Alvard personally. RT 506. He never did send a written consignment agreement to Palmer, however, because the car could be sold at Stevens only if it passed a smog and safety check, the car failed to pass such a test, and Palmer refused to authorize Alvard to spend the money needed to reinstall Palmer's smog control equipment. RT 506-509, 516-518.

At this point, Alvard offered to try to sell the car personally for Palmer — without the smog equipment — and Palmer agreed to this. RT 510. Palmer placed no restrictions on the manner in which Alvard might sell the car. RT 514. Palmer placed no restriction on Alvard's authority to consign the car to another dealer in order to facilitate selling the car for Palmer. RT 514. Palmer did not tell Alvard not to take the car to Ferrari of Los Gatos for sale. RT 510. Alvard denied that Palmer ever told him that he did not wish to sell the car. RT 495.

When Alvard arranged for Ferrari of Los Gatos to sell the car, he did not then tell Palmer of this (though he did tell him this after the car was sold). RT 495. Alvard ended his employment with Ted Stevens in 1984, before the trial began. RT 490.

Respondent called *Ted Stevens* as a witness. RT 436. Stevens is the president and owner of Appellant Honda and of 6 other auto dealerships. RT 436-437. Alvard was the used car manager for Honda in 1982. RT 474. Ferraris have been sold at the Honda dealership (RT 444), and a Ferrari was displayed in the showroom there (RT 452). Stevens has never spoken to Palmer. RT 476.

By asking Stevens a single question, Respondent's counsel sought to establish that Stevens was denying the existence of a contract between Palmer and Honda:

> Q. Do you deny that Mr. Palmer had a contract, a consignment contract, with Ted Stevens Honda for his Ferrari?

> A. Yes, I do. [RT 476:11-13]

Respondent's counsel did not explain what he meant by "consignment contract" in his question, and there is no evidence that Stevens had any training in the law or had any reason to know that the oral agreement which Palmer made with Alvard could be considered a "consignment contract" as a technical, legal matter. The record shows only that Stevens considered "consignment contract" to be a *written* agreement, not an oral agreement.

On one occasion, Stevens had orally agreed to do a favor for a friend, William Geggatt, by selling his Ferrari for him at the Honda dealership. RT 446. Stevens did not consider this arrangement to be a "consignment," because no written consignment contact was made. RT 471. Respondent's counsel pressed Stevens to concede that the arrangement was nevertheless a "consignment," as he was selling the car on behalf of Geggatt. But Stevens made it clear that this was not *his* understanding of the term "consignment."

Q. So what you had was a consignment sale, would you agree with me?

A. No. I disagree because I had nothing signed as a consignment sale. When we consign an automobile we would have him sign the documents and a consignment form which were not signed.

Q. In this instance you had an oral agreement to consign; would you agree with me?

A. If that is your way of giving me the verbiage I have to agree, but I don't agree, in my way of thinking a consignment is.

Q. Mr. Stevens, you don't agree with me? You did not have an oral consignment?

A. I agree we had an oral agreement, but I had nothing to consign the automobile.

Q. Did you have an oral consignment agreement with Mr. Geggatt? The answer is yes or no.

A. Yes. [RT 473:8-25]

Respondent presented evidence that, in 1984, Appellant had gross sales of $23,359,759 and a net after-tax profit of $886,965. RT 705, 708.

Appellant's Evidence

Appellant's evidence was, for the most part, consistent with Respondent's evidence. There was no disagreement with Palmer's testimony that Palmer first approached Alvard personally for the purpose of selling his car, that Palmer and Alvard initially contemplated that Honda (rather than Alvard) would take the car on consignment, that Palmer never had a written consignment agreement with Honda, that Alvard phoned Palmer to tell him that Honda could not sell the car because it lacked smog control equipment, that Alvard later took the car to Ferrari of Los Gatos for sale, that Alvard told Palmer that a buyer had been found and Palmer should send him the pink slip, that Palmer then sent the pink slip to Alvard, and that Ferrari of Los Gatos sold the car and then went bankrupt.

All of Respondent's evidence of these facts was (and is) undisputed. Appellant sought to prove, however, that Alvard was acting on his own account, and not for Honda, when Alvard finally agreed to sell the car for Palmer.

Appellant called *Donald Alvard* back to testify again, and he confirmed these facts. RT 662-685. He denied, however, that Palmer told him on

November 3 or 4 to reinstall the smog equipment, testifying instead that Palmer had refused to spend any more money on the car. RT 667. He also testified that, after Alvard told Palmer that Honda could not sell the car, Palmer said "that I should take the car home and attempt to sell the car privately by word of mouth, by newspaper advertising, by any means in which I could, including moving the car about to anyplace." RT 669:12-16.

Alvard's placing the car with Ferrari of Los Gatos was in conformity with his arrangement with Palmer. RT 670. After the car was sold by Ferrari of Los Gatos, Alvard obtained the pink slip from Palmer and took it to Ferrari of Los Gatos. RT 671. However, he did not leave the pink slip with them, because they failed to give him a check for the proceeds of the sale. RT 672. Alvard denied that he ever tried to avoid taking phone calls from Palmer. RT 673.

Appellant presented several witnesses to show that — contrary to the possible implications of Mr. Schonig's testimony for Respondent — Palmer's car was never displayed for sale at the Honda dealership.

Rudy Esquivel was a sales manager at Honda during 1982, and was in charge of keeping track of Honda's inventory: "My job was to know what was in stock as far as new cars and used." RT 629-630. Mr. Esquivel never saw a car like Palmer's — which had distinctive Florida license plates and wire wheels — for sale at Honda. RT 630.

Pamela Dinning, a saleswoman at Honda, never saw a car like Palmer's for sale at Honda during 1982 — though she did see another red Ferrari there. RT 636-637. *George Ament*, a sales manager at Honda, never saw a car like Palmer's for sale there in 1982. RT 626-628. *Robert Ducharme*, shop foreman at Honda, never saw a car like Palmer's for sale there in 1982 (though he did see another red Ferrari there). RT 647-649. *Richard Warren*, service manager at Honda, never saw a car like Palmer's for sale there in 1982 (though he too saw another red Ferrari there). RT 654-657. *Gary Manning* (a salesman), *Larry Bethel* (a salesman), and *Arnold Fried* (a parts manager) all testified that they never saw a car like Palmer's at the Honda dealership during 1982. RT 584-591, 642-646, 658-661.

Appellant also called *Brian Burnett* as a witness. RT 591. Mr. Burnett was the owner of Ferrari of Los Gatos. RT 591-592. While Alvard was working for him, Alvard sold the car to Palmer, and Alvard and Palmer became friendly. RT 593-594. In 1982, after Alvard had left his employment with Burnett, he returned with the car. RT 596. Alvard consigned the car to Ferrari of Los Gatos for sale, and Alvard personally signed a written consignment agreement to that effect. RT 598. There was no evidence that the document or Alvard stated that Alvard was acting on behalf of Honda in making this consignment.

Burnett admitted that Ferrari of Los Gatos was responsible to Palmer for the proceeds of the sale of his car: "Ferrari of Los Gatos has never denied for a moment that the money is not due Mr. Palmer from us." RT 599:7-16.

There was no evidence that, at the time Alvard consigned the car to Ferrari of Los Gatos, Alvard (or Stevens or any of his employees) had any reason to believe that Ferrari of Los Gatos was in any financial trouble or might go bankrupt.

There was no evidence that Alvard or Appellant took any fee or commission from the sale of Palmer's car, or that they otherwise profited from that sale in any way.

SUMMARY OF ARGUMENT

Appellant concedes that Respondent presented substantial evidence (though barely substantial) that, through Alvard, Honda had made an agreement with Palmer to sell his car for him. The testimony of Palmer and Frank Schonig may be read to imply this. Because the car was sold, Honda owes Palmer $29,500, less the $18,141 already paid to Palmer in the bankruptcy action.

Appellant denies, however, that there was substantial evidence supporting either of the theories — bad faith denial of the existence of a contract, and fraud — which Respondent has invoked to justify an award of punitive damages. There was no evidence that either Alvard or Stevens ever denied that Palmer had a contract with Alvard, let alone evidence of bad faith. There was no evidence that Alvard or Stevens intended to harm Palmer in any way, and therefore neither malice nor oppression was proved. There was no evidence that Alvard or Stevens ever intended to or did in fact defraud Palmer of his car, the proceeds of the sale, or anything else.

The fact that the jury awarded punitive damages to Respondent in spite of this paucity of evidence may be attributed to the improper introduction of certain evidence which was irrelevant: evidence that Appellant had invoked pretrial litigation devices, evidence that it had taken two and one-half years to get to trial, and evidence that Respondent had incurred over $50,000 in attorneys fees in this lawsuit. There is no authority in law for admitting such evidence in a "bad faith" case, and the consequence of allowing such evidence would be to expand every breach of contract action into a jury trial on the wisdom and propriety of lawyers' litigation tactics.

The improper admission of this evidence was highly prejudicial to Appellant on the matter of punitive damages, because Respondent presented very little evidence tending to show the "malice" needed to support an award of punitive damages.

Finally, exclusion of evidence that Respondent in fact recovered $18,141 of the $29,500 from the bankruptcy proceeding was improper, as this money came directly from Alvard's cosignee. The "collateral source" rule invoked by Respondent has no application to this recovery, because Ferrari of Los Gatos was not a source "wholly independent" of Honda.

Exclusion of this evidence was highly prejudicial to Appellant. The jury was misled into believing that Palmer's loss was the full $29,500, and the jury was instructed by the trial court to consider Palmer's actual loss in setting any punitive damage award. The resulting award of $150,000 in punitive damages — about 5 times the $29,500 — might well have been only $56,795 (5 times $11,359) had the jury been allowed to hear the whole truth.

ARGUMENT

I. THERE IS NO SUBSTANTIAL EVIDENCE IN THE RECORD SUPPORTING AN AWARD OF PUNITIVE DAMAGES AGAINST APPELLANT.

We concede that the record, viewed in a light most favorable to Respondent, does support a finding that Respondent at some point made a consignment agreement with Appellant, through Appellant's agent Alvard — even though this evidence was thin and heavily disputed. Therefore, the judgment was proper to the extent that it awarded $11,359 to Respondent ($29,500 minus the $18,141 paid through the bankruptcy proceeding), for breach of the consignment contract (by failing to pay this money to Palmer).

We contend, however, that the record does not contain substantial evidence supporting the portion of the judgment which awarded $150,000 in punitive damages against Appellant.

A. THERE WAS NO SUBSTANTIAL EVIDENCE SHOWING THAT APPELLANT COMMITTED THE TORT OF BAD FAITH DENIAL OF THE EXISTENCE OF A CONTRACT.

To establish that a defendant has committed the tort of bad faith denial of the existence of a contract, a plaintiff has the burden of proving *each* of the following: (1) that the defendant denied the existence of a contract with plaintiff, (2) that this denial was without probable cause, and (3) that this denial was in bad faith. *Seaman's Direct Buying Services, Inc. v. Standard Oil Co.* (1984) 36 Cal. 3d 752, 769. In the case at bench, the record fails to show substantial evidence of *any* of these 3 elements of the tort.

1. There Was No Substantial Evidence That Appellant Denied The Existence of a Contract.

There was no evidence that either Alvard or Stevens ever denied that Palmer had a contract with Alvard. In fact, Appellant has never disputed the fact that Palmer did have such a contract with Alvard. What *was* disputed was whether this contract was binding on Appellant *Honda*, i.e., whether Alvard made the contract on his own or in his capacity as Appellant's agent. Appellant did not deny the existence of the contract, but only whether Appellant (as opposed to Alvard) was liable under it.

In *Seaman's*, the defendant denied the *very existence* of a contract with plaintiff, not merely whether an admitted contract extended to defendant. It would take an extension of *Seaman's* to apply its newly-adopted tort to the case at bench.[1]

---

[1] Respondent's counsel did try to elicit testimony from Stevens that Stevens denied that Palmer had a "consignment contract" with Honda, but it seems clear that Stevens denied *only* that Palmer had a formal, *written* contract with Honda. *See* Pages 12-13 of this brief, *supra*.

In *Seaman's*, however, the Supreme Court cautioned *against* any extensions of tort law further into the area of commercial contracts.

> When we move from such special relationships [as insurance contracts] to consideration of the tort remedy in the context of the ordinary commercial contract, we move into largely uncharted and potentially dangerous waters. * * * *

> In such contracts, it may be difficult to distinguish between breach of the covenant [of good faith and fair dealing] and breach of contract, and there is the risk that injecting tort remedies will intrude upon the expectations of the parties. *This is not to say that tort remedies have no place in such a commercial context, but that it is wise to proceed with caution in determining their scope and application. [Id. at 769, emphasis added.]*

In *Quigley v. Pet, Inc.* (1984) 162 Cal. App. 3d 233, the court interpreted *Seaman's* as including a warning against "judicial adventurism" (*id.* at 235), and the court added its own notes of caution:

> The risk of a contract-tort action may have negative consequences of varied kinds, such as hesitancy to contract in the first place, or later, fear of defending energetically against uncertainties or mistakes. [*Id.* at 237]

> General and punitive damages may be appropriate judicial sanctions for those who in bad faith deny the contract itself, but may be much less well chosen for those whose fault lies only in having inadequate grounds to challenge contract terms. *An unrestricted rule of tort liability for unfair dealing could convert routine contract cases into contract-tort jury trials, issues of fact regarding perceived tortious conduct being so easily raised*

[*Id.* at 238; *emphasis added*]

We submit that *Seaman's* does not apply to the case at bench, as Appellant did *not* deny the existence of a contract. We also submit that this Court should not extend *Seaman's* to encompass denials of liability under commercial contracts, for the sound policy reasons discussed in *Seaman's* and *Quigley*.

2. There Was No Substantial Evidence That Appellant Lacked Probable Cause To Deny Liability.

As discussed above, this case could fall within *Seaman's* new tort only if *Seaman's* is extended to cover Mr. Stevens' denial that Palmer's contract was with Honda (as opposed to Alvard). But even if *Seaman's* were so extended, Appellant would still not be liable for that tort, because Respondent has failed to sustain his burden of proving that Stevens' denial was *without probable cause.*

As we conceded earlier, Respondent presented evidence that Alvard made the consignment agreement on behalf of Honda. But Appellant presented very strong evidence to the contrary, and we submit that this shows strong "probable cause" supporting Mr. Stevens' conclusion that Honda was *not* a party to that contract.

Don Alvard testified that he told Palmer that Alvard could not and would not sell the car on behalf of Honda, because Honda could sell a car *only* if it passed a smog and safety test, and Palmer's car failed to do so. RT 506-509, 516-518. Alvard also testified that, after he told Palmer that Honda could not sell the car, Palmer asked Alvard to do so, and Alvard agreed. RT 669.

Respondent presented a single witness (Frank Schonig) to testify he saw Palmer's car at the Honda lot for sale (though he admitted that he saw no stickers on the car that would indicate that it was for sale). RT 556-571. Appellant, however, presented no less than *eight* witnesses who testified that Palmer's car was *not* displayed for sale at Honda. These witnesses were Rudy Esquivel (RT 629-630), Pamela Dinning (RT 636-637), George Ament (RT 626-628), Robert Ducharme (RT 647-649), Richard Warren (RT 654-657), Gary Manning (RT 584-591), Larry Bethel (RT 642-646), and Arnold Fried (RT 658-661).

While the jury was within its rights in preferring Respondent's evidence over Appellant's evidence on this issue, it seems clear that Appellant's evidence was quite substantial, and thus showed probable cause for Mr. Stevens' belief that Alvard did not make the contract on Honda's behalf. As lack of probable cause — an essential element of *Seaman's* new tort — was missing, Appellant cannot be held liable under *Seaman's*.

3. There Was No Substantial Evidence That Appellant's Denial of Liability Was In Bad Faith.

Respondent also had the burden of proving the presence of the third element of *Seaman's* new tort: bad faith. But there is no evidence in the record showing that Mr. Stevens' denial of liability on the part of Honda was in bad faith. To infer bad faith, one would have to infer *all* of the following: that Alvard was lying when he testified that he told Palmer that Honda could not sell the car,[2] that all eight witnesses who testified that Palmer's car was not for sale at the Honda lot were lying, and that Mr. Stevens knew that all these people were lying. Such inferences would not be based on any evidence in the record, but on pure speculation.

To constitute "substantial evidence" of a fact, the evidence must be "reasonable in nature, credible, and of solid value." *Estate of Teed* (1952) 112 Cal.

---

[2] If *Alvard* had lied on the witness stand, this might now bad faith on *Alvard's* part. Such bad faith could not, however, be attributed to Appellant *Honda*, as *Alvard's* employment with Honda was *terminated* in 1984 (RT 490) — well before he testified in this case, in June of 1985.

App. 2d 638, 644. *See also Krause v. Apodaca* (1960) 186 Cal. App. 2d 413, 417. No such evidence of bad faith denial of a contract appears in the record before this Court.

B. EVEN IF APPELLANT HAD COMMITTED THE TORT, PUNITIVE DAMAGES SHOULD NOT HAVE BEEN AWARDED, BECAUSE THERE WAS NO SUBSTANTIAL EVIDENCE SHOWING MALICE, OPPRESSION OR FRAUD.

"It is well settled in this state that punitive damages may not be awarded in an action based on breach of contract, even though the defendant's breach was willful or fraudulent." *Dryden v. Tri-Valley Growers* (1977) 65 Cal. App. 3d 990, 999. *See also Quigley v. Pet, Inc., supra*, 162 Cal. App. 3d at 232-233.

When the defendant's act goes *beyond* breach of contract and becomes the tort of bad faith denial of the existence of a contract, punitive damages may be awarded, *if and only if* the plaintiff *also* proves that the denial was fraudulent or malicious.

> It does *not* follow that because plaintiff is entitled to compensatory damages that he is also entitled to exemplary damages. In order to justify an award of exemplary damages, the defendant must be guilty of oppression, fraud or malice. * * * * While we have concluded that defendant violated its duty of good faith and fair dealing, this alone does *not* necessarily establish that defendant acted with *the requisite intent to injure*. [*Silberg v. California Life Ins.Co.* (1974) 11 Cal. 3d 452, 462-463; *emphasis added*. See also *Wallis v. Superior Court* (1984) 160 Cal. App. 3d 1109, 1118, fn. 4; *Mason v. Mercury Cas. Co.* (1976) 64 Cal. App. 3d 471, 474.]

This holding of our Supreme Court would also apply to the new tort of bad faith denial of the existence of a contract, as it is closely related to the tort of breach of the duty of good faith and fair dealing.

Even if the record in this case did show that Appellant committed a bad faith denial of the existence of Palmer's contract, the record fails to show that Appellant acted with the "requisite intent to injure" Palmer (i.e., that Appellant acted maliciously or oppressively) or that any fraud was involved in this case. Therefore, the record does not support an award of punitive damages.

1. There Was No Substantial Evidence of Malice or Oppression.

As indicated by the above quote from *Silberg*, the malice and oppression needed to support punitive damages consists of *an intent to injure the plaintiff*. "[I]t is the wrongful personal intention to injure that calls forth the penalty." *Davis v. Hearst* (1911) 160 Cal. 143, 162; *Wolfsen v. Hathaway* (1948) 32 Cal. 2d 632, 647-648. "Proof of a violation of the duty of good faith and fair dealing does not establish that the defendant acted with the requisite intent to injure the plaintiff." *Beck v. State Farm Mut. Auto. Ins. Co.* (1976) 54 Cal. App. 3d 347, 355.

Here, there is simply no evidence that Stevens' denial of Honda's liability was motivated by any desire to injure Palmer in any way. Stevens was simply protecting the interests of his company, Honda. He may have been mistaken, and we may assume — for purposes of this argument only — that his denial was in bad faith. Such bad faith protection of his own interests would *not* be equivalent to an intent to injure Palmer. Proof of malice "cannot be based on mere speculation; it depends instead on a *definite showing* of a willingness to vex, harass or injure consistent with a wrongful intent to injure." *Kendall Yacht Corp. v. United California Bank* (1975) 50 Cal. App. 3d 949, 958-959; *emphasis added*. See also *Henderson v. Security Nat. Bank* (1977) 72 Cal. App. 3d 764, 771 ("malice will never be established by 'mere speculation'"). No such "definite showing" was made here.

Respondent presented evidence that he and Appellant had been involved in discovery motions before trial, that it had taken two and a half years to get to trial, and that he had incurred $56,000 in attorneys fees in this action. RT 284-289. Later in this brief we will explain why the admission of this evidence was error. But even assuming that this evidence was admissible, it does not tend to show that Appellant's denial of liability was malicious or oppressive. Defensive litigation tactics, by themselves, show no more than a desire to avoid liability. They do not show a desire to gratuitously inflict harm on a plaintiff. Nor do they show a desire to commit "oppression," which is defined by Civil Code § 3294(c)(2) as "subjecting a person to cruel and unjust hardship in conscious disregard of the rights or safety of others." Such desires could be shown by statements of the defendant that he meant to harm the plaintiff merely for the pleasure of doing so, but there was *no* evidence of any such statements in the case at bench.

The distinction between tactics used to avoid liability (even in bad faith) and the intent to injure needed to support a punitive damage award was carefully drawn in a recent, excellent law review article:

> The substantive standards for punitive damages emphasize the actor's intent to injure the plaintiff, and fix that motive as the justification for punitive damages. Bad faith, in contrast, emphasizes the actor's attempt to evade litigation of liability on the merits, or to gain advantages which litigation might not support. An actor that breaches the implied covenant need not intend to harm plaintiff or to consciously disregard plaintiff's rights. It is sufficient that he act unreasonably and with the knowledge that he is asserting an invalid claim. In short, a violation of good faith and fair dealing does not reach a level of culpability high enough to merit punitive damages. [Cohen, *Reconstructing Breach of the Implied Covenant of Good Faith and Fair Dealing As A Tort*, 73 Calif. L. Rev. 1291, 1327-1328 (1985).]

The evidence in case shows only that Stevens' actions to avoid liability were done to protect Honda — no more. There is no evidence of any *motive* which Stevens might have had to injure Palmer. There was no history of any animosity between the two men. Indeed, Stevens had never even spoken to Palmer. RT 476.

There being no evidence of intent to injure Palmer, there was no evidence of malice which would support the award of punitive damages.

2. There Was No Substantial Evidence of Fraud.

At trial, Respondent's counsel made no argument that any fraud was committed by Mr. Stevens. He did argue, however, that fraud was committed by Alvard. RT 724-725, 778.

As stressed by Respondent's counsel (at RT 778), there was evidence tending to show that Alvard asked Tony Schwager to testify falsely in this case. RT 424. But this occurred in 1985 — when Alvard was *no longer employed by Honda.* Any fraudulent activity committed by Alvard after termination of his employment at Honda may not be attributed to Appellant Honda.

Respondent's only effort to persuade the jury that Alvard committed fraud *while* he worked for Honda was an argument that Alvard (1) concealed from Palmer the fact that the consignment to Honda was conditional on the car passing a smog test, and (2) told Palmer that he intended to sell the car at a Stevens location, when he in fact intended to take it to Ferrari of Los Gatos for sale. RT 724:18-725:7. But there was no substantial evidence showing any fraudulent intent by Alvard in either of these two matters.

Regarding the first, the record shows no more than a dispute in the testimony regarding whether Alvard ever told Palmer that the consignment to Honda was subject to the car passing a smog test. Alvard testified that he told this to Palmer (RT 506:4-14; 664:17-665:1), and Palmer testified that Alvard did not tell him this (RT 262:23-263:2). It may be inferred from the verdict that the jury believed Palmer's testimony over Alvard's. But there was *no* evidence showing that Alvard *intentionally and fraudulently concealed* from Palmer some secret plan to cancel the consignment if the car did not pass a smog test. Fraud cannot be presumed; a plaintiff alleging fraud must sustain his burden of proving it by competent evidence. *Liodas v. Sahadi* (1977) 19 Cal. 3d 278, 292 ("[W]hen the circumstances shown are equally consistent with fraud and with innocence, the plaintiff has failed to carry his burden of proving the fact of fraud by a preponderance of the evidence.")

Regarding Respondent's second contention, there was testimony by both Palmer and Alvard that Alvard told Palmer on October 30, 1982, that he planned to try to sell the car at one of Stevens' dealerships (RT 261:1-5; 506:4-14) and there was also evidence that he later took the car to Ferrari of Los Gatos for sale. RT 596-598. Once again, however, there was *no* evidence showing that when Alvard made that statement, he did not intend to try to sell the car at one of Stevens' dealerships. "The presumption is against fraud [citations] and is not overcome by shadowy evidence [citations]." *Shapiro v. Equitable Life Assur. Soc.* (1946) 76 Cal. App. 2d 75, 91. See also *Goldstein v. Enoch* (1967) 248 Cal. App. 2d 891, 895. Respondent failed to present more than the most "shadowy evidence" of fraud.

In addition, it should be noted that Alvard had *no motive* to conceal any intent to take the car to Ferrari of Los Gatos for sale. There was no evidence that Palmer ever told Alvard of his poor opinion of Ferrari of Los Gatos, and Palmer admitted that he did not instruct Alvard not to deal with Ferrari of Los Gatos. RT 299:13-17.[3] There was no evidence that Alvard knew that Palmer would refuse to deal with Alvard if Palmer thought that Alvard might have dealings with Ferrari of Los Gatos. There was no evidence that Alvard (or Honda) might receive a greater fee or profit by placing the car with Ferrari of Los Gatos. There was no evidence that the $29,500 which Palmer would receive from the sale would in any way be diminished if the car were sold by Ferrari of Los Gatos. And there was no evidence that Alvard (or anyone else at Honda) then had any information indicating that Ferrari of Los Gatos was in any financial difficulty or might go bankrupt. In short, there was *no reason* for Alvard to conceal from Palmer an intent to deal with Ferrari of Los Gatos if he were unable to sell the car through a Stevens dealership.

Respondent has claimed that Appellant was guilty of *constructive* fraud, under Civil Code § 1573(1), which provides that constructive fraud exists:

> In any breach of duty which, without an actually fraudulent intent, gains an advantage to the person in fault . . . by misleading him to his prejudice. . . .

As discussed above, there is no evidence that Alvard gained any advantage over Palmer. No is there any evidence that Alvard intentionally "misled" Palmer.

As there was no substantial evidence of fraud, the award of punitive damages cannot be sustained on that ground.

C. THIS COURT SHOULD MODIFY THE JUDGMENT BY STRIKING THE AWARD OF PUNITIVE DAMAGES.

The attitude of California courts towards punitive damages was summed up by our Supreme Court in *Egan v. Mutual of Omaha Ins. Co.* (1979) 24 Cal. 3d 809, 828:

> Our courts have recognized that the law does not favor punitive damages, granting them only in the most outrageous cases. [Cita-

---

[3] Palmer knew, of course, that Alvard was acquainted with people at Ferrari of Los Gatos, because Palmer knew that Alvard used to work there. RT 237.

tions.] In *Gombos v. Ashe* (1958) 158 Cal. App. 2d 517, 526-527, Justice Peters enunciated the limited basis for punitive damages award: "Punitive damages are allowed in certain cases as a punishment of the defendant. They are not a favorite of the law and the granting of them should be done with the greatest caution. *They are only allowed in the clearest of cases.*" [*emphasis added*]

The case at bench is far from clear. There was no evidence — let alone *clear* evidence — that Stevens, Alvard, or anyone at Honda intended to injure or defraud Palmer.[4]

In reversing an award of punitive damages, the court in *Woolstrum v. Mailloux* (1983) 141 Cal. App. 3d Supp. 1, issued a severe critique of the tendency of jurors — through inexperience and "susceptibility to passion, prejudice and the histrionics of counsel" — to award punitive damages too freely. *Id.* at 11. After noting that "The misuse of punitive damages can become intolerable," the court stated:

> Trial and appellate courts have demonstrated their realization that a tighter rein should be employed in punitive damage cases, as compared to other civil cases by the frequency in which courts have cut down the *amounts* of punitive damage awards or granted new trials if remittitur is not accepted, as distinguished from the general hands off attitude the courts take toward jury decisions as to compensatory damages. [Citations] Judges should exercise the same care in monitoring the merits of punitive damages. [*Id.* at 11. *See also* Mallor & Roberts, *Punitive Damages: Toward A Principled Approach*, 31 Hastings L.J. 639, 642 (1980) ("Because of the danger of an excessive or inappropriate imposition of punitive damages, courts must supervise punitive damage awards closely to ensure that they are imposed only when justified.")]

Where there is no substantial evidence in the record showing malice, oppression, or fraud, an appellate court may modify the judgment by striking an award of punitive damages. *McInerney v. United Railroads* (1920) 50 Cal. App. 538, 549. We submit that this Court should strike the punitive damage award from the judgment below.

---

[4] It should also be noted that, even if substantial evidence of malice or fraud were present here, there would be little need to impose punitive damages in order to deter wrongdoing in the auto sales industry, because that industry is heavily regulated by the state. Each auto dealer must have a license. Vehicle Code §11700. The state may refuse to issue a license to any dealer who has outstanding an unsatisfied judgment stemming from the sale of a car. Vehicle Code §11703.2 The state may suspend or revoke the license of any dealer who commits fraud in the operation of the dealership. Vehicle Code §11705.

II. THE PUNITIVE DAMAGE AWARD OF $150,000 WAS EXCESSIVE AS A MATTER OF LAW.

In the trial court, Appellant challenged the size of the punitive damage award, by a motion for new trial.[5] See Code of Civil Procedure § 657(5) (allowing a motion for new trial on the ground of excessive damages). This motion was denied.

If this Court should reject each of our contentions above that there was no substantial evidence justifying any punitive damage award in this case, we nevertheless contend that the evidence was so weak that it does not support an award of $150,000 — more than 13 times Respondent's actual damages of $11,359.

The purpose of punitive damages is "to serve as an example or warning to others not to engage in such conduct." *Wetherbee v. United Ins. Co. of America* (1971) 18 Cal. App. 3d 266, 270. *See also Neal v. Farmers Ins. Exchange* (1978) 21 Cal. 3d 910, 928, fn. 13 ("The purpose of punitive damages is to punish wrongdoers and thereby deter the commission of wrongful acts").

This purpose is important where the wrongful conduct is not an isolated instance, but is part of a policy the defendant or a common practice of others in the industry. Thus, in *Neal, supra,* and in *Egan v. Mutual of Omaha Ins. Co.* (1979) 24 Cal. 3d 809, punitive damages were awarded to deter a practice common in the insurance industry: wrongful refusal to pay claims. In *Ferraro v. Pacific Fin. Corp.* (1970) 8 Cal. App. 3d 339, punitive damages were awarded to deter a corporate policy of repossessing cars despite third party claims. In *Zhadan v. Downtown L.A. Motors* (1976) 66 Cal. App. 3d 481, punitive damages were awarded to discourage a car repairer from billing owners for car repair work done without authorization.

In the case at bench, however, there is no indication that the conduct which led to the punitive damage award is at all common. There was no evidence that Appellant handles consignments on a regular basis or is likely to do so in the future. Indeed, there was not even evidence that consignments are common in the automobile sales industry.

The situation which arose here appears to be unique. There is little need to set an example to deter Appellant or others in his industry. There is no need to impose an award of $150,000 against Appellant to discourage wrong-

---

[5] Respondent claimed that this motion was filed too late, beyond the 15 days after entry of judgment allowed by Code of Civil Procedure § 659. The original judgment was filed on August 5, 1985, and the motion for new trial was filed on August 26, 1985. CT 707-708, 730. But Respondent filed an *amended* judgment on August 13 (CT 709-710), and time to file a motion for new trial thus began on August 13. *See Bond v. United Railroads* (1915) 169 Cal. 273, 275; *Machinery, etc. Co. v. University City Synd.* (1934) 3 Cal. App. 2d 425, 426-427. Therefore, the motion filed on August 26 was timely.

ful conduct in this area, when Appellant will have to pay actual damages and his attorneys fees in any event.

While an appellate court may reverse the *granting* of a new trial only upon finding an abuse of discretion, the appellate court must make an *independent* determination as to the propriety of the *denial* of a motion for new trial. *Los Angeles v. Decker* (1977) 18 Cal. 3d 860, 871. We submit that a review of the record in this case and the purpose of punitive damages show that the punitive damage award of $150,000 was excessive and the judgment should be amended or reversed to reflect this.

III. THE TRIAL COURT COMMITTED PREJUDICIAL ERROR BY ADMITTING EVIDENCE THAT APPELLANT HAD LITIGATED PRETRIAL DISCOVERY ISSUES, THAT IT TOOK OVER TWO YEARS TO BRING THE CASE TO TRIAL, AND THAT RESPONDENT HAD INCURRED $56,000 IN ATTORNEYS FEES.

A. THIS EVIDENCE WAS INADMISSIBLE.

In view of the paucity of evidence of malice or fraud, it may seem surprising that the jury awarded punitive damages here. This award might be due, however, to certain prejudicial evidence which the trial court erroneously allowed the jury to hear.

The court allowed Palmer to testify that there had been over 12 "law and motion matters in this lawsuit in an attempt to bring it to trial," that "We have had to battle, take depositions too, forever to get information," that Respondent was awarded sanctions against Appellant, that it had taken about two and a half years to get to trial, and that Palmer had incurred attorneys fees of about $56,000 in this lawsuit. RT 284-289.

The court overruled Appellant's objection to the admission of this evidence, ruling that it was relevant to the issue of whether Appellant's denial of liability was in good faith. RT 17-18, 31-32, 285-288. We submit, however, that this evidence had no reasonable bearing on the good faith of Honda in choosing to defend this case, and therefore it was irrelevant.

Discovery and other pretrial litigation techniques are usually handled by lawyers, not by clients. Absent evidence that the client knowingly directed the lawyer as to whether and how to use these techniques, it cannot be presumed that the client was so involved.

As the court stated in *Daley v. County of Butte* (1964) 227 Cal. App. 2d 380, 392:

> Pretrial procedures are the cabalistic rituals of the lawyers and judges who serve as priests and high priests. The layman knows nothing of their tactical significance. He knows only that his case remains in limbo while the priests and high priests chant their lengthy and arcane pretrial rites. He does know this much: that

several years frequently elapse between the commencement and trial of lawsuits. Since the law imposes this state of puzzled patience on the litigant, it should permit him to sit back in peace and confidence without suspicious inquiries and incessant checking on counsel.

In the case at bench, there was no evidence that Mr. Stevens or anyone else at Honda was actively involved in the pretrial litigation decisions of Appellant's trial lawyer, or that they understood their legality or tactical significance. Therefore, evidence that Appellant's lawyer used certain pretrial devices is not relevant to whether Appellant's denial of liability was in bad faith.

In addition, it should be noted that pretrial litigation tactics which are frivolous or conducted in bad faith are *already* made punishable by sanctions, under Code of Civil Procedure § 128.5, and such sanctions were apparently imposed in this case. CT 35, 159; RT 288. If evidence of such tactics were *also* used to impose punitive damages on Appellant in the underlying action, Appellant would be punished twice for the same conduct. As the court stated in *Troensegaard v. Silvercrest Industries, Inc.* (1985) 175 Cal. App. 3d 218, 228, had the Legislature "intended a double recovery of punitive and penal damages for the same willful, oppressive, malicious, and oppressive [*sic*] acts, it would in some appropriate manner have said so."

The evidence that Palmer incurred $56,000 in attorneys fees in this lawsuit was also inadmissible.[6] The mere fact that Palmer incurred these fees casts *no* light on the question of whether Honda defended this lawsuit *for the purpose of causing* Palmer to incur this expense. If the fact that a plaintiff in a breach of contract suit incurs attorneys fees tends to show that a defendant is acting in bad faith by defending the claim, then evidence of the plaintiff's attorneys fees is admissible in *every* breach of contract action. This cannot be the law.

We might pause to consider the potential consequences of the trial court's ruling that evidence of pretrial litigation tactics and attorneys fees are admissible in a *Seaman's*-type action.

If pretrial litigation tactics were allowed into evidence, then the defendant would have the right to present evidence (testimonial and documentary) fully explaining exactly what was done and why it was done — including evidence of the *plaintiff's* litigation tactics to which defendant was reacting or anticipating. As the court noted in *Daley, supra*, laymen (such as jurors) usually know nothing of the tactical significance of the arcane practices of the high priests of the law. Therefore, expert testimony would be

---

[6] The attorneys fees themselves were not recoverable in this action, as there was no evidence apportioning the fees between those attributable to work toward recovering the amount due under the consignment agreement and those attributable to work toward recovering punitive damages. *See Brandt v. Superior Court* (1985) 37 Cal. 3d 813, 819-820.

necessary to explain to the jury the full meaning, wisdom, and ethics of taking depositions, serving interrogatories, filing and resisting motions for summary judgment, and every other procedure allowed by the Code of Civil Procedure or the common law.

In short, every breach of contract trial could include a mini-trial which would take the jurors through a law school curriculum of Civil Procedure, Evidence, and a Civil Litigation Clinic. This mini-trial might dwarf the rest of the trial — and still leave the jury mystified as to why the lawyers did what they did before trial.

Jurors might also be subjected to defense evidence that the attorneys fees incurred by the plaintiff were unreasonable in amount. This might include testimony that the hourly rate of the plaintiff's attorney was higher than the prevailing rate in the area, that the plaintiff's attorney did unnecessary work, and that his work was of poor quality. Expert testimony on these questions could be presented by both sides.

Lawyers engaged in pretrial litigation, of course, would have to adapt their tactics to the danger that evidence of these tactics could be used against their clients at trial.

Is this what the Supreme Court in *Seaman's* intended? We think not.

For any and all of these reasons, the trial court's ruling admitting this evidence was in error.

B. THIS ERROR WAS PREJUDICIAL.

Admission of the evidence of pretrial litigation tactics and how long it took to get to trial was highly prejudicial to Appellant. Palmer testified to this (RT 287-289), and his lawyer stressed this both in his opening statement (RT 188) and in his closing argument:

> We are requesting punitive damages. The reason why there's two and a half years of litigation Mr. Palmer has taken to prove to you the existence of the contract, a contract that existed two and a half years ago that they ignored, a contract that they made him go through 16 law and motion matters to get it her to you to trial. [RT 728]

As lay people, the jurors would naturally know little about discovery and other "law and motion matters", and they would naturally carry a layman's preconception that any lawyer who uses them is merely a trickster seeking to use technicalities to delay justice. Admission of this evidence permitted Respondent to exploit this preconception and persuade the jury to award punitive damages, despite the paucity of evidence of malice on the part of Appellant.

Admission of the evidence that Palmer had incurred large attorneys fees was highly prejudicial for a different reason: it invited the jury to compensate Respondent for non-recoverable attorneys fees in the guise of a punitive damage award.

As the court's admission of this evidence was erroneous and prejudicial, the judgment should be reversed for this reason also.

IV. THE TRIAL COURT COMMITTED PREJUDICIAL ERROR BY EXCLUDING EVIDENCE THAT PALMER RECEIVED $18,141 IN THE BANKRUPTCY PROCEEDING.

A. THE COLLATERAL SOURCE RULE DOES NOT BAR THE ADMISSION OF THIS EVIDENCE.

Although Respondent's complaint alleged that he recovered $18,141 from Ferrari of Los Gatos in the bankruptcy action (CT 418), Respondent filed a pretrial motion to exclude any evidence of this fact, relying on the "collateral source" rule (RT 17-19). Nevertheless, Respondent conceded that the $18,141 should be deducted from any award against Appellant. RT 19. Appellant opposed the motion, but the court granted it, invoking Evidence Code § 352. RT 34-35.

Evidence of Palmer's recovery of the $18,141 was relevant and admissible under well established California law.

Where two parties are jointly liable to a plaintiff, evidence that plaintiff recovered money from one of the parties is admissible in an action against the other. "Since the plaintiff can have but one satisfaction, evidence of such payments is admissible for the purpose of reducing *pro tanto* the amount of the damages he may be entitled to recover." *Laurenzi v. Vranizan* (1945) 25 Cal. 2d 806, 813. *See also Helfend v. Southern Cal. Rapid Transit Dist.* (1970) 2 Cal. 3d 1, 8, fn.7.

Under this rule, evidence that Palmer recovered $18,141 from Ferrari of Los Gatos was admissible. Assuming that Palmer's agreement with Alvard ran to Honda, so that Honda was liable to Palmer for the proceeds of the sale of Palmer's car, then Ferrari of Los Gatos was also liable for those proceeds, because Ferrari sold the car and *had* the proceeds.[7]

The collateral source rule simply has no application here. That rule provides:

> [I]f an injured party receives compensation for his injuries from a source wholly independent of the tortfeasor, such payment should not be deducted from the damages which the plaintiff would otherwise collect from the tortfeasor. [*Helfend v. Southern Cal. Rapid Transit Dist.* (1970), *supra*, 2 Cal. 3d at 6.]

This rule applies only to payments from someone who has *no connection* with the defendant or with anyone who acted on defendant's behalf. In fact,

---

[7] Mr. Burnett, owner of Ferrari of Los Gatos, admitted that his company owed the proceeds to Palmer. RT 599:7-16. Palmer testified that Burnett had told him this. RT 374:10-12.

the primary purpose of the rule is to enable plaintiffs to retain insurance proceeds on insurance taken out by plaintiffs.

> The collateral source rule expresses a policy judgment in favor of encouraging citizens to purchase and maintain insurance for personal injuries and for other eventualities. [*Id.* at 10][8]

The $18,141 received by Palmer bears no resemblance to insurance proceeds on a policy bought by Palmer.[9] Ferrari of Los Gatos was not "a source wholly independent" of Honda. Assuming that Alvard was acting for Honda when he reconsigned the car to Ferrari of Los Gatos, that company thereupon became the *agent* of Honda for the purpose of selling the car and obtaining the proceeds. When Ferrari's trustee in bankruptcy paid $18,141 to Palmer, that payment was — in effect — a payment from Honda itself.[10]

Respondent — and the trial court — admitted as much when they conceded that the $18,141 should be deducted from any jury award against Appellant. If this payment were from a source independent of Appellant, there would be no reason to deduct this amount from the award.

B. EXCLUSION OF THIS EVIDENCE UNDER EVIDENCE CODE § 352 WAS AN ABUSE OF DISCRETION.

The trial court invoked Evidence Code § 352 in excluding this evidence, stating that:

> It was not even clear that you [Appellant's counsel] could make a claim of what the issue was in this bankruptcy, and it would just be inordinately confusing and time consuming to allow such issues to go before the jury. And generally speaking it would be my rule to never let the proceedings of another tribunal go to a jury unless I absolutely had to. [RT 34:16-25]

---

[8] At pages 13-14, *Helfend* noted that the rule would also cover payments which are similar to such insurance proceeds:

> We therefore reaffirm our adherence to the collateral source rule in tort cases in which the plaintiff has been compensated by an independent collateral source — such as insurance, pension, continued wages, or disability payments — for which he had actually or constructively . . . paid or in cases in which the collateral source would be recompensated from the tort recovery through subrogation, refund of benefits, or some other arrangement.

[9] This $18,141 was essentially damages for breach of contract, and to our knowledge the collateral source rule has never been applied to contract damages. In *United Protective Workers v. Ford Motor Co.* (7th Cir. 1955) 223 F.2d 49, 54, the court held:

> We have been unable to find a single case in which [the collateral source rule] has been carried over to contract damages. In the absence of any binding precedent to the contrary we prefer to follow here the ordinary contract measure of damages rather than the rule in tort cases.

[10] Our case is similar to *Turner v. Mannon* (1965) 236 Cal. App. 2d 134, where the court held that the collateral source rule did not apply to payments to plaintiff made by defendant's insurance company. See also *Krusi v. Bear, Stearns & Co.* (1983) 144 Cal. App. 3d 664, 675; *Kirtland & Packard v. Superior Court* (1976) 59 Cal. App. 3d 140, 144-145.

This statement reveals that the court misunderstood Respondent's motion to exclude. Respondent did not move to exclude evidence of the bankruptcy *proceedings*, but to exclude the simple, uncontested fact that Palmer *received payments* from the bankruptcy proceeding. RT 17:19-21 (Respondent moved for "the exclusion of any payments plaintiff received through the adversary proceeding, exclusion of evidence that any payments [were] received through distributions of the bankruptcy.")

Appellant's counsel made it clear that he had no desire to introduce evidence regarding the bankruptcy proceedings. He simply wanted the jury to understand that Palmer received $18,141 from Ferrari of Los Gatos.

> Well, maybe the court misunderstood me. I wasn't going to produce any evidence as far as the proceeding, but the evidence that I wanted to elicit and I am still asking to be able to produce, the fact that $18,000 has been paid. [RT 34:26-35:4]

There was nothing complicated, confusing, or time-consuming about the fact that Palmer recovered $18,141 from the bankruptcy. A single question to Palmer would have elicited this fact. As the fact was not disputed by Respondent, it might even have been handled by a stipulation. Indeed, it might have been handled *simply by reading to the jury paragraphs 18-20 of Respondent's complaint!*[11]

In addition, it must be noted that the trial court *allowed Respondent to tell the jury that Ferrari of Los Gatos had filed for bankruptcy*. RT 60-62, 193. In view of this, it can hardly be said that telling the jury the single, added fact that Palmer recovered money from that bankruptcy would be "confusing and time consuming."

The trial court abused its discretion by thus allowing the jury to be *misled*. Telling a group of lay people that a company went bankrupt is equivalent to telling them that the creditors of that company went wholly unpaid. Telling the jury that Ferrari of Los Gatos went bankrupt was equivalent to telling them that Palmer received *nothing* from his claim to the proceeds of the sale of his car.[12] This was simply false.

Evidence Code § 352 provides:

> The court in its discretion may exclude evidence if its probative value is substantially outweighed by the probability that its admission will (a) necessitate undue consumption of time or (b) create sub-

---

[11] Paragraph 18 states that Palmer filed an adversary proceeding against Ferrari of Los Gatos in the bankruptcy action, "seeking to trace the proceeds of the sale of the Ferrari." Paragraph 20 states that "Palmer entered into a Settlement Stipulation with Ferrari of Los Gatos and the other defendants in the Adversary Proceeding and received $18,141 in partial satisfaction of his claims as set forth therein." CT 417-418.

[12] Respondent's counsel reinforced this misimpression by telling the jury that "the defendants deprived Mr. Palmer of his car and the proceeds from the sale of his car. The defendants deprived him of this *and gave him nothing*." RT 188:18-22, *emphasis added*.

stantial danger of undue prejudice, of confusing the issues, or of misleading the jury.

Here, the "probative value" of the evidence is very high, as it would show that Palmer's actual damages ($11,359) were less than half of the actual damages he was claiming ($29,500). Because the amount of actual damages is a key factor in setting punitive damages — as will be further explained in the next section of this brief — the fact that Palmer suffered only $11,359 actual damages was very probative on the issue of punitive damages, which is the critical issue in this case.

In *Kessler v. Gray* (1978) 77 Cal. App. 3d 284, 292, the court stated:

> Where the evidence relates to a critical issue, directly supports an inference relevant to that issue, and other evidence does not as directly support the same inference, the testimony *must* be received over a section 352 objection absent highly unusual circumstances. [*emphasis added*]

There were no such "highly unusual circumstances" here. It cannot be said that the probative value of the excluded evidence was "substantially outweighed" by "undue consumption of time," as it would have taken less than a minute to bring out the uncontested fact that Palmer received the $18,141 from Ferrari of Los Gatos. It cannot be said that this probative value was "substantially outweighed" by a "substantial danger of undue prejudice, of confusing the issues, or of misleading the jury," because allowing Respondent to tell the jury that Ferrari *went bankrupt* — *without also* telling them that Ferrari paid $18,141 to Palmer in spite of the bankruptcy — tended to mislead and confuse the jury, much to Appellant's undue prejudice.

It thus appears that *none* of the factors listed in Evidence Code § 352 applies here. "The discretion granted the trial court by § 352 is not absolute [citations] and must be exercised reasonably in accord with the facts before the court." *Brainard v. Cotner* (1976) 59 Cal. App. 3d 790, 796. Therefore, the trial court's exclusion of this evidence was an abuse of discretion.

C. THIS ERROR WAS HIGHLY PREJUDICIAL ON THE MATTER OF PUNITIVE DAMAGES.

The trial court properly instructed the jury that punitive damages must bear a reasonable relation to actual damages. CT 690. It must be presumed that the jury followed this instruction, and that its erroneous assumption that actual damages were $29,500 played a role in its decision to set punitive damages at $150,000. Misleading them as to the correct amount of actual damages, therefore, was prejudicial error. In *Foster v. Keating* (1953) 120 Cal. App. 2d 435, 455, the court stated: "it would be improper and premature to assess [punitive] damages until or concurrently with the assessment of 'the actual damages.'"

In addition, it should be noted that the jury fixed the punitive damages at $150,000, which is almost exactly 5 times $29,500 — the figure which they were told was the actual damages. Had the jury known the truth — that actual damages were only $11,359 — it might well have used this same multiplier of 5 and set punitive damages at $56,795 instead of $150,000.

In *Liodas, supra,* the court held that where compensatory damages are improperly determined, the defendant is entitled to a new trial on the issue of punitive damages. 19 Cal. 3d at 284-285. The same remedy is appropriate here.

As the exclusion of evidence that Palmer received the $18,141 was both erroneous and prejudicial, the judgment should be reversed.[13]

CONCLUSION

A recent Roper poll asked a cross-section of American adults how they rated people in several professions for "honesty and ethical standards." Out of 17 professions listed, "car salespeople" were ranked 17th — at the bottom. 54% of the people believe that the honesty and ethical standards of car sales people are low or very low. See Appendix I, attached.

We can assume that the jury below — another cross-section of American adults — shared this attitude.

Thus, this case was laden with prejudice against Appellant from the beginning, and it is not surprising that the jury awarded punitive damages against Appellant on "shadowy" (at best) evidence of malice, fraud, and the underlying tort itself. In law, however, such latent prejudice and shadowy evidence are not sufficient to support such an award.

We submit that this is a case where *Seaman's* has been extended well beyond its carefully defined limits, and some of the fears expressed in *Quigley* may have materialized.

For any and all of the reasons set out in this brief, the judgment should be reversed or modified by striking the punitive damage award.

Respectfully submitted,
Myron Moskovitz
E. Day Carman
Attorneys for Appellants

May 1, 1986   by:_____

Myron Moskovitz

---

[13] Alternatively, this Court could rectify this error by modifying the judgment, reducing the punitive damages portion of the judgment *pro tanto* down to $56,795 (*see Krusi v. Bear, Stearns & Co.* (1983) 144 Cal. App. 3d 664, 681) — *if* the exclusion of this evidence were the only reversible error committed in this case. However, several other reversible errors (discussed in this brief) were committed, so it would be more appropriate for this Court either to reverse outright or to strike the punitive damage award entirely.

Sample Brief #2

AN APPELLANT'S OPENING BRIEF IN A CRIMINAL CASE

[A] THE CONCEPT BEHIND THIS BRIEF

This brief was filed in a criminal case, *People v. McNally*.[4] Jim McNally drove his Ford Bronco into a Volkswagen, killing a young woman and severely injuring a young man. McNally was convicted of vehicular manslaughter (with "gross negligence") and drunk driving. He was sentenced to six years in prison.

McNally wanted to appeal. But an appellate attorney told him to serve his time and save his money — there were no grounds for appeal. When he came to me, that was my initial reaction too. The evidence showed that he was intoxicated when he drove his car into the Volkswagen. But there was something about the case that bothered me. Somehow, the final result seemed unfair.

This was an unusual crime — it was based on negligence, not intent. McNally did not intend to hurt anyone. It may be fair to punish people for negligence, but it does not seem fair to punish them very much. They are simply not as culpable as those who intentionally hurt people. Six years imprisonment for negligence rubbed me the wrong way. Perhaps it would also rub appellate judges the wrong way. I decided to take the case.

There were also some peculiar facts. McNally was a businessman, with no prior criminal record. He went to a company party, had a few drinks, and then had this accident. He was not your typical career criminal. Perhaps the judges might identify with him somewhat. (This may seem unfair to poor defendants with whom the judges could *not* identify, but that's not my problem. My duty is to my client.) Also, the accident occurred in a small community, where the young woman who died was well known and very popular. The "righteous anger" of the community might well have influenced both the jurors and the sentencing judge. It might also influence the appellate judges, but there might be a way to *turn* this to our advantage — to imply that McNally was a victim of a type of "vigilante justice." I couldn't *prove* this, as the record didn't really have evidence that the jurors or judge were influenced by it. But I could state what we had and raise some inferences.

So this would be the core of our brief: the result was unfair. This couldn't be our *legal* argument. Neither the Constitution nor any statute forbids

---

[4] The name has been changed. Even though the decision is published, I'd rather not broadcast my client's name across the country.

"unfair" results. But this would be our *emotional* argument — the means of getting the judges to *want* to reverse the judgment. My next job would be to search every nook and cranny of the trial transcripts for some legal "hooks" on which the appellate court could hang its reversal.

I could find only one: a jury instruction that just didn't seem right. As you'll see, the brief argues that this instruction was not consistent with what the Legislature intended. This argument didn't seem too promising. The instruction was a standard "CALJIC" (California Jury Instructions, Criminal) instruction which had been approved for cases of this type. Also McNally's trial counsel had not objected to the instruction. To get over this second hurdle, I would have to convince the court that the defect in the instruction was so fundamental that the judge should have fixed it even without an objection. This would be difficult, but if the court *wanted* to reverse, it could.

Even if we failed to get the verdict set aside, we might have a shot at the sentence, in two ways. First, the brief would methodically go through the sentencing rules and try to show that the trial court abused its discretion — both in denying probation and imposing a 6-year term instead of a 4-year term. Second, I would make a constitutional argument — that the 6-year sentence was "cruel or unusual" punishment. It is rare for a court to find any punishment short of execution or torture to be "cruel or unusual," and I didn't really expect this court to buy it. But this challenge permitted the inclusion of some arguments about the basic fairness of the sentence that I would have had difficulty including elsewhere. These arguments might put the judges in a mood to accept my more traditional claims based on the sentencing rules.

I decided to use one more tactic — a very important one. With my client's consent, I would tell the court that my client was guilty — not of the crime charged, but a lesser one (vehicular manslaughter *without* "gross negligence"). This concession would make me appear reasonable and McNally appear remorseful. In fact, this wouldn't give up much, because the evidence of this lesser crime was quite strong, and we had virtually no chance of knocking out a conviction on *that* charge. But if this concession could help us persuade the court to reverse the conviction on the higher charge, we would gain a lot, as the possible sentence for the lesser crime was significantly lower.

The process by which this strategy was developed might seem strange to you. Rather than begin with the law and use "justice" arguments to bolster my legal arguments, I did it the other way around. Looking back on it, it seems strange to me too. It certainly is not what I learned in law school. In my practice over the years, I've done it the other way too, and sometimes it worked. Sometimes there *aren't* many justice factors, and just arguing the law is sufficient. But that is more unusual than you might imagine. As the other two Sample Briefs show, justice issues crop up even in business cases.

Usually, I'm reluctant to bring a client to oral argument. I don't want to be tempted to flatter or impress the client, instead of focusing on persuading the court. But I brought McNally to the oral argument — and had him sit right behind me, so the judges could see that the person described in my brief was in fact the clean-cut businessman I said he was.

The Court of Appeal reversed both the verdict and the sentence. *See* 181 Cal. App. 3d 1048 (1986). The opinion is quite traditional, applying the law to the facts, not directly mentioning the "justice" and emotional points in my brief. The court accepted almost every argument in the brief — except my "cruel and unusual punishment" argument. Did the court just dutifully follow the law, or was it influenced by my stratagems? We'll never know.

[B] WHAT TO WATCH FOR WHILE READING THIS BRIEF

You might get the most out of this section by reading it *after* you read — or at least skim — the brief. *Note*: To save space in this Book, the brief is single-spaced. Most court rules require double or 1.5 line spacing.

As you read the brief, note that — on the surface — it seems very traditional. Every argument is framed as a legal argument, simply applying the law to the facts. But threaded through all this is an undertone, constantly playing the same justice theme: "Jim McNally was unfairly tried and unfairly sentenced. He deserves to be punished, but not this much."

[1] The Statement of the Case

Little things can mean a lot. The Statement of the Case mentions that McNally was released on bail of $5,000 pending the appeal. This has nothing to do with the arguments raised in the appeal, so why include it? Because it shows that the trial judge felt that he was not dangerous and that his ties to the community were so strong that he would not take off — even after he was convicted! A small thing, but it's one more item tending to show that McNally was not such a bad guy. Keep an eye out for little things like this as you read the brief.

[2] The Statement of Facts

Trial lawyers do not present evidence in a neat, orderly, chronological story. One witness might testify first not because his part of the story comes first, but because he is available to testify that day and going on vacation the next day. Another witness might testify to facts occurring at the beginning and end of the story, but not the middle. Facts come out in a disorderly, sloppy manner, and the trial attorneys use their closing arguments to put them into a logical order.

Your job as an appellate lawyer is to gather in the facts — scattered throughout the transcripts, mingled in with objections, repetitions, and irrelevancies — and mold them into a story that makes sense, reads well, and helps you win the appeal. You have many choices on how to do this, so long as you comply with the rules. If you plan to argue that no substantial evidence supports the verdict, the rules of appellate review require you to include all facts that tend to support the verdict. If you plan to argue that a jury instruction was prejudicial (as I do in this case), the rules of review allow you to include evidence that was disputed (so you may show that this was a "close case," and but for the erroneous instruction, the jury might have decided otherwise).

How you *arrange* the facts is totally up to you. In this Statement of Facts, I chose to begin *not* with the facts of the *crime*, but with facts about the *defendant*. Why? Because the facts about McNally are very favorable. He was a decent citizen, going about his life, just as you, me, or an appellate judge might. Then he made a mistake — just as one of us might have done. The underlying message to the judge is: "This could have been you."

Usually, the Statement of Facts includes only the out-of-court real-life facts, not facts about what happened in court, which belong in the Statement of the Case. The rules don't say this, but "custom" does. I normally follow custom, as judges are used to it. But when custom conflicts with what I think is the best way to present my case, to hell with custom. The last part of the Statement of Facts is about in-court facts, because it sets up my Argument. Indeed, I try to do even more: to use these facts to *persuade* the appellate court, right in the Statement of Facts itself.

Where the situation permits, it's nice to break up the Statement of Facts into subsections, to make it more readable. Here, it made sense to break it up into "The Crime" and "The Sentence." But some of the facts in the first part of "The Crime," about what a great guy McNally was, are taken from the *sentencing* portions of the trial transcripts.

Note the use of words like "only" and "nevertheless" in the Statement of Facts. While mildly argumentative, they highlight certain facts and factual connections.

Certain language from the record is *quoted* rather than paraphrased. These little things add impact to key facts. Finally, note that the appellant is always called by his name, not "the appellant" — he is a human being, not a faceless party.

[3] The Summary of Argument

The Summary of Argument spells out the guts of my case. It is *not* just a repetition of my Table of Contents. It is meant to be *persuasive* — all by itself, in a very short space. It might convince a judge too busy or lazy to read the rest of my brief, and it might put a more diligent judge in a mood to be receptive to the more detailed argument which follows.

[4] The Argument

While emotional factors are important — even crucial — it is also essential to do a good job on the law. Much as the judges may want to do "justice" — as they see it — they can't do so if they will look patently arbitrary or careless about established law. Show them a way to rule in your favor while writing an opinion that appears merely to follow established precedent. This is what I tried to do here.

This Argument contains 29 footnotes. That's a lot. I tend to use footnotes more than most lawyers. Some judges say they don't like footnotes: "I don't like bobbing my head up and down. If it's important enough to put in the brief, put it in the text." They have a point. But as you read the footnotes, I think you'll find it hard to decide whether they should be put in the text or omitted entirely. Putting them in the text would break the flow of my argument, while omitting them would leave out something helpful, even if not crucial. Footnotes are a compromise. I don't think a footnote ever cost me a case, but I can remember victories where the court used the material in my footnotes in their opinions. If footnotes give the judge a neckache but help you win the case, use them. You work for your client, not the judge.

Footnote 21 refers to "Appendix A" to the brief — a study of sentencing practices in Los Angeles. It is highly unusual to attach such a study to an appellate brief. I could certainly have *cited* this study, but I knew it was very unlikely that a study like this could be found in the Court's law library. The Court *might* take the trouble of asking its law librarian to send for it — but then again, it might not. If you really want the Court to see something like this, why not do the Court (and yourself) a favor by simply attaching a copy of it to your brief?

[5] The Conclusion

There are no *rules* about Conclusions. By *custom*, many lawyers use them simply to summarize their legal arguments. I try to do more.

You've *already* given your legal arguments — in your Argument. The Conclusion is your chance — indeed, your *last* chance — to pull out the stops and lay out your *emotional* arguments. This way, the Conclusion has some *independent* persuasive value. As this is the last thing the judge reads, maybe this is what the judge will mull over tonight before he goes to sleep — and what he'll be thinking about tomorrow when he writes his opinion.

I tried to make this Conclusion persuasive by including my emotional arguments.

IN THE COURT OF APPEAL OF THE STATE OF CALIFORNIA
FIFTH APPELLATE DISTRICT

THE PEOPLE OF THE STATE OF CALIFORNIA,

Plaintiff and Respondent,

vs.

JAMES BRYAN McNALLY,

Defendant and Appellant

No. F004598
(Tulare County Superior
Court No. 22291)

APPELLANT'S OPENING BRIEF

On Appeal from the Judgment of the Superior Court of the State of
California for the County of Tulare

HONORABLE DAVID L. ALLEN, JUDGE

Myron Moskovitz
536 Mission St.
San Francisco, Calif. 94105
Phone: (415) 442-6646

James T. Wilson
Wilson, Alschule & Sigmund
3714 W. Mineral King Avenue
Visalia, CA 93291
(209) 627-3666

Attorneys for Appellant

TABLE OF CONTENTS

TABLE OF AUTHORITIES

Page

Cases

STATEMENT OF THE CASE

On March 16, 1984, an Information was filed in Tulare County Superior Court charging Appellant with three crimes, allegedly committed on January 21, 1984:

> Count I: Vehicular manslaughter of Karen Walker, with gross negligence, in violation of Penal Code § 192(3)(c).

> Count II: Driving under the influence of alcohol and causing bodily injury to Karen Walker and Russell Biggs, in violation of Vehicle Code § 23153(a).

> Count III: Driving with .10 or above blood alcohol and causing bodily injury to Karen Walker and Russell Biggs, in violation of Vehicle Code § 23153(b). CT (Clerk's Transcript) 1.

Appellant pled not guilty to the charges. CT 2. After a jury trial, Appellant was found guilty on all three counts. CT 74-76.

The Presentence Report recommended that probation be denied, but also recommended that Appellant receive only the lower term of four years on Count I. PR (Presentence Report) 10. (The presentence report has been filed as part of the record on appeal. It appears at the back of the Clerk's Transcript.)

On December 4, 1984, the trial court, however, not only denied probation, but also rejected the recommendation that the lower term be imposed. It imposed the middle term of 6 years. CT 145. In addition, the trial court imposed a consecutive sentence of 8 months on Count II. CT 145. A sentence on Count III was stayed pursuant to Penal Code § 654. CT 145.

Appellant was released on bail of $5,000 pending appeal. CT 146.

Notice of Appeal was filed on December 7, 1984. CT 150.

STATEMENT OF FACTS

The Crime

For 20 years, Jim McNally has been a highly respected and responsible member of his community. He is married and the father of two teenaged boys. PR 1-2. He is a college graduate and a military veteran. *Id.* He is a businessman, the sole owner of California Gun Specialties, Inc., a wholesale gun distributor employing 30 people in the Tulare County community of Lindsay. PR 2. His "criminal record" consists of one ticket for failing to stop at a stop sign. *Id.* The record shows no indication of any alcohol or drug problems of any kind. *Id.* He has served his community as a 4-H Community Leader, High 4-H Advisor, California Hunter Safety Instructor, Livestock Project Leader, and Area Chairman of Ducks Unlimited. CT 105, 106, 108, 117, 119, 123, 127, 128, 130, 137.

He has contributed time, money and materials to the Lindsay Community Theater, the Lindsay Athletic Boosters, the Key Club, Little League, and other community projects. CT 117, 140, 142, 143. He is widely respected and admired as "a fine, fine man," a "concerned citizen," a "loving, caring individual" with "a keen concern for humanity" and "high moral character." CT 103-143.

On January 21, 1984, Jim McNally made a mistake — a serious mistake, with tragic consequences.

On Friday, January 20, and Saturday, January 21, 1984, California Gun Specialties held its annual sales meeting at the Lampliter Inn in Visalia. RT 521-524. As President of the company, McNally attended all of the sessions of the meeting. RT 521-524.

On Saturday night, at the end of the business meetings, a cocktail party (from about 6:30 to 8:30 p.m.) and dinner (from about 8:00 to 10:30 p.m.) were held. RT 526-527. McNally drank some beer and wine before and during the cocktail party (RT 579, 598), some wine at dinner (RT 546, 603), and perhaps a drink after dinner in the Inn's lounge. RT 603, 604, 629. Both prosecution and defense witnesses testified that McNally did not appear to be intoxicated at any time that evening at the Lampliter Inn. RT 123, 529, 562, 605-606.

At about 11:30 p.m., McNally left the Lampliter, driving alone in his 1979 Ford Bronco toward his home in Lindsay. RT 605-606. Soon after midnight, while driving down County Center Drive, he failed to stop at a stop sign at the Caldwell Avenue intersection. RT 285-286. Just at that moment, a small Volkswagen "bug" driving along Caldwell came through the intersection. RT 14-16, 20, 90. The Bronco struck the Volkswagen broadside. RT 247. The driver of the Volkswagen, Russell Biggs, was seriously injured. RT 16 17. His passenger and girlfriend, 19-year-old Karen Walker, was killed. RT 12-13, 91. McNally was unhurt. RT 92, 164.

McNally was intoxicated. He failed field sobriety tests (RT 95-96, 169-179), and a blood alcohol test showed his alcohol level to be .15. RT 148-149.

The posted speed limit on County Center Drive was 30 miles per hour, and on Caldwell it was 45 miles per hour. RT 155, 188. Under California's Basic Speed Law, however, greater speeds are permitted if conditions make it safe. RT 189, 190. The clear conditions that night (RT 189) did permit a greater speed, and a speed five to ten miles per hour over the posted speed would have been safe. RT 188.

At trial, there was little or no dispute regarding any of the above facts. What was disputed — extensively — was the speed at which each vehicle was actually traveling when the collision occurred.

Three witnesses who saw or heard the Bronco driving down County Center Drive before the accident estimated its speed to be between 50 and 60 miles per hour. RT 29, 41, 60. Two accident reconstruction experts for the prosecution gave varying estimates of the Bronco's speed: 60.9 MPH (RT 250), between 55 and 64 MPH (RT 251), and 52.46 MPH (RT 318). Defense experts, however, testified that the Bronco was traveling at 41.39 MPH (RT 382, 396) or between 35 and 42 MPH (RT 453).

The Volkswagen was also exceeding the posted speed limit, though here too the prosecution experts could not agree on how fast the car was actually traveling. Prosecution experts testified that it was traveling at 58.6 MPH (RT 251), between 53 and 59 MPH (RT 251, 287), and between 48 and 55 MPH (RT 336).

At closing argument, defense counsel conceded that the basic elements of vehicular manslaughter had been established, and that Appellant had never claimed otherwise. He argued extensively, however, that the prosecution had failed to prove the additionally charged element of "gross negligence." RT 685-686. In particular, he conceded that McNally had been intoxicated (RT 690) and that McNally had failed to stop at the stop sign (RT 696), but argued that Appellant's speed had not been excessive (RT 696-706).

The prosecutor, during his closing argument, argued at one point that gross negligence was shown solely by the fact that McNally had driven while intoxicated. RT 709. At other points in his argument, he argued that gross negligence was shown by McNally's failure to stop at the stop sign, including his failure to slow down, look for side traffic, and yield the right of way. RT 679-683. At other points, he stressed McNally's alleged speeding as establishing gross negligence. RT 680-684, 713-714. Summing up, the prosecutor told the jury that a verdict of guilty of vehicular manslaughter without gross negligence would "congratulate" McNally for "killing an 18 year-old girl." RT 715:5-13. He repeated his "congratulations" argument several times. RT 19:4-7.

The trial court gave the jury standard jury instructions defining vehicular manslaughter (CALJIC 8.90.1) and gross negligence (CALJIC 8.92).

CT 45-48. However, the jury was not instructed that it could not base a finding of gross negligence on facts which satisfied the elements of vehicular manslaughter. Also, the jury was not given CALJIC 17.01, requiring that the jury unanimously find certain acts it relied on to establish the elements of vehicular manslaughter and gross negligence. This instruction apparently was considered and rejected by the trial court. CT 71.

The jury returned a verdict of guilty on Count I, with gross negligence, as well as on Counts II and III. RT 747-748.

The Sentence

On November 21, 1984, Tulare County Probation Officers Robert Duncan and Robert Sharley filed a Presentence Report, a copy of which is part of the record on appeal. The report reviewed McNally's social, family, and employment history. PR 1-2. Regarding use of alcohol, the report found that "Prior to the instant offense, the defendant consumed alcoholic beverages daily in extreme moderation," and that McNally "has discontinued his use of alcohol since causing the death of Karen Walker." PR 3. Other than a single traffic ticket (failure to stop), a record check turned up no prior convictions (PR 3).

Regarding his feelings about the instant offense, McNally said he was "tremendously sorry" about causing the collision and that it was the "worst thing that could have possibly happened." PR 4. He had contacted the Walker family and tried to express his remorse. PR 4. He took the matter to trial only because he believed that he was not grossly negligent. PR 4.

No matter what sentence is imposed, McNally's felony conviction might cause his federal licenses to sell guns to be revoked, and this may cause California Gun Specialties to be sold or liquidated. PR 4. A prison sentence would increase the likelihood of such revocation. PR 4-5. This might cause the 30 people who work for him to lose their jobs, and cause his older son to quit college to come home and help his mother. PR 5.

The Presentence Report also described Karen Walker. She was a cheerleader at the local high school, graduated in the top third of her class, was very active in church and school activities, and was chosen to be listed in Who's Who Among American High School Students. PR 5. Karen's parents were severely affected emotionally by Karen's death, and they obtained counseling and medication for depression for several months after her death. PR 5-6. Their "deepest concern" was "that the defendant's punishment fits his crime." PR 6.

Russell Biggs was badly injured and was hospitalized for six days by the collision. PR 6. He was also very depressed by Karen's death. PR 7. His father, Vern Biggs, told the probation department that "defendant's punishment must be commensurate with the crime." PR 7. The Presentence

Report noted that the probation department had received 31 letters supporting McNally, and summed them up as follows:

> In summary, those letters indicated the defendant is considerate, compassionate, caring, sincere and a good father to his sons. Furthermore, Mr. McNally is noted to be an active member of the community, noting his extensive involvement in 4-H, Ducks Unlimited and as an instructor in the State Hunter Safety Program. It was noted Mr. McNally has a high regard for public safety, a love for children and that he has suffered a tremendous amount of mental anguish as the result of his involvement in these crimes. One writer questioned whether a commitment to prison would benefit anyone: the defendant; his family; friends; employees; the community; or, the Walker family. Other writers asked the court to consider that Mr. McNally has been an asset to his community in the past. [PR 7.]

The Presentence Report found two circumstances in mitigation under Rule of Court 423(b): (1) that McNally had no prior criminal record, and (2) that McNally was willing to make restitution for any loss not paid by his insurance company. PR 7.

Under the heading "Circumstances In Aggravation," the report stated, "None." PR 8.

Therefore, the probation officers recommended that on Count I, the vehicular manslaughter charge, McNally be sentenced to the mitigated term of 4 years in prison. PR 9. The report also noted that on January 1, 1984, only 3 weeks before the crime, the Legislature had increased the penalties for vehicular manslaughter. PR 9.

Regarding probation, the report listed seven factors under Rule of Court 414(d) which favored probation: (1) McNally had no prior criminal record, (2) he was willing to comply with terms of probation, (3) he was well educated and had strong ties to Tulare County, (4) he had a stable employment history, (5) "having never served a period of incarceration and facing the possibility of liquidating his family's business, the likely effect of imprisonment on the defendant and his dependents may be significant," (6) he may lose his federal licenses to run his business, and (7) he has expressed remorse. PR 8.

The report listed only two factors under Rule of Court 414(c) against probation: (1) Karen Walker was killed and Russell Biggs was injured, physically and psychological, and (2) McNally inflicted bodily injury. PR 8.

Nevertheless, the report recommended that probation be denied (PR 8), noting that "denial of probation is consistent with recent Legislative intent focusing on increased punishments for those convicted of causing death while driving under the influence of alcohol." PR 9.

Because the crime involved multiple victims and injuries, the report also recommended that a consecutive sentence be imposed on Count II. PR 8. In addition, the report recommended that a restitution fine of $3,000 be imposed. PR 8.

In response to the Presentence Report, the prosecutor filed a Statement In Opposition to the Mitigated Sentence. CT 79. In this document, the prosecutor contended that the Presentence Report had omitted a circumstance in aggravation: that the victim was "particularly vulnerable," as the Volkswagen could not have avoided the collision. CT 79-80. Therefore, this aggravating circumstance balanced out the mitigating circumstances, and the prosecutor urged that the middle term of 6 years should be imposed on Count I. CT 81.

McNally's attorney then submitted a Statement in Support of Probation. CT 85. This statement elaborated upon the factors relevant to probation which were listed in the Presentence Report, and it attached and summarized 35 letters attesting to McNally's contributions to the community and how a prison sentence would affect his family and employees. CT 86-94. The statement requested that McNally's be granted probation, subject to ten conditions, including the following: (1) that McNally's serve a term in county jail, (2) that McNally pay a fine, (3) that McNally not drink alcohol during probation, and (4) that McNally serve in community programs designed to deter drunk driving. CT 95-96.

At the sentencing hearing, the court began by noting "the large number of people here." RT of 12/4/84 hearing, page 1. Several members of the Walker and Biggs families then addressed the court regarding Karen's value to them and to the community, and the effect which her death had on them. *Id.* at 2-38. These statements said little about McNally, except to repeat the circumstances of the crime and to "demand that Mr. McNally be given the maximum sentence allowable by law for killing Karen." *Id.* at 7. These statements did not include any allegations that the Presentence Report or the letters supporting McNally had misstated or overstated in any way McNally's contributions to the community. Nor was any other evidence introduced which attacked this information.

McNally's attorney, Mr. Wilson, then addressed the court, pointing out that the six-year sentence on Count I sought by the prosecutor would be much harsher than that imposed on a recent defendant (Ruiz) by the same court for vehicular manslaughter, even though Ruiz had stolen the car, had no license, was speeding, failed to stop at a stop sign, and struck a car containing a family of four — injuring two children and killing both parents. *Id.* at 40-41.

Mr. Wilson also pointed out that McNally's conviction has caused revocation of his driver's license for at least three years, and that McNally has not touched alcohol since the accident. *Id.* at 45-46. Therefore, placing McNally on probation would not impose a danger on society. *Id.* Mr. Wilson also made it clear that he was requesting a county jail sentence of one year as a condition of probation. *Id.* at 47. Mr. Wilson noted that the Legislature had precluded the availability of probation for certain offenses, but vehicular manslaughter was not one of them. *Id.* at 49-51. If McNally's case was not suitable for probation, Wilson said, then *no* case under Penal Code § 192(3)(c) was suitable for probation. *Id.* at 51. After discussing factors listed in Rule 414(d) as relevant to probation, Mr. Wilson concluded that "Mr. McNally meets every single one of those. *Id.* at 52.

In response, the prosecutor argued that granting probation, even if conditioned on a year in county jail, would "fly in the face" of the Legislature's intent, as the Legislature had recently doubled the penalties for vehicular manslaughter as of January 1, 1984. *Id.* at 62-63. He also argued that the fact that McNally committed this single crime showed that he was a danger to society. *Id.* at 65. In rebuttal, Mr. Wilson pointed out that although the Legislature had indeed doubled the penalties for vehicular manslaughter, it had not eliminated the availability of probation for this crime. *Id.* at 67.

After hearing these arguments, the court announced its sentence.

First, probation was denied. *Id.* at 69-73. In applying Rule of Court 414 — "Criteria Affecting Probation" — the court relied on subdivision (c)(1), "the nature, seriousness and circumstances of the crime, and subdivision (c)(2) "the vulnerability of the victim and degree of harm or loss to the victim. *Id.* at 69-73. While the court found that McNally would not be a danger to society under Rule 414(b) (*Id.* at 79-80), no mention was made of any of the remaining subdivisions of Rule 414. No mention was made of the other six subdivisions of subsection (c), or of subsection (d), "Facts Relating to the Defendant", even though the Presentence Report and letters submitted by Mr. Wilson discussed these factors extensively. Indeed, the facts inherent in the crime of which McNally was convicted appeared to dominate the court's decision to deny probation:

> It was a killing, a homicide, and it was caused by somebody who was driving under the influence, and it was done with gross negligence. That one factor almost standing by itself could almost preclude the granting of probation, and the nature and seriousness of the circumstances of this particular offense. [*Id.* at 70. *See also id.* at 81:3-8, where the court expressed similar sentiments.]

Next, the court selected the middle term of six years as the proper sentence for Count I, vehicular manslaughter with gross negligence, rejecting the Presentence Report recommendation that the mitigated term of four years be imposed. *Id.* at 73-74, 79. While the Presentence Report had found no aggravating circumstances under Rule of Court 421, the trial court found "at least three or more circumstances in aggravation." *Id.* at 74. Later, the court identified two of these as "the nature and circumstances and type of offense for which he has been convicted" (*id.* at 80), and "deterring others." *Id.* at 80:8-9. The second factor is not listed as an aggravating factor in Rule 421, but it is indicated as one of the general objectives in sentencing in Rule 410. Earlier, while explaining its decision to impose a consecutive sentence on Count II, the court did cite three aggravating factors listed in Rule 421: the crime involved great bodily harm, the victim was particularly vulnerable, and the crime involved multiple victims. *Id.* at 75:24-76:2. As the circumstances in aggravation balanced out the circumstances in mitigation, the court imposed the middle term of six years on Count I. *Id.* at 79.

On Count II, the court again denied probation because of the nature and circumstances of The crime, to wit, driving under the influence with gross negligence, the vulnerability of the victim (Russell Biggs), and the fact that McNally inflicted serious bodily injury on Biggs. *Id.* at 74.

The court then ruled that the sentence on Count II should be consecutive to that imposed on Count I. *Id.* at 75-77. Applying Rule of Court 425, the court relied on the facts that the crime involved multiple victims and great bodily harm, and that the victim was particularly vulnerable. *Id.* at 75:19-76:4. In accordance with Penal Code § 1170.1, a consecutive sentence of one-third the middle term for Count II, specifically eight months, was imposed to run consecutively with the six years imposed on Count I. *Id.* at 77:12-14.

The court selected a middle term of two years on Count III, but stayed imposition of sentence on that count because of the prohibition against double punishment for the same act, as provided by Penal Code § 654. *Id.* at 77:15-23, 85:7-11.

The court also imposed a fine of $3,000 (*Id.* at 78:4-12) on McNally, and advised him that after he served his term in prison he would be on parole for an additional three years. *Id.* at 78:13-21.

SUMMARY OF ARGUMENT

The sole defense at trial was that, although McNally was guilty of vehicular manslaughter of some sort, his crime did not include the added element of gross negligence. For the jury to give him a fair trial on this issue, it was crucial that it be instructed that the element of gross negligence cannot be found solely from facts satisfying the essential elements of Penal Code § 192(3)(c) — drunk driving and a traffic offense. The jury was not so instructed.

Even assuming the conviction of this count was proper, the sentence of six years imprisonment was not. The trial court abused its discretion by denying probation, because an uncontradicted Presentence Report showed that McNally met every one of the criteria specified in the Rules of Court which are relevant to this case. In addition, selection of the middle term of six years violated the Rules of Court and — in this case constituted cruel or unusual punishment.

The trial court also abused its discretion by denying probation and imposing a consecutive sentence on Count II.

ARGUMENT

I. REGARDING COUNT I, THE TRIAL COURT COMMITTED PREJUDICIAL ERROR BY NOT FAILING TO INSTRUCT THE JURY THAT IT COULD NOT BASE A FINDING OF GROSS NEGLIGENCE SOLELY ON FACTS INHERENT IN THE CRIME OF VEHICULAR MANSLAUGHTER.

A. Such An Instruction Is Essential In A Prosecution Under Penal Code § 192(3)(c).

Count I of the Information filed against McNally charged him with violating Penal Code § 192(3)(c). CT. 1. That section defines vehicular manslaughter, in relevant part, as:

> Driving a vehicle in violation of § 23152 [driving under the influence] or § 23153 [driving under the influence and causing bodily injury] of the Vehicle Code *and* in the commission of an unlawful act, not amounting to felony, and with gross negligence. . . . [*Emphasis added.*]

Subsection 3(d) of § 192, however, prohibits a slightly different type of vehicular manslaughter:

> Driving a vehicle in violation of § 23152 or 23153 of the Vehicle Code *and* in the commission of an unlawful act, not amounting to felony, but without gross negligence. . . . [*Emphasis added.*]

The only difference between these two subsections is that subsection 3(c) requires "gross negligence" and subsection 3(d) does not. The difference in punishment, however, is substantial. Subsection 3(c) carries a penalty of four, six or eight years in state prison, while subsection 3(d) carries a penalty of only 16 months, two or four years in state prison. Penal Code § 193.

The basic elements of subsection 3(d) are, one, driving under the influence, and, two, the commission of an unlawful, nonfelonious act (presumably a traffic violation). The language of subsection 3(c) is identical, though it adds a third element, gross negligence.

Therefore, it seems clear that the Legislature intended that elements one and two would not be sufficient to support a finding of the third element, for otherwise subsection 3(c) would merely duplicate subsection 3(d). Thus, a finding of gross negligence *cannot* be based solely on the facts that the defendant was driving under the influence, and committed a traffic offense. Something *more* is needed to show "gross negligence." Otherwise, the Legislature's decision to establish two different subsections with two different penalties would be rendered meaningless.

To carry out this legislative intent, juries should be specifically instructed that they may not base a finding of "gross negligence" merely on the facts that a defendant drove under the influence and committed a traffic offense. Unless juries are so instructed, the legislative intent might easily be frustrated. The term "gross negligence" is an imprecise one, even to lawyers and judges. Lay people — jurors — might well view someone who drives while intoxicated as "grossly negligent" by that fact alone. If, in addition, the defendant committed a traffic violation while so driving, it is even more likely that jurors would consider this "grossly negligent" conduct. A jury instruction which merely defines "gross negligence" in general terms invites jurors to make just this mistake.

In the case at bench, the jurors were encouraged — by the prosecutor as well as the court's instructions — to make exactly this mistake.

B. Failure To Give Such An Instruction Was Highly Prejudicial In The Instant Case.

In this case, the trial court instructed the jury that if it first found that the basic elements of vehicular manslaughter were present, "you must also find whether the act causing the death was done with or without gross negligence; and you must declare your finding in that respect in your verdict." RT 733:24, 734:1; CT 46. The definition of "gross negligence" which followed, however, was only a very general one:

> The term "gross negligence," as used in the definition of manslaughter given in these instructions, means the failure to exercise any care, or the exercise of so little care that you are justified in believing that the person whose conduct is involved was wholly in different to the consequences of his conduct to the welfare of others. [RT 734:16-22; CT 48.]

This definition — without a further explanation — was highly misleading in the context of Penal Code § 192(3)(c), because it invited the jury to find gross negligence based solely on the facts that McNally was driving under the influence and failed to stop at the stop sign — facts which would satisfy only the *first two* elements of the statute.

The misleading nature of the court's instruction on "gross negligence" was exacerbated by the prosecutor's closing argument.

While the prosecutor discussed evidence that McNally was intoxicated, ran the stop sign, and speeded, at various points in his closing argument, the prosecutor never made it clear which of these allegations would support a finding of "gross negligence." In fact, *the prosecutor never told the jury that the mere fact that McNally was intoxicated was sufficient to show "gross negligence"*:

> Do you feel based on the evidence in this case and what took place at the intersection that the alcohol did not cause the accident? Are we talking about a stone cold sober person driving a vehicle down County Center? No. Did it cause the accident? *That is what gross negligence deals with, facts.* Did it cause the accident? Absolutely, alcohol caused this accident. [RT 709:14-20; *emphasis added*.]

We grant that the prosecutor, in other parts of his closing argument regarding gross negligence, also discussed other traffic offenses alleged to have been committed by McNally. *See, e.g.*, RT 680-683, where the prosecutor argued that McNally was speeding, did not slow down, and did not look down Caldwell before he went by the stop sign.

It is *possible* that the jury based its finding of gross negligence on *all* of the infractions McNally was alleged to have committed. It is equally possible, however, that defense experts convinced the jury that there was a reasonable doubt as to whether McNally was speeding. It is also quite possible that the jury paid scant or no attention to disputed evidence as to whether McNally slowed down before the stop sign, and simply based its finding of gross negligence on the fact that McNally was intoxicated (as the prosecutor urged it to do) or on that fact plus the additional fact that McNally did not stop at the stop sign. If the jury did either of those things, its verdict of "gross negligence" was incorrect, as it found only the first one or two elements of Penal Code § 192(3)(c), and *not the third*.

We do not know the basis for the jury's finding. We do know, however, that if the jury was properly instructed, it might well have found that there was a reasonable doubt as to whether there was gross negligence in this case. If the jury was instructed that negligent conduct *over and above* intoxication and a single traffic offense is required for gross negligence, it might well have found that such conduct was missing, insubstantial, or inherent in running the stop sign.

Thus, failure to so instruct the jury was prejudicial error by the trial court, and the judgment of the court should be reversed and remanded for a new trial under proper instructions.

C. The Trial Court Had A Duty To So Instruct The Jury On Its Own Motion.

While no request was made for the instruction discussed above, this does not preclude Appellant from raising this issue on appeal, because the trial court was required to give such an instruction *sua sponte* — on its own motion.

In *People v. Wade* (1959) 53 Cal. 2d 322, the court set out the basic rule on this matter:

> In determining what instructions a trial court is required to give without request, the rule is usually stated to be that the court has a duty to give instructions on the general principles of law governing the case, even though not requested by the parties, but it need not instruct on specific points developed at the trial unless requested. . . . The judge need not fill in every time a litigant or his counsel fails to discover an abstruse but possible theory of the facts. . . . The most rational interpretation of the phrase "general principles of law governing the case" would seem to be as those

principles of law commonly or closely and openly connected with the facts of the case before the court. [*Id.* at 334; *see also People v. Henry* (1972) 22 Cal. App. 2d 951, 957-958; *People v. Hamilton* (5th Dist., 1978) 80 Cal. App. 3d. 124, 132-133.]

The notion that "gross negligence" — as that term is used in Penal Code § 192(3)(c) — cannot be founded on the other elements of that subsection is *not* an "abstruse but possible theory of the facts" of this case. Instead, this concept is fundamental to the statutory scheme which establishes distinct definitions and penalties for subsections 3(c) and 3(d) of Penal Code § 192, and it is a crucial distinction raised by the evidence in this case — as shown in section IB of this brief. Therefore, the proposed instruction involved a principle of law "commonly or closely and openly connected with the facts of the case before the court."

This case is very similar to *People v. Burns* (1948) 88 Cal. App. 2d 867. There, the appellant had been convicted of violating Penal Code § 273(d), which made it a felony for a husband to inflict on his wife an injury resulting in "a traumatic condition." The court held that the trial court's failure to instruct the jury — on its own motion — as to the definition of "traumatic condition was a reversible error. *Id.* at 873-875. Thus:

> The words, "a traumatic condition" are not commonplace words. We cannot say, as a matter of law, that their meaning is within the knowledge of jurors. The difficulty the legal profession and the courts have had with the meaning of the word "traumatic" clearly indicates that the term is a technical one. . . . An instruction defining "a traumatic condition" was on a principle of law pertaining to the offense charged. It was not on a point developed through the evidence introduced at the trial. It should have been given by the court on its own motion. [*Id.* at 874-875; *see also People v. Smith* (1978) 78 Cal. App. 3d. 698, 710-713 (failure to define "assault" *sua sponte* is reversible error); *People v. Pailla* (1964) 64 Cal. 2d 560, 563-565 (failure to define "felony" *sua sponte* is reversible error].)

Here, the term "gross negligence" is also highly technical in the context of Penal Code § 192(3)(c). While it might have some meaning to lay people in another context, here it has an unusual meaning. A lay person might easily believe that one who drives while intoxicated is — for that reason alone — "grossly negligent," especially if the defendant also commits a traffic offense (such as failing to stop at a stop sign). But these facts cannot satisfy the "gross negligence" element of subsection 3(c) without violating the intent of the Legislature in setting out "gross negligence" as an additional element of this subsection. This "principle of law" should have been explained to the jury on the court's own motion.

As this Court has noted, "It cannot be overemphasized that instructions should be clear and simple in order to avoid misleading the jury." *People v. Carrasco* (1981) 118 Cal. App. 3d 936, 944. In the case at bench, the trial court misled the jury by giving it the standard instructions on vehicular manslaughter (CT 45-46 and RT 732-734) and gross negligence (CT 48 and RT 734), without explaining the technical manner in which "gross negligence" is used in Penal Code § 192(3)(c). This error was highly prejudicial to McNally, and his conviction should be reversed and the case should be remanded for a new trial on proper instructions.

II. THE TRIAL COURT ERRED BY SENTENCING APPELLANT TO SIX YEARS IN PRISON ON COUNT I.

A. Denial of Probation Was An Abuse of Discretion.

Rule of Court 414, "Criteria Affecting Probation," sets out 20 criteria which the court should consider regarding probation. In the case at bench, the trial court considered only two of these in denying probation — ignoring all of the other criteria. We will show that the two criteria relied on by the court did not properly apply to this case. We will also show that all of the other 18 criteria which are relevant to this case favor the grant of probation to McNally. Therefore, the trial court's denial of probation was an abuse of discretion. The trial court mentioned only two of the twenty criteria in denying probation: "the nature, seriousness and circumstances of the crime" (Rule 414(c)(1)), and "the vulnerability of the victim and the degree of harm or loss to the victim" (Rule 414(c)(2)). RT [12/4/84] 70:15-73:6.

In applying the first criteria to this case, the court said only this:

> One of the primary reasons for that is the nature, the seriousness, and the circumstances of the crime. It was a killing, a homicide, and it was caused by some body who was driving under the influence, and it was done with gross negligence. That one factor almost standing by itself could almost preclude the granting of probation, and the nature and seriousness of this particular offense. [RT [12/4/84] 70:15-22.]

This statement does no more than recount the basic elements of Penal Code § 192(3)(c). It says nothing to indicate that the circumstances of *this* case show greater culpability on McNally's part than the "normal" § 192(3)(c) case, every one of which *must* involve drunk driving, a traffic offense, gross negligence, and a death. If probation may be denied in a § 192(3)(c) case simply because the court takes a dim view of this particular offense, then the intent of the Legislature that probation be allowed in § 192(3)(c) cases — where otherwise appropriate — would be frustrated. In order for the language of Rule 414(c)(1) to comport with the Legislature's intent, "the nature, seriousness, and circumstances of the crime" must refer to the particular manner in which the defendant committed the crime on this occasion. This, however, is not how the trial court applied that language in this case.

The second criteria found present by the trial court was "the vulnerability of the victim and the degree of harm or loss to the victim." Rule 414(c)(2). Here, the court relied on evidence showing that because of McNally's speed and running the stop sign, Karen Walker and Russell Biggs "were vulnerable and had little or no chance whatsoever to avoid any kind of collision" (RT [12/4/84] 72:2-4), and that the harm to the victims — death and serious bodily injury — were "enormous" (*Id.* at 72:24-26).

This ruling was erroneous for much the same reason that the first ruling was: these particular consequences are inherent in every violation of Penal Code § 192(3)(c). To use them to deny probation is to frustrate the Legislature's intent that one convicted under that statute be considered for probation. "All victims of drunk drivers are 'vulnerable victims,' but it is precisely because they are all vulnerable that [the victim] cannot be considered to be vulnerable in a special or unusual degree, to an extent greater than in other cases." *People v. Bloom* (1983) 142 Cal. App. 3d 310, 322, holding that such "vulnerability" cannot be considered a factor in aggravation in a vehicular manslaughter case. Similarly, "enormous" harm to victims is suffered by all victims in prosecutions under Penal Code § 192(3)(c).

While the trial court relied on subsections (c)(1) and (c)(2) of Rule 414, it failed to apply any of the other 18 subsections. This might be unimportant in a case where none of those subsections is relevant. Here, however, most of them are quite relevant, as can be seen from an examination of the other subsections of Rule 414:

Subsection (a): "Statutory provisions authorizing, limiting or prohibiting the grant of probation."

Penal Code § 1203 authorizes probation here. The limitation and prohibition of probation contained in Penal Code § § 1203(e) and 1203.06 do not apply to vehicular manslaughter.

Subsection (b): "The likelihood that if not imprisoned the defendant will be a danger to others."

At another point in the sentencing hearing, the court stated that "I don't think that the Defendant necessarily would be a danger to society if he were granted probation at some point and given 90 days or six months or a year in jail and released, counsel." RT [12/4/84] 79:25-80:2.

Subsection (c)(3): "Whether the defendant was armed with or used a weapon."

There was no evidence that McNally carried any weapon in the Bronco or on his person.

Subsection(c)(4): "Whether the defendant inflicted bodily injury. "

Obviously, McNally inflicted bodily injury. But — as discussed above — bodily injury is inherent in every case of vehicular manslaughter, so it should play no part in a decision regarding probation in a vehicular manslaughter case.

Subsection (c)(5): "Whether the defendant planned the commission of the crime, whether he instigated it or was solicited by others to participate, and whether he was an active or passive participant."

This criterion was meant to apply to crimes committed by groups. It has no application here.

Subsection (c)(6): "Whether the crime was committed because of an unusual circumstance, such as great provocation, which is unlikely to recur."

The Presentence Report states that prior to the crime McNally drank only moderately, and after the crime he stopped drinking entirely. (PR 3.) His license to drive has been suspended for at least 3 years. (RT [12/4/84] 45:19-46:20.) There was no evidence to the contrary. There is no indication that this crime is likely to recur.

Subsection (c)(7): "Whether the manner in which the crime was carried out demonstrated criminal sophistication or professionalism on the part of the defendant."

There is no evidence of this here.

Subsection (c)(8): "Whether the defendant took advantage of a position of trust on the part of the defendant."

There is no evidence of this here.

Subsection (d)(1): "Prior record of criminal conduct. . . ."

The Presentence Report stated that "defendant has reached the age of 44 without becoming involved in criminal conduct." PR 8.

Subsection (d)(2): "Prior performance on probation or parole and present probation or parole status."

McNally has never been on probation or parole.

Subsection (d)(3): "Willingness and ability to comply with terms of probation."

McNally's attorney proposed conditions of probation. RT [12/4/84] 47:1-6, 58:12-59:21. The Presentence Report states that "defendant has expressed a willingness and ability to comply with any terms of probation." PR 8. There was no evidence to the contrary.

Subsection (d)(4): "Age, education, health, mental faculties, and family background and ties."

The Presentence Report states that McNally "is well educated and has significant ties to Tulare County." PR 8. There was no evidence to the contrary.

Subsection (d)(5): "Employment history. military service history, and financial condition."

These are also discussed in the Presentence Report, and, again, they show nothing unfavorable to McNally or to a grant of probation.

Subsection (d)(6): "Danger of addiction to or abuse of alcohol, narcotics, dangerous drugs, or other mood or consciousness-altering substances."

McNally drank only moderately before the crime, and has not consumed alcohol since the crime. PR 3. The record contains no suggestion of any danger of addiction or abuse.

Subsection (d)(7): "The likely effect of imprisonment on the defendant and his dependents."

The Presentence Report concludes that: "Having never served a period of incarceration and facing the possibility of liquidating his family's business, the likely effect of imprisonment on the defendant and his dependents may be significant."

Subsection (d)(8): "The possible effects on the defendant's life of a felony record."

The Presentence Report concludes that: "Having been convicted of a felony, the defendant may not have the Federal license renewed that he requires to operate his business." PR 8. He has also lost his driver's license. (RT [12/4/84] 45:19-46:20. There was no evidence to the contrary.

Subsection (d)(9): "Whether the defendant is remorseful."

The Presentence Report concludes that "defendant has expressed remorse." PR 8. McNally did not disclaim criminal responsibility for the collision; he took the case to trial over the "gross negligence" issue. PR 4. There was no evidence to the contrary.

Subsection (d)(10): "Whether a financially able defendant refuses to make restitution to the victim."

The Presentence Report states that "defendant has indicated his willingness to make restitution for tangible losses not paid to the victim by his insurance company." PR 7. There was no evidence to the contrary.

Thus, it appears that *every one* of the criteria which properly apply here to the question of probation points toward a grant of probation to McNally.

The Advisory Committee Comment to Rule 414 states:

> The decision whether to grant probation is normally based on an overall evaluation of *the likelihood that the defendant will live successfully in the general community.* Each criterion points to evidence that the likelihood of success is great or small. A single criterion will rarely be determinative; in most cases, the sentencing

judge will have to balance favorable and unfavorable facts. [*Emphasis added.*]

In the case at bench, we respectfully submit that the sentencing judge did not properly "balance favorable and unfavorable facts" in seeking to determine "the likelihood that [McNally] will live successfully in the general community." There were no unfavorable facts not already inherent in the crime of which McNally was convicted, and the favorable facts were numerous and substantial. Even if the Presentence Report (or this brief) has in some way overstated the factors in favor of probation, they still remain overwhelming.

We recognize that trial courts have broad discretion regarding probation. But — as with every other area of the law involving discretion — there are limits. The discretion to deny probation must be based upon "sound principles of law, . . . free from partiality, not swayed by sympathy or warped by prejudice. . . ." *People v. Belton* (1979) 23 Cal. 3d 208, 216.

If probation is not proper here, then it is hard to conceive of *any* case involving a conviction under Penal Code § 192(3)(c) where it would be proper. This result does not accord with the intent of the Legislature to allow probation in § 192(3)(c) cases.

McNally has proposed severe conditions (including a year in county jail) on a grant of probation in this case. RT [12/4/84] 47:1-6, 58:12-59:21. We submit that the trial court's refusal to grant probation on these conditions — or on conditions — was an abuse of discretion.

B. The Trial Court Erred In Selecting The Middle Term of Six Years Imprisonment As The Base Term.

In its Presentence Report, the probation department stated that there were two circumstances in mitigation — McNally had no prior record and was willing to make restitution — and no circumstances in aggravation. PR 7-8. Therefore, a lower term of four years imprisonment was recommended. PR 10.

The trial court rejected this recommendation, based on its finding that there were three circumstances in aggravation, and that these offset the mitigating circumstances. Thus, it ruled that the middle term of six years was appropriate. RT [12/4/84] 73:15-74:14.

Later, the court specified three circumstances in aggravation: great bodily harm (Rule of Court 421(a)(3)), the victim was particularly vulnerable (Rule 421(a)(3)), and there were multiple victims (Rule 421(a)(4)). RT [12/4/84] 75:22-76:2.

Individually and collectively, however, none of these three factors may properly be considered as an aggravating factor in this case.

The first — great bodily harm — is included in one of the elements of vehicular manslaughter, to wit, death of a human being. Rule 441(d) provides that: "A fact which is an element of the crime may not be used to impose the upper term." *See also People v. Reeder* (1984) 152 Cal. App. 3d 900, 921-922. While no upper term was imposed here, the *effect* of the trial court's use of an element of the crime as an aggravating factor was exactly the same. It raised the level of the basic term up a notch from the lower term to the middle term. Therefore, the rationale of Rule 441(d) should apply here too.

The second factor — vulnerability of the victim cannot be considered as an aggravating factor in a vehicular manslaughter case, as "all victims of drunk drivers are 'vulnerable victims.'" *People v. Bloom, supra,* 142 Cal. App. 3d at 322.

The third factor — multiple victims — is also inappropriate to consider as an aggravating factor in a vehicular manslaughter case. The defendant in such a case has no control over the number of occupants in the vehicle he hits, and he does not intend to hit the vehicle. The "multiple victims" factor bears no rational relationship to the defendant's degree of culpability. *See People v. Lobaugh* (1971) 18 Cal. App. 3d 75, 79, and *People v. Leavitt* (1984) 156 Cal. App. 3d 500, 516-517.

In addition, *none* of the three factors may be used as aggravating factors here for an entirely *separate* reason: the trial court used these identical three factors as a basis for imposing a consecutive sentence on Count II. RT [12/4/84] 75:19-76:4. Rule 441(c) provides: "A fact used to enhance the defendant's prison term may not be used to impose the upper term." This Court has held that imposition of a consecutive sentence is an "enhancement." *People v. Lawson* (1980) 107 Cal. App. 3d 748; *see also People v. Garfield* (1979) 92 Cal. App. 3d 475, 478-479; *People v. Skenamore* (1982) 137 Cal. App. 3d 922, 924.

While no upper term was imposed here, the effect of the trial court's use of the three factors was the same: by using these factors to offset the mitigating factors, the court raised the base term up a notch from the lower term to the middle term. This violates the "dual use" rationale of Rule 441(c).

C. On The Facts Of This Case, A Sentence Of Six Years In State Prison Constitutes Cruel Or Unusual Punishment.

The California Supreme Court has held on several occasions that a punishment violates the California Constitution "if, although not cruel or unusual in its method, it is so disproportionate to the crime for which it is inflicted that it shocks the conscience and offends fundamental notions of human dignity." *In re Lynch* (1972) 8 Cal. 3d 410, 424; *People v. Dillon* (1983) 34 Cal. 3d 441, 478.

In determining whether the punishment is "so disproportionate to the crime," one of the techniques used by the courts is to examine "the nature of the offense and/or the offender, with particular regard to the degree of danger both present to society." *In re Lynch, supra,* 8 Cal. 3d at 425.

Regarding the nature of the offense, we do not deny that drunk driving poses a serious danger to society. This does not dispose of our contention, however, for first degree murder (*Dillon*), child molesting (*In re Rodriguez* (1975) 14 Cal. 3d 639), and sale of heroin (*In re Foss*) (1974) 10 Cal. 3d 910) are just as dangerous, but sentences for each of these crimes have been set aside as cruel or unusual punishment.

The particular circumstances of McNally's case do involve inexcusable wrongful conduct on his part. As vehicular manslaughter cases go, however, this one does not show especially high culpability. Compare, e.g., *People v. Bloom, supra*, 142 Cal. App. 3d 315, where the defendant had a .31 blood alcohol, and sped and cut across center divider into oncoming traffic; *People v. Hutson* (1963) 221 Cal. App. 2d 751, where the defendant had .24 blood alcohol, drove between 70 and 120 miles per hour, and ran 3 red lights; and *People v. Jones* (1985) 164 Cal. App. 3d 1173, where the defendant had .22 blood alcohol, drove up to 95 miles per hour, and ran a stop sign.)

Regarding the nature of the offender, it is hard to imagine a stronger case for the Appellant on this score. McNally has no prior criminal record, has no history of alcohol abuse, is not a danger to the community (according to the trial court — RT [12/4/84] 79:25-80:2), and has an impeccable record of service to his family and community. Clearly, McNally "is not the proto-type of one who poses a grave threat to society" — in the language used by our Supreme Court in *In re Reed* (1983) 33 Cal. 3d 914, 924.

In addition to the circumstances of the offense and offender, the court may examine "the penological purposes of the prescribed punishment" when considering the question of cruel or unusual punishment. *In re Foss, supra*, 10 Cal. 3d at 919-920.

In the case at bench, those purposes, to the extent that they are discernable, do not justify a punishment of six years in state prison.

If McNally had engaged in the identical conduct he engaged in here, but — for any of a variety of reasons — had not caused any death or injury, he would have been guilty of violating Vehicle Code § 23152(a) (driving under the influence) or § 23152(b) (driving with .10 or more blood alcohol). Vehicle Code § 23160(a) provides that one convicted of a first violation of § 23152 shall be imprisoned not less than 96 hours nor more than six months, although § 23161 permits probation on certain conditions.

To our knowledge, the only study of sentencing practices under these statutes was one prepared in 1983 by the Los Angeles County Municipal Courts Planning and Research Department. This study was based on a survey of over 4,000 driving-under-the-influence cases handled in eight Los Angeles judicial districts in July of 1982. On pages 14-15 of the report, the following results appear:

First Offenders

Vehicle Code § 23160, 23161 provide three alternative penalties for first offenders. The percentage of first offenders sentenced under each penalty provision was as follows:

a. In 74% of these cases, the sentence was a 90-day license restriction, a fine, an alcohol program, and three years of probation.

b. In 23% of these cases, the sentence was 48 hours in jail, a fine, an alcohol program, and three years of probation.

c. In 3% of these cases, the sentence was 96 hours in jail, a fine, and a six-month license suspension (no probation).

McNally was charged with speeding and running a stop sign, as well as driving under the influence. Therefore, let us assume that, because of these alleged infractions, he would have received the harshest penalty: the 96 hour jail term meted out to only 3% of the first offenders.

The six year sentence imposed on Jim McNally is *over 540 times* the 96 hour sentence he would have received had Karen Walker not been killed. If McNally receives good behavior and work credits and serves only 3 years, he will have served over 270 times the 96 hours.

This, we contend, is cruel punishment, as it is arbitrary, imposing an extraordinary additional sentence which is based on a fortuity not under McNally's control and which has no bearing on his culpability.

This, we contend, is unusual punishment, for no other California crime carries such a disparity in punishment between conduct which causes harm and identical conduct which causes no harm.

The leading article on this issue in American legal literature is by Professor Schulhofer, *Harm or Punishment: A Critique of Emphasis on the Results of Conduct in the Criminal Law*, 122 U. Penna. L. Rev. 1497 (1974). In this article, the author considers whether the imposition of a harsher penalty solely because harm results serves any of the fundamental purposes of the criminal law — giving particular attention to vehicular homicide statutes, as there the disparity in penalty is usually the greatest. He concluded that the purpose of deterrence is not served, as one who is not deterred by the penalty for driving under the influence *and* the risk of injury or death to himself from this particular crime is unlikely to be deterred by the very slight risk that he will cause another's death and thereby be punished for vehicular manslaughter. *Id.* at 1543-1544.

Schulhofer also says that "selection of those who cause harm [for a stiffer punishment] is a kind of lottery, just as selection of those born on certain days, determined at random, would be a kind of lottery." *Id.* at 1567. While retaliation seems to loom as the dominant motive for a punishment based on results — an eye for an eye — "most American jurisdictions exclude retaliation from the legitimate goals of the criminal law." *Id.* at 1510.

Regarding vehicular homicide, he states that "emphasis on results seems devoid of support in the arguments considered," and he concludes that, "The crime of vehicle homicide or involuntary manslaughter should for practical purposes disappear from the statute books."

While there is support in California for Schulhofer's position that sentencing should turn on culpability, not results, there is also support for the position that retribution or retaliation may play some role in establishing punishments in this state. In any event, we are *not* asking this court to invalidate California's vehicular manslaughter statute, as Schulhofer might.

We are willing to assume that it is permissible — for whatever reason — to impose a higher penalty on wrongful conduct because it happens to cause an injury or death. The question then becomes: how much higher? In California, for almost every crime, the answer to this question is twice as high — not 270 or 540 times as high.

Under Penal Code § 664, one who *attempts* a crime but fails in its accomplishment — i.e., fails to cause harm — receives one-half the punishment for the completed crime. Thus, while one who murders is no more culpable than one who attempts murder, the "successful" murderer receives only twice the punishment that the attempted murderer receives. The robber receives only twice what the attempted robber receives. The rapist receives only twice what the attempted rapist receives. And the same is true of arson, burglary, sale of heroin, and a host of other serious crimes.

Note that all of these crimes are *intentional* crimes, involving much higher culpability than an unintentional crime such as involuntary manslaughter. What possible valid penological purpose can there be in telling one who *plans* a killing, "If you succeed, your penalty will be *doubled*" and telling a drunk driver who does *not* intend to kill, "If you 'succeed' in causing a death, your penalty will be increased *540 fold*"?

We do not deny that high penalties on drunk driving may deter drunk driving and decrease traffic fatalities. If the Legislature chooses to *increase* the penalties for all such culpable conduct which might lead to such fatalities — i.e., *drunk driving itself* — we see no problem with this, as it will apply to *all* defendants who have the same culpability. When, however, the Legislature selects a small handful of these defendants — no more culpable than the others — and increases their penalty 540 times, this is cruel and unusual. It is not necessary to do this in order to add to the deterrent effect of the law, as the Legislature could accomplish this purpose simply by increasing the penalty for drunk driving.

In *In re Lynch, supra,* the court observed that "isolated excessive penalties may occasionally be enacted, e.g., through honest zeal [citation] generated in response to transitory public emotion. . . ." 8 Cal. 3d at 426; *see also In re Foss, supra,* 10 Cal. 3d at 927, fn. 13.) The sentence meted out to Jim McNally, we submit, is the result of such "honest zeal" — by the Legislature in authorizing a four to eight year penalty, and by the trial court in choosing to impose a six-year penalty on McNally.

If this court agrees with our contention that six years in prison is cruel or unusual punishment in this case, we propose the following remedy. We do not ask that Penal Code § 192(3) or § 193 be invalidated. We do not ask that McNally go unpunished. The most appropriate remedy is to grant probation to McNally on the conditions his trial counsel proposed, including one year in jail ("only" 90 times the 96 hours imposed on no-injury drunk drivers). CT 95-96; RT [12/4/84] 47. This would be in addition to a fine, community service work, and probation (*Id.*), as well as the effects that the conviction could have on his life — including "the disgrace of being stigmatized" as a felon, a drunk driver, a manslaughterer.

III. DENIAL OF PROBATION AND IMPOSITION OF A CONSECUTIVE SENTENCE ON COUNT II WAS IMPROPER.

For all the reasons discussed in section IIA of this brief, the trial court's denial of probation on Count II was an abuse of discretion.

The trial court also erred in ruling that the sentence on Count II should run consecutive to the sentence on Count I. The court so ruled for the following three reasons: the crime involved great bodily harm, the victim was particularly vulnerable, and the crime involved multiple victims. RT [12/4/84] 75:19-76:4.

These factors are mentioned in Rule 421 ("Circumstances in Aggravation"), which is incorporated into the list of criteria in Rule 425 relevant to the question of whether a sentence should be concurrent or consecutive.

As we discussed earlier in this brief, at section IIB, none of these three factors may properly be used to enhance a sentence in a vehicular manslaughter case.

In addition, *multiple victims* may not be used as a factor to impose consecutive sentences unless at least one of the counts involves multiple victims. *People v. Humphrey* (1982) 138 Cal. App. 3d 881. Here, while Counts II and III each alleged that both Karen Walker and Russell Biggs were *injured* by McNally, the allegations in these counts regarding Karen Walker were barred by Penal Code § 654, as Count I was based on an allegation that she was *killed* in the same accident. Therefore, *none* of the three counts can be said to have properly involved multiple victims, and use of this factor to impose a consecutive sentence was improper for this

additional reason. Even if this were the only one of the three factors which were improper, the error could not be said to be harmless, for *none* of the *other* factors listed in Rule 425(a) is present here.

CONCLUSION

This is a sad case. It is sad because a fine young woman has been killed and a fine young man injured. It is sad because their families have suffered a grievous loss. It is sad because an outstanding member of the community, Jim McNally, has made a mistake — a single, tragic, inexcusable error in judgment — which has cost him and will cost him dearly no matter how this case is resolved. The impact on McNally — emotionally, financially, and through effects on his reputation and his family and employees — has been and will continue to be severe, even if he never sees the inside of a state prison. It is sad because, in addition to McNally's mistake, fate decided that the Volkswagen should enter the intersection at the moment McNally went through the stop sign, and the Volkswagen was a small car affording little protection to the occupants.

This case will be sadder still if it appears that McNally's punishment has been dictated by emotions — by the understandable desires of Karen Walker's family and friends for retribution — rather than by the law. When the emotions of a community run high, the need for calm application of principles of law is the greatest.

Jim McNally has committed a crime, and he should be punished for it. He contends, however, that he was not "grossly negligent," as that term is used in Penal Code § 192(3)(c), when he committed the crime, and he is entitled to a fair trial by a jury properly instructed on that issue. If convicted, he is entitled to consideration for probation and sentence based on the law as set out in the Rules of Court — not on emotions, sympathy, or the demands of the victim's family and friends for retribution. The judgment of the court below should be reversed.

Respectfully submitted,
Myron Moskovitz
James T. Wilson
Attorneys for Appellants

Date: June 11, 1985   by:_____

                               Myron Moskovitz

Sample Brief #3

A RESPONDENT'S BRIEF

[A] THE CONCEPT BEHIND THIS BRIEF

This sample brief is a respondent's brief filed in a civil case, *Weiss Associates, Inc. v. Crawford*.

Crawford (a lawyer) represented some farmers suing a tire factory for polluting a nearby landfill that allegedly drained polluted water into the farms. Crawford hired Weiss (a hydrologist) to testify as an expert witness about how the water found its way to the farms. When Crawford failed to pay Weiss, Weiss said he would not testify. Crawford got another law firm (Stemple & Boyajian) to promise Weiss to pay his fees, and Weiss testified. Crawford won the suit, but neither he nor Stemple & Boyajian paid Weiss, so Weiss retained counsel to try to collect his fees — about $64,000.

When Weiss's attorney obtained evidence that Stemple and Boyajian had *never intended* to pay Weiss, what began as a simple collection suit turned into a complex fraud suit. In a long non-jury trial, the judge became so enraged by Stemple & Boyajian's conduct (both in court and out) that she not only awarded Weiss his $64,000, she slammed Stemple and Boyajian with $4 million in punitive damages. Stemple and Boyajian appealed, and Weiss retained me to represent him.

Before writing the brief, I told this simple story to several lawyers I happened to run into. (This is a good habit — it's very helpful to get people's reactions to a story before you write your brief. Their responses might well be those of the appellate judges.) The feedback was unanimous: "$4 million punitives on top of only $64,000 compensatory? Forget it! The appellate court will reverse, or at least cut the punitives way down." I could see that we had a serious problem.

Usually, a respondent has a substantial advantage. The appellate judges start with the assumption that the trial court was correct, and they don't like to impose the expense of a retrial on the parties or the system. So in most jurisdictions, over 75% of all civil appeals result in affirmance.

But this case was different. My opposing counsel (a very experienced, savvy appellate lawyer) would surely argue that the trial judge had lost her objectivity and had gone overboard, and it was up to the appellate judges to bring some "common sense" into the case and set aside such a "ridiculously excessive" award.

My strategy became two-fold. I would try to show that (1) the trial judge was experienced, sensible, and very fair-minded, and (2) she was outraged by conduct that *should* have outraged her — and that should also outrage the appellate judges. These things would have to be shown with *facts*, not just legal arguments. So I read the voluminous transcripts (about 7,000 pages) with an eye toward supporting these two points. I carefully looked for examples of the judge's fairness. (See footnotes 1 and 42.) And I painstakingly sought every tiny example I could find showing the defendants' venality. For example, take a look at footnote 8, which describes Stemple & Boyajian's methods of getting clients and servicing their cases. I put this in a footnote rather than in the text because, strictly speaking, it was not really relevant to the legal issues in the appeal. I wanted it in the brief, but not in a way that would give my opponent too much ammunition to accuse me of directly arguing irrelevancies.

In an unpublished opinion, the appellate court affirmed the entire $4 million punitive damage award, making little effort to hide its distaste for the defendants' conduct. (In its opinion, the court recited the facts set out in footnote 8 — in the *text* of its opinion!)

This case is a good example of the principle that, even in an appeal, *emotions* may be just as important as *law*. I believe our legal arguments in *Weiss* were correct, but *no* argument based solely on the law could have persuaded this court to uphold such a large punitive damage award. On an issue like this, an appellate court has wide discretion — there are no cases holding that it *must* uphold such an award. To win, it was essential to enrage the judges.

Stemple and Boyajian's opening brief is not included in this book, because it is too long. But I think you will know what was in it from reading my respondent's brief. The beginning of each section summarizes the appellant's arguments to which I will respond. I *don't want* the judge to read my opponent's brief any more than he has to. The more times he reads it, the more chances my opponent has to get to him. So if I do a decent job of telling the *whole* story — including my opponent's arguments — the judge might rely on *our* brief and look at other briefs less than he otherwise would.

In any event, just in case our brief came up short on that score, I've included for you the Table of Contents of the Appellants' Opening Brief (omitting the parts of the Table that deal with Crawford and "Olfacto," another expert whom defendants had failed to pay, whose suit was consolidated with Weiss's.)

[B] WHAT TO WATCH FOR WHILE READING THIS BRIEF

You might get the most out of this section by reading it *after* you read — or at least skim — the brief. *Note*: To save space in this Book, the brief is single-spaced. Most court rules require double or one and a half line spacing.

[1] The Introduction

This "Introduction" is a bit unusual — starting with a quote from the trial judge about how she saw defendants' conduct. But I wanted to shock the court a bit, and this quote is concise, sober, and very shocking. It's very common for *lawyers* to say things like this about their opponents, but it's quite unusual for a *judge* to say them. To persuade the appellate judges to uphold such a large punitive damage award, I had to get them angry at the defendants. So the brief starts with a bang.

[2] The Statement of the Case

The Statement of the Case is normally a rather dry recitation of the procedural facts. So is this one, though note that it includes a few marginally-relevant procedural facts that put the defendants in a rather bad light (such as their claim that Judge Sutter, a well-respected judge, was "biased," and their fight for a jury trial, which they then withdrew).

[3] The Statement of Facts

This Statement of Facts is pretty long. Part of this is due to the complex nature of the case and the very lengthy reporter's transcript. But it is also due to my view that I had to use the facts to make the defendants look like very bad people if we were to have any chance of sustaining the punitive damage award. I did *not* accept my opponent's Statement of Facts. I never do. I want the story told my way, with the facts I choose from the transcripts.

Not only do I refuse to accept my opponent's Statement of Facts, I attack it — right off the bat. Appellants who claim insufficiency of the evidence have a duty to recite all *adverse* evidence, but they seldom do. So make them pay the price. This discrediting can be a pretty effective way to begin a respondent's brief.

Putting together this Statement of Facts was a lot of work. As you can see from the citations to the record, I rearranged testimony and exhibits scattered all over the record, in order to reassemble them into the story *I* wanted to tell.

At several points in the Statement of Facts, I put my own spin on the facts. This is a bit argumentative, and perhaps it presses the "rule" (more a custom than a rule) against arguing in the Statement of Facts to its outer limits. Note, however, that the argumentative comments are always *backed up* with solid evidence and specific citations to the record.

The brief cites not only page numbers, but line numbers too: "See RT 23:7-11." This is not required in all jurisdictions, but I do it anyway, to make it easier for the judge to find the exact testimony we rely on.

[4] The Argument

My recitation of the facts did not end with the Statement of Facts. *Throughout* this brief, in virtually every section on virtually every topic, I continuously weave into my argument nasty little facts about the defendants. All of these repeat facts already set out in the Statement of Facts, but so what? It is certainly appropriate to *apply* the law to the facts in the Argument section of the brief, and if you have some particularly juicy facts, it doesn't hurt to burn them into the judge's mind. If you've got 'em, use 'em!

The appellants attacked the constitutionality of California's punitive damage procedure. My response is very short, simply referring to some decided cases and a case then pending before the California Supreme Court. There was no point in doing more, as I knew the Court of Appeal would not rule on this issue while it was pending before the California Supreme Court. The appellants knew this too, and were simply preserving the issue for a further appeal to the United States Supreme Court (which later denied certiorari — *see Boyajian v. Olfacto-Labs*, 515 U.S. 1103 (1995)).

There are many footnotes in this brief — possibly too many. Read each footnote and consider whether you think it should be (1) included as is, (2) deleted, or (3) moved to the text.

[5] The Conclusion

I tried to end this brief with some short, powerful statements. Many lawyers use the Conclusion to summarize their *legal* arguments. I go further, using it to summarize my *emotional* arguments: the appellants were very bad guys, and a reversal would have bad effects on society. This has a more persuasive impact.

My opponent had quoted Dickens' *Bleak House*: "The lawyers have twisted it into such a state of bedevilment that the original merits of the case have long disappeared from the face of the earth." I responded with Shakespeare. Some judges have a literary bent, and literary allusions might have an effect where cases and statutes fall flat. I usually don't go out of my way researching such tomes to find catchy quotes, but when my opponent invites such a response and I have it somewhat close at hand (I had recently seen *King Richard III* and recalled the line), I'll put it in. I also keep a couple of books of famous quotations near at hand, and occasionally I'll insert a particularly appropriate quote from Mark Twain, Dr. Johnson, or the like in a brief. It can't hurt, and it might help with a particular judge.

IN THE COURT OF APPEAL OF THE STATE OF CALIFORNIA
FIRST APPELLATE DISTRICT
DIVISION THREE

WEISS ASSOCIATES

Plaintiff and Respondent

vs.

ROBERT K. CRAWFORD, et. al.,

Defendants and Appellants

No. A055789

APPELLANTS' OPENING BRIEF

* * * *

Table of Contents

* * * *

IN THE COURT OF APPEAL OF THE STATE OF CALIFORNIA
FIRST APPELLATE DISTRICT
DIVISION THREE

WEISS ASSOCIATES

Plaintiff and Respondent

vs.

ROBERT K. CRAWFORD, et. al.,

Defendants and Appellants

No. A055789

RESPONDENT WEISS ASSOCIATES' BRIEF

On Appeal from the Judgment of the Superior Court of the State of
California for the County of Alameda

Honorable Jacqueline Taber, Judge

Myron Moskovitz
536 Mission St.
San Francisco, Calif. 94105
Phone: (415) 442-6646

Donald Jelinek
Jelinek & Samsel
1942 Addison St.
Berkeley, Calif. 94704
Phone: (510) 841-4787

Attorneys for Respondent
Weiss Associates

TABLE OF CONTENTS

Page

TABLE OF AUTHORITIES

Cases

Page

INTRODUCTION

"This court has never before experienced such deceit, willful disregard of clients' protection and rights, overreaching in dealing with other attorneys, indifference to and avoidance of payments of business creditors, and outright disregard of the truth, whether under oath or not, as demonstrated by the two individual partners of Stemple & Boyajian in the conduct of their professional affairs concerning which they testified in this case."

— Superior Court Judge Jacqueline Taber, March 12, 1991[1]

STATEMENT OF THE CASE

On June 17, 1988, Respondent Olfacto-Labs filed a complaint for damages against Appellants Stemple & Boyajian (S&B) and Robert K. Crawford, alleging breach of contract and fraud. CT 1. S&B answered this complaint in pro per (CT 15) and also filed a cross-complaint alleging that Olfacto had committed fraud and conspiracy. CT 19, 24; Ex. 66. This cross-complaint also sought damages against Robert Glynn and Crawford. CT 19.

On October 12, 1988, Respondent Weiss Associates filed a complaint for damages against S&B and Crawford, alleging breach of contract, fraud, and related causes of action. CT 45. S&B answered this complaint in pro per (CT 78) and also filed a cross-complaint alleging that Weiss had committed fraud and conspiracy. CT 59, 67. This cross-complaint also sought damages for fraud and conspiracy against Glynn, Crawford, and Stephen Vonder Haar (a Weiss employee). CT 59. S&B demanded a jury trial. CT 120.

On March 26, 1989, the court consolidated the Olfacto and Weiss cases for trial. CT 232-247.

On September 11, 1989, S&B moved to continue the trial. CT 305. This motion was denied. CT 331.

S&B filed an Issue Conference Statement, stating that S&B had contracted with Olfacto and Weiss "under duress," that the contracts were "adhesion contracts," and that Olfacto and Weiss had breached their obligations and overcharged for their services. CT 391, 396-397. S&B also asserted that it "has been the most cooperative party to this action," that it "had every right to reject arbitration," and that its attempt to coordinate these cases with another case pending in Monterey was proper. CT 398-399.

S&B also demurred to Glynn's cross-complaint, on the ground that there was another action pending between S&B and Glynn, an action initiated by Robert D. Smith, who was also claiming that S&B had failed to pay for

---

[1] CT 1514. At the time of trial, Judge Taber's "experience" included 13 years on the Municipal Court bench and another 12 years on the Superior Court bench. See Ex. A, attached to this brief. Before becoming a judge, she had practiced law for 18 years. RT 760:11.

expert witness services. CT 402, 406. This demurrer was sustained. CT 496.

S&B claimed that Judge Sutter was biased (C.T. 1136), so he was disqualified, and the case was assigned to Judge Taber. RT 3.

S&B had demanded a jury trial, but Glynn claimed that S&B had waived its right to jury trial. RT 10. S&B disagreed, and the court ruled for S&B and held that "Therefore there will be a jury trial." RT 17:9. Two weeks later, however, when the parties appeared in Judge Taber's court for the jury trial, S&B announced that "We're hereby withdrawing our request for a jury." RT 110:18-19. Judge Taber ruled that the case would proceed as a non-jury case. RT 112-113.

The trial began on November 2, 1990, with Weiss's presentation of evidence. RT 216:11-14. (In S&B's brief, at page 2, S&B incorrectly assert that *Crawford* presented his case first. Crawford did not begin until December 31, 1990. RT 3404:12-18.)

On November 8, 1990, in the middle of the trial, S&B moved to withdraw its fraud and conspiracy claims against the other parties (both in its affirmative defenses and in its cross-complaint), admitting that it did not have the evidence to prove them. RT 752-755. The court denied the motion as untimely (RT 758), and S&B then withdrew the motion (RT 761).

On December 17, 1990, Olfacto moved to amend its complaint, in order to add Stemple and Boyajian as individual defendants. CT 1291, 1335. Weiss filed a similar motion on December 19, 1990. CT 1324. The court granted the motions. RT 2525.

After 36 days of trial (CT 1488), on March 12, 1991, the court issued a Memorandum of Decision, ruling for the plaintiffs. CT 1508. On September 6, 1991, the court issued its Statement of Decision (CT 2789) and signed its Judgment (CT 2780). S&B and Crawford moved for a new trial. CT 2931, 2899. With Weiss's agreement, the motions were granted to the extent that Weiss's damages for fraud against S&B were reduced by almost $400,000, and Weiss's damages for fraud against Crawford were reduced by almost $150,000. CT 3345-3346. These changes were reflected in a Modified Statement of Decision (CT 3349) and Modified Judgment (CT 3354), both entered on November 27, 1991.

Weiss moved for an order imposing sanctions against S&B under CCP § 128.5. CT 1784-1790. The court granted the motion, finding that both Stemple and Boyajian had "engaged in bad faith actions or tactics that were frivolous or solely intended to cause unnecessary delay." CT 2875-2877. The court listed the following examples supporting its finding:

- S&B's defenses to the lawsuit were spurious.

- S&B filed an unfounded cross-complaint against Weiss.

- S&B engaged in "questionable" pretrial and trial tactics, including wrongfully refusing arbitration, filing in inappropriate venues, demanding a jury trial (thereby requiring plaintiffs to *prepare* for a jury trial) and not withdrawing their request until the day of trial, protracting the trial by admitting facts one day and denying them the next, refusing to stipulate to conceded facts, changing positions on issues, demanding repeated discovery of the same material, and creating spurious defenses and cross-complaints which they themselves had never believed in. CT 2876-2877.

Though the court granted the motion for sanctions, it decided not to impose monetary sanctions, "because of the hardship of the multi-million dollar punitive damage award against these Defendants in this lawsuit". CT 2877.

S&B filed notices of appeal from both the original judgment (CT 3339) and the modified judgment (CT 3380).[2]

STATEMENT OF FACTS

S&B's Opening Brief claims that the evidence does not support the trial court's awards of compensatory and punitive damages, but their brief fails to provide a fair summary of the overwhelming evidence which supports those awards.[3] We now present a brief condensation of the evidence contained in the 36 volumes (almost 7,000 pages) of testimony and 174 exhibits before the trial court.

Richard Weiss is president of respondent Weiss Associates. RT 2001:19-24. He is a geologist, specializing in hydrology. RT 2001:19-22; 2003:13-16. In December of 1986, Weiss was contacted by Ken Aaron, a scientist working for lawyer Robert Crawford. RT 259:6-12, 2005:2-14. Crawford was representing the plaintiffs in the "Crazy Horse" case, a lawsuit pending in Monterey County Superior Court. RT 220:1-3. The plaintiffs in that case were farmers suing Firestone Tire Co. for dumping toxic chemicals into the "Crazy Horse" landfill, which allegedly drained into plaintiffs' water supplies. RT 220:1-222:17. The City of Salinas and a disposal company (Rossi) were also defendants. RT 221:10-20. Aaron asked Weiss to serve as an expert witness regarding the flow of water from the Crazy Horse site to the plaintiffs' properties. RT 266:25-267:10, 2006:6-15. Weiss agreed to do so, and on January 8, 1987, he signed a written agreement (called a "Service

---

[2] Crawford filed a notice of cross-appeal from the original judgment, the order for attorneys fees, and the modified judgment. CT 3403. The cross-appeal was dismissed after the parties stipulated to such dismissal and that the judgment for fraud against Crawford would be vacated and the judgment for contract damages against Crawford would survive Crawford's bankruptcy.

[3] When an appellant's brief fails to state the evidence fairly but presents only the evidence favorable to himself, this Court may treat as waived any contention that the judgment is not supported by substantial evidence. *Handy v. Shiells* (1987) 190 Cal. 3d 512.

Agreement") to this effect with Crawford. RT 2010:6-21; Ex. 7. Weiss contracted with Dr. Stephen Vonder Haar to serve as Project Manager for this job. RT 2012:24-28.

John Amoore and Robert O'Neill are the principals of Olfacto-Labs, which consults on the effects of vapors given off by toxic chemicals. CT 2793-2794. They were also asked by Crawford to serve as experts in the Crazy Horse case (RT 267:12-270:9), and they orally agreed to do so on January 9, 1987. CT 2794.

Weiss began work on the case, as instructed by Crawford. Weiss worked nights and weekends, putting in overtime to get ready to testify in time. RT 5119:20-28. Weiss submitted bills to Crawford, which Crawford paid. By June, however, Crawford had become delinquent in paying Weiss's bills, causing Weiss to threaten to stop work (Ex. 9, 142, 156), and by September, Crawford had stopped paying entirely, owing a balance of $31,135. CT 2795. Weiss told Crawford that he and Dr. Vonder Haar would not testify at the Crazy Horse trial unless the bill was paid. CT 2795.

Olfacto was owed $60,195, and Mr. Amoore told Crawford that he would not testify unless the bill was paid. Exhibit 65. Several other experts were also unpaid, and they told Crawford the same thing. RT 275:20-277:15, 292:18-24.

When Weiss told Crawford that Weiss would not testify unless the bill was paid, Crawford told Weiss to contact the law firm of Stemple and Boyajian (S&B), whose partners are Gordon Stemple and Berj Boyajian. RT 280:10-18; 2030:5-11; 2105:3-5. Weiss did so. Ex. 10. Weiss told S&B that Weiss would not provide testimony in Crazy Horse unless he was paid. RT 2035:21-25. S&B initially refused to agree to pay the bill (RT 918:2-14), and Crawford told Weiss that an attorney named Robert Glynn would agree to pay it (RT 919:3-13; 2041:8-2042:12). Weiss said he would accept Glynn instead of S&B (RT 2042:13-15). Weiss was not happy with the prospect of signing with Glynn (RT 2123:24-2124:4), as Weiss preferred to have S&B sign, because he had heard of S&B through their work on toxic lawsuits (RT 2044:11-18), and he thought that S&B "was a prosperous and profitable firm and could pay the bill" (RT 2110:1-4).[4] Weiss had a contract prepared for Glynn to sign, but before Glynn could sign it, Crawford told Weiss that S&B would agree to pay, so "forget Glynn." RT 920:2-22; 1050:16-22; 2044:5-10; 2111:20-27. So Weiss did not have Glynn sign the agreement. RT 2045:3-15.

To keep Weiss working on the case, on September 14, 1987, Stemple signed a "Service Agreement" with Weiss, agreeing that S&B would pay Weiss $10,000 immediately, the $21,135 balance by October 1, and all future

---

[4] Weiss had not encountered payment problems with other clients, and he was not very sophisticated in collection matters. RT 2125:16-24.

billings within 30 days. CT 574-584,[5] 2796; Ex. 23. S&B intentionally failed to send Weiss the last page of the agreement, which contained Stemple's signature, in order to frustrate any later attempts by Weiss to collect on the agreement. CT 2795-2796, 2805. Weiss Employee Beth Springston noticed that the page was missing, and obtained it from S&B on September 14. RT 923:19-926:21.

After Olfacto told Crawford that it would do no more work unless it was paid, an S&B attorney called Dr. Amoore of Olfacto and asked how much "we" owed. RT 2145:3-2147:6. To keep Olfacto working on the case, on September 16 Stemple offered to sign a written contract with Olfacto (RT 2276:8-12), by which S&B would promise to pay Olfacto $15,000 immediately, the $45,195 balance by October 15, and any future billings within 30 days. CT 2794-2795. Amoore had never used a written contract with clients before (RT 2216:12-18), so he obtained a sample "service agreement" from Weiss and sent it to Stemple. RT 2159:19-2160:11; 2222:4-27. Stemple phoned Amoore and asked for certain changes, which Amoore agreed to. RT 2161:15-2164:15; 2168:20-2169:1; 2262:1-21. Stemple signed the agreement with Olfacto on September 16, 1987. (Ex. 24; CT 2795.) After signing the agreement, Stemple told Amoore to "make yourself available to testify in the Crazy Horse case", and Amoore replied that he was continuing to prepare his testimony. CT 2795.

Pursuant to these agreements, both Weiss and Olfacto continued working on the Crazy Horse case, doing studies in preparation for their testimony, and Vonder Haar and Amoore then testified at the trial. CT 2796-2797. Stemple drove Vonder Haar to court, watched him testify, and was "very enthused about his testimony". RT 291-292, 952:4-9. Plaintiffs won, and they would not have won without Olfacto's and Weiss' work. CT 2798.

In fact, the work done by Olfacto and Weiss was exceptionally skillful, and they performed in an outstanding manner. CT 2797-2798. In addition, their billings were reasonable and fair. CT 2798. S&B *never complained* about the quality of their work or the amount of their bills. RT 295:9-23, 955:25-956:4, 970:22-971:1; 2179:1-18. Crawford testified that their work was "special" and that "We beat the best experts that Firestone and anybody could buy, and they were top rate in the country, if not the world. They brought in the biggest guns in the country and we beat them because of our experts." RT 295:24-296:9. The judge in Crazy Horse awarded the plaintiffs almost $4 million. RT 300:16-25.[6] In making this award, the judge relied on the testimony of Weiss and Olfacto: "Testimony from the hydrogists [*sic*] called by plaintiffs and corroborated by much of the independent data collected from the test wells on site convincingly show the existence of clay layers and

---

[5] In our copy of the Clerk's Transcript, page 584 appears after page 521.

[6] Most of the award was affirmed by the Court of Appeal for the Sixth District (*Potter v. Firestone Tire & Rubber Co.* (1990) 9 Cal. App. 4th 881), but the California Supreme Court has granted a hearing in the case. Supreme Court No. 5018831.

underground channeling as readily available pathways from module one to the plaintiffs' wells." Ex. 20, at 4:12-17.

With S&B's knowledge and assistance, Crawford included all of the bills submitted by Weiss, Olfacto, and other experts as part of the plaintiff's cost bill in the Crazy Horse case — a total of $482,000. RT 301:21-304:14. S&B expressly told the Monterey Superior Court that the expert witness fees were "reasonable." RT 470:15; Ex.12, at 2:3. The court awarded all of those bills as costs, except for $8,000. RT 302:8-18.

S&B was happy with the quality and quantity of Weiss's work, and happy with the result which Weiss helped to achieve in the Crazy Horse case. Thus, it came as quite a shock to Weiss when — after making the initial payment of $10,000[7] — S&B failed to make any further payments. S&B failed to pay Weiss the $21,135 due on October 1, or any of Weiss's later billings. CT 2798; Ex. 40. The total of these unpaid bills owed to Weiss eventually amounted to $63,956. Ex. 40.

When Weiss's business manager (Beth Springston) called S&B's office to ask for payment, S&B would not even return her calls. Ex. 10. This occurred about 15 times. RT 882:11-21, 975:2-8; Ex. 38. Mr. Stemple was "never available." RT 930:9-11. At one point, Stemple's secretary said that they would be sending a check to Weiss, but no check ever arrived. RT 909:17-24. Nor did S&B reply to Weiss's letters. Ex. 32, 33. Weiss was "given the runaround" by S&B. RT 2049:1-6.

Unbeknownst to either Weiss or Olfacto, S&B and Crawford had *never intended* to pay them. Much later, Weiss and Olfacto finally learned of the fraudulent scheme concocted by S&B and Crawford.

Stemple and Boyajian are lawsuit brokers. Somehow, they find thousands of people who have been exposed to asbestos and other toxic substances, and they obtain contingent-fee retainer agreements from them. CT 2792.[8] They file suit and then farm the cases out to other lawyers for trial, either as co-counsel with S&B or independently. CT 2792; RT 1691:6-22. After farming the cases out, Stemple and Boyajian do no further work on the cases — they simply sit back and wait to receive their cuts from the

---

[7] S&B made the initial $10,000 payment from a trust account which S&B held for Glynn — essentially paying Weiss with Glynn's money. RT 1642, 3266.

[8] Stemple is the founder, director, and coordinator of the "National Tire Workers Litigation Project." RT 3856:17-27. Harry Gamotan was president and spokesman of the Local 726, the tireworkers' union at the Firestone plant in Salinas. RT 3794:4-7, 4870:13-21, 5770:15-24. Stemple hired Gamotan to work as "field coordinator" of the Litigation Project and as a paralegal for S&B. RT 1961:21-1963:18; 2022:21-2023:26; 2813:12-23; Ex. 81. Gamotan's work for S&B required him to "sign up tireworkers to become part of the National Tireworker Litigation Project." RT 5801:1-5. The Project sent out "screening station mobiles" to screen between 30,000 and 40,000 tireworkers to see if they would be appropriate plaintiffs for lawsuits. RT 6646:22-28. This resulted in the filing of between 4,000 and 5,000 lawsuits. RT 6649:4-18.

resulting settlements and judgments. CT 2792. At the time of trial, they had between 4,000 and 5,000 viable cases farmed out in this manner. RT 6616:18-27. Glynn is an attorney who finds trial lawyers for S&B to try their cases, sometimes financing the case for the trial lawyer and splitting the resulting attorneys fees with the trial attorney and S&B. CT 2792; RT 1510:24-1511:23.[9]

These lawyers treat clients and lawsuits as commodities, designed to produce profits through the work of other lawyers.[10]

As these cases all involve technical, scientific issues, they require expert witnesses. This assistance is expensive, but Stemple and Boyajian have found a way to minimize this expense: they delay payment, procrastinate, and sometimes refuse payment outright to their experts, as well as to other outside personnel they hire to assist them (such as court reporters). RT 257:1-260:13, 487:17-19, 751:1-4, 1529:18-26, 1530:18-1532:1, 2475:17-21, 3438:17-3440:14, 3513:3-20; CT 3202-3206.

Most unpaid bills involve amounts under $10,000 — not enough to justify the expense of a collection lawsuit. For example, Stemple asked Dr. Marvin Legator to testify for the plaintiffs in Crazy Horse. Stemple had been late paying Legator in previous cases, but Stemple assured him that "it won't happen again." RT 4621:9-18. Legator accepted this assurance, and he testified. RT 4608:11-13. But Stemple again failed to pay Legator, and Legator phoned Stemple several times about $10,110 in unpaid bills. Ex. 134. Each time, Stemple assured him that "the money would be forthcoming" — but it never came forth. RT 4611:10-4616:22. (Stemple had even told Legator that "the check is in the mail." RT 4620:13-19; Ex. 134). After spending $200 on phone calls to Stemple, Legator hired an attorney to try to collect his fees. RT 4616:23-4617:2. The attorney wrote to Stemple, evoking no response, so Legator "just dropped" the matter. RT 4617:3-12; Ex. 135.

When creditors such as Dr. Legator gave up, the resulting savings went straight into S&B's profits, which have been rather sizeable. From 1986 to 1989, Stemple and Boyajian drew a combined total of $7,750,000 out of their law firm. Ex. 172; CT 2807. In 1989, the law firm's net worth was $40 million. RT 6528:4-7. Stemple's net worth (including his interest in the law firm) was over $20 million. RT 6656:24-28; Ex. 173.[11] Boyajian's net worth (including his interest in the law firm) was over $29 million in 1990. RT

---

[9] Previously, Glynn had a contract with Stemple whereby Stemple was to refer personal injury plaintiffs to Glynn, in return for 40% of the attorneys fees collected. R.T. 4247:13-4248:9.

[10] See, e.g., CT 429-435, an agreement whereby S&B assigned 623 of their asbestos clients to Glynn, in return for $242,600 in cash plus 40% of the contingent fees realized.

[11] This Exhibit includes a "Personal Financial Statement" which Stemple submitted to the Bank of America on May 8, 1990 with a loan application, in which Stemple certified that his net worth (assets minus liabilities) was $20,130,824.

6516:24-27; Ex. 171;[12] CT 2808. Thus, this tiny law firm (consisting of only 2 partners and 2 associates — RT 1171:4-23) has generated rather sizable profits.[13]

After S&B signed retainer agreements with the Crazy Horse plaintiffs (with S&B agreeing to advance expenses — RT 708:23-27; Ex. 103, 148), Stemple asked Glynn to try the case. RT 4263:319. Stemple said that plaintiffs' discovery had been completed, that the City of Salinas would admit liability and was ready to settle, that liability was clear, and that the City was offering to settle for $1.5 million. RT 4264:1-12; 4273:15-17. Glynn said he was too busy, and he suggested that Stemple contact Crawford. RT 4264:1-9.

Crawford met with Stemple on November 30, 1986. RT 241:13-26. At that meeting, Stemple persuaded Crawford to take the Crazy Horse case. He did so by making some of the same representations he had made to Glynn. Stemple told Crawford that S&B had completed almost all trial preparation, that S&B had spent $100,000 "in hard costs" preparing the case for trial (RT 243:12-18; 1886:15-1887:5), that two of the defendants (the City of Salinas and a disposal company) had already offered $1.5 million to settle and would admit liability, and that experts had already been retained and were willing and able to testify. CT 2793; RT 243:8-244:23, 1727:20-24; 4811:20-4812:5. Relying on these representations, Crawford agreed to assume responsibility for financing the case himself and to accept only a small cut of the contingent fee (only 30% of S&B's one-third). C.T. 2793, RT 247:5-249:16. Crawford agreed to split this 30% with Glynn 50-50. RT 249:8-10. Crawford was to try the case, and Glynn was to finance the costs. RT 252:6-10. Glynn was upset with the 70/30 split, and he persuaded S&B to increase the 30% to 40%. RT 251:9-252:10.[14]

In fact, the representations which Stemple made to Glynn and Crawford were false. Crawford later learned that Stemple and Boyajian had laughed at how they had taken advantage of him. RT 253:9-22. When Crawford began working on the case, he discovered that, in fact, S&B had put only $16,000 into the case, not $100,000 (RT 287:7-15, 4020:24-4021:2, 4305:2-4), that several designated experts were not prepared to testify (RT 256:10-26), that S&B had failed to pay about 20 experts, who refused to testify until paid (RT 257:1-260:13, 751:1-4), and that — far from ready to

---

[12] This Exhibit includes a "Personal Financial Statement" which Boyajian submitted to the Bank of America on April 9, 1990, with a loan application, in which Boyajian certified that his net worth (assets minus liabilities) was $29,951,000.

[13] The firm owns a half-interest in an airplane. RT 6520:21-6521:23. Stemple and Boyajian also own a $75,000 Porsche, a Mercedes, a Jeep, an MBZ 500, and a Jaguar. RT 6553:3-12; 6662:2-4; Ex. 171, 173.

[14] Stemple testified that S&B's agreement with Crawford *released* S&B from its obligation to its Crazy Horse clients to advance costs in that case, even though S&B's retainer with its clients (Ex. 55) expressly required S&B to advance costs. R.T. 1294:4-8; 1309:6-21. He later modified this, claiming that his clients could seek payment from S&B only if Crawford and Glynn failed to advance costs. RT 1310:2-16.

settle — the City of Salinas was ready to fight. The City served Crawford with a list of the City's experts "a mile long", and it became clear that it was "stoutly defending" the case. RT 260:14-261:5, 265:6-11; Ex. 74. Crawford considered this "a real shocker" (RT 265:9), so he asked the City's attorney (Mr. Lankes) about the City's supposed settlement offer to Stemple. Mr. Lankes said that "Gordon [Stemple] likes to hear himself talk. He knew he was not ready to go to trial. We're not going to pay anything on this case. And we're going to stoutly defend it." RT 261:18-21. In fact, Lankes had never told Stemple that he would recommend that the City settle the case for $1.5 million. RT 4497:16-4498:14; 4533:5-12.[15]

As Crawford put it, "we had been snookered." RT 287:19-20. After Glynn learned of this, he persuaded Stemple to increase Crawford/Glynn's cut to 50% of the attorneys fees. RT 262:18-22.

Later, when Crawford and Glynn failed to pay Weiss and Olfacto, and Crawford told S&B that the experts would not testify unless paid, Boyajian told Stemple not to sign the agreement to pay Weiss. Despite the effect this would have on S&B's Crazy Horse clients, Boyajian said, "If he doesn't want to testify, let him not testify." RT 2607:7-16. Stemple nevertheless signed the agreements with Weiss and Olfacto. Ex. 23.

On February 23, 1988, Weiss employee Beth Springston was finally able to speak to Boyajian. CT 2800. During their phone conversation, Springston took notes of what was said. RT 885:18-23; Ex. 38. Boyajian told Springston that back when S&B signed the contract with Weiss and made the first $10,000 payment, S&B had *never intended* to make another payment on it. RT 884:1-11; Ex. 38; CT 2800. Boyajian also told Springston that S&B would refuse arbitration (even though the contract provided for arbitration) and that if Weiss sued to collect for his work, S&B would "make that litigation long, protracted, and expensive." CT 2800. Boyajian told Springston "that if we were to file for arbitration, they were going to cross-sue against Robert Crawford and Robert Glynn, and this would prevent arbitration from happening, and it would have to go to court, and it would be in court forever." RT 883:3-24.

Boyajian told Crawford the same thing. He said that "he had no intention to pay" Weiss and Olfacto. RT 716:28-717:25, 829:5-9. He also told Crawford that if Weiss, Olfacto, or other Crazy Horse experts sued S&B for payment, "he was going to drag this through the courts, that there would be no payment from his office, that he would appeal this matter to the Supreme Court of the United States, if it took that." RT 430:20-431:13. Boyajian also told Crawford that if Weiss and Olfacto sued S&B, "he would drag them through the courts around [sic] pursue all types of appeals." RT 718:3-5.

---

15 On September 14, 1987, Crawford knew that S&B had lied to him. RT 5694:7-5695:1. Nevertheless, Crawford told Weiss and Olfacto to sign a contract with S&B — without telling them that S&B had already lied to Crawford about the Crazy Horse case. RT 5705:11-17; 5714:3-6; 5951:5-27.

When Weiss heard what Boyajian had told Springston, he "felt like a fool." RT 2053:12-14. "I felt like I was stupid for believing and giving them the benefit of the doubt. I should have known when the contract came back without the important page signed that this was a real sign that these people were not serious. So I felt very stupid. * * * * I was enraged that these guys would threaten us basically to avoid paying at all, using the legal system, and being lawyers and all, it being a lot easier for them to do that than for us." RT 2053:12-25.

S&B delivered on its threat. When Weiss finally did file suit to collect what S&B never denied they owed him, S&B did not hesitate to manipulate the court system in an effort to cheat Weiss and other people S&B had hired to work for them.

Before filing this lawsuit, Weiss and Olfacto followed the provisions of their contracts with S&B by requesting arbitration by the American Arbitration Association. Ex. 60, 63, 146; RT 1832:18-22; 2054:13-14; 5122:27-5123:15. Olfacto paid $1,600 in fees to the American Arbitration Association. RT 5000:22-25. S&B refused to submit the cases to arbitration, claiming that its contracts with Weiss and Olfacto were "contracts of adhesion", that the requests that the arbitrations be heard in San Francisco were invalid due to "improper venue," and they should be heard in Los Angeles. Ex. 61; RT 1421:17-26.[16]

Weiss filed suit in the court below on October 12, 1988. CT 45. S&B then did all they could to move the case to a forum far from Weiss and his attorney.

First, S&B tried to move the case to Los Angeles. On September 30, 1988, S&B filed a lawsuit in Los Angeles Superior Court against Weiss,[17] Olfacto, Crawford, and Glynn. Ex. 22. S&B sought to rescind its agreement with Weiss, claiming that the agreement was "a contract of adhesion," that Weiss had falsely represented to S&B that Weiss would not perform unless S&B signed, and that Weiss had procured S&B's agreement "by duress and fraud." Id. at 3-5. S&B also alleged that "Weiss failed to provide said services." Id. at 11. S&B sought compensatory and punitive damages against all defendants. Id. at 15.

The allegations against Crawford in the L.A. suit were identical to those raised in S&B's cross-complaint against Crawford in the Alameda County suit. RT 495:9-27. Nevertheless, plaintiff S&B tried to persuade Crawford to file an answer to the L.A. suit, in order to move the Alameda County

---

[16] At trial, Stemple abandoned his "adhesion contract" argument (RT 1631:11-16), but he added a new one: that the arbitration provisions were not mandatory. RT 1835:24-1836:4.

[17] And against Dr. Stephen Vonder Haar, a Weiss employee who was not even a party to the contracts with Crawford and S&B.

action to L.A. RT 494:3-25; Ex. 70.[18] Crawford testified: "And if I were to answer in Los Angeles they were hoping to get the matter moved down to Los Angeles away from the Superior Court for Alameda County. And I refused to do that." RT 494:22-26. Weiss was forced to pay his lawyer to defend that action, where his demurrer to the complaint was sustained on the ground that the issues were already being litigated in the instant case, in Alameda County. CT 684-685; Ex. 64.

Next, S&B tried to move the case to Monterey. Crawford had failed to pay a court reporter in Monterey, and the reporter filed suit against Crawford in Monterey Superior Court. S&B then paid the reporter, "purchasing" the lawsuit. RT 1530:19-1532:1. S&B then used this lawsuit as a vehicle for filing (on April 21, 1989) an unsuccessful motion to *coordinate* that suit with 6 other collection suits then pending against S&B in Alameda and San Francisco counties. CT 2802; RT 486:14-489:25, 1529:18-26, 2475:17-21; Ex. 21. This included the Olfacto and Weiss suits, which had been filed in Alameda County. S&B asserted that Glynn and Crawford — and not S&B — were responsible for paying these "alleged creditors of whom Stemple & Boyajian knew nothing." Ex. 21 (Points & Authorities, page 4).[19] The purpose of this baseless effort to coordinate was to make it difficult and expensive for claimants to pursue their claims against S&B. CT 2802:13-22. Even to oppose the motion to coordinate, these other claimants would have to pay their attorneys to travel to Monterey. Most did not — essentially giving up their claims — but Olfacto and Weiss did. RT 2055:15-18.

When these schemes failed, S&B defended the instant action with spurious after-the-fact fabrications, including conspiracy, fraud, allegations that S&B had not approved certain work, that Weiss had padded his bills, and that Weiss had done poor work. RT 5965:13-5968:1; CT 2801. Not only were these assertions false and without any basis in fact, both Stemple and Boyajian *knew* that they were false and without foundation, eventually admitting in open court that they did not have sufficient evidence to go forward with those claims. RT 752:5-755:27; CT 2801-2802.

Nevertheless, Stemple took the witness stand and testified under oath that Weiss, Olfacto, and Vonder Haar had *conspired* with Crawford and Glynn to trick S&B into signing contracts with Weiss and Olfacto. RT 1330:11-1331:8; 1335:2-12. His alleged belief that Weiss and Olfacto had so conspired was supposedly based on evidence "there was a great commonality of the series of events that were happening at the same time." RT

---

[18] S&B wrote to Crawford: "We would like you to appear by answering and assisting us in bringing the matter down here, where we feel we can do a better job proceeding, a [sic] defending against Weiss's claim." Ex. 70.

[19] At another point, S&B did appear to concede that they had made agreements with Weiss and Olfacto to pay them, but claimed that Weiss and Olfacto "used coercion to obtain Gordon Stemple's agreement to pay outstanding amounts for their asserted services to the Crazy Horse litigation." Ex. 21, Points & Authorities, page 5.

1347:18-25. This "commonality" consisted of the facts that the proposed contract which Weiss sent to S&B was the same form sent by Olfacto (RT 1348:13-20) and that both Weiss and Olfacto refused to do further work until S&B paid them (RT 1350:16-1351:5), showing that Weiss and Olfacto had "some discussion between them." RT 1362:4-1363:3. Stemple also found it very significant that Olfacto had apparently used Weiss's FAX machine. RT 1626:19-23. Vonder Haar was part of this alleged conspiracy because he had picked up the signed Weiss contract from Stemple, and this made him an "instrumentality" of the conspiracy (even though Stemple had no evidence that Vonder Haar intended to defraud S&B). RT 1334:5-1335:26. The "lynchpin" that supposedly convinced Stemple of the "conspiracy" occurred later, when Glynn asked Stemple why he had signed the contracts with Weiss and Olfacto, and Glynn told Stemple that Glynn had been willing all along to sign them. RT 1361:13-26. This caused both Stemple and Boyajian to go "through the roof." RT 1361:23-24; 1595:2-20. As Stemple put it, "There's an old Mideastern parable I once heard that, you know, you don't mind that somebody should make a donkey out of you, but you don't have to pin the ears on." RT 1806:17-21.

At his deposition, when asked why he did not pay Weiss and Olfacto, Stemple gave the "conspiracy" justification, and *only* the "conspiracy" justification. RT 1809:16-25. Nevertheless, at trial, Stemple invoked several *new* justifications for his failure to pay. He testified that Weiss had no right to refuse to testify until S&B paid what it owed him, as Weiss had failed to provide the 30-day notice of suspension required by § 17.1 of their agreement (Ex. 23A). RT 1340:10-16. Stemple also testified that S&B had "transferred" its obligation to pay Weiss to Crawford and Glynn, and that Weiss must seek payment from Crawford and Glynn rather than S&B. RT 1340:10-25.

Even though S&B had never before said that they were dissatisfied with Weiss's work (RT 2057:17-2058:2), they defended this suit by claiming that Weiss's work was unsatisfactory. RT 432:15-433:3. Crawford told them that "you guys are crazy to raise that kind of a defense. What evidence do you have of that? Because we had filed our 998 motion to tax costs bill [in the Crazy Horse case], where we certified everything was reasonable and necessary." RT 433:6-10. S&B's reply: "Well, discovery is continuing, or we might come up with something." RT 433:17-23.

Even though S&B had never before claimed that Weiss had worked without S&B's prior approval (RT 434:12-18; 2058:3-6; 5152:14-19), they defended this lawsuit on that basis. RT 1176:16-19. Even though S&B had never before claimed that Weiss's bills had improperly included charges for another project which Weiss performed for Crawford (the Marina project), S&B defended the suit on that basis. RT 5152:1-7. Even though S&B had never before claimed that its contract with Weiss was obtained by "economic duress" (RT 1032:25-1033:2), they defended Weiss's suit on this basis. CT 391, 396-397.

This was no accident. S&B treated Olfacto the same way: refusing arbitration (Ex. 62) and fabricating defenses which both Stemple and Boyajian knew were false, in order to drag out the litigation and make collection of a legitimate claim difficult. CT 2801-2802. S&B claimed that Olfacto had deceived S&B by not disclosing that the $45,000 in its contract contained improper amounts, but S&B had never complained about this to Olfacto. RT 1564:20-1565:16. S&B claimed that Olfacto had performed work without S&B's prior approval (as required by their contract), but Stemple admitted that he *knew* Olfacto was going to perform this work (rubber testing), but never called Olfacto to express any disapproval. RT 1585:11-22.

During trial, S&B finally *admitted* that both Weiss and Olfacto "did a very professional job." RT 1120:3-16. S&B also admitted that the bills submitted by Weiss and Olfacto were "proper billings for the services they performed." RT 1122:6-21. Nevertheless, they refused to concede that they were liable to Weiss and Olfacto for their billings, and insisted that Weiss and Olfacto had performed work which was not authorized by S&B. RT 1122:23-1123:8. This was part of a pattern of obstinate refusal caused the trial to go on for 36 days.

During Stemple's testimony, he admitted that S&B had the funds to pay Weiss the $21,000 it owed Weiss after it paid the first $10,000 payment, but deliberately chose not to pay. RT 1175:21-26. While S&B had alleged in its cross-complaint that Weiss's services were not properly performed, Stemple admitted that this was not true. RT 1176:5-13. Stemple initially testified that he had refused to pay because S&B had not authorized Weiss's work (RT 1176:16-19), but later backed off from this, admitted that he had approved that work (RT 1183:18-21), and testified that "I don't have any problem with this $21,000." RT 1177:20-21. Stemple then testified that he did not pay Weiss the $21,000 because Weiss had defrauded him into believing that its invoices covered work only on the Crazy Horse case, whereas they in fact included some work on the Marina Landfill project.[20] RT 1195:10-23; Ex. 30A. Stemple then admitted, however, that even though he supposedly became "quite upset" when he discovered this, he never called Weiss or wrote him about it. RT 1202:19-1203:5; 1205:1-19. Nor did he discuss this with Crawford or Glynn. RT 1211:22-1214:6.[21] When Weiss phoned and wrote Stemple asking for payment, Stemple never told Weiss that he was not paying because he thought Weiss had defrauded him. RT 1214:15-1215:3. Stemple testified that, instead of assuming that some mistake

---

[20] In fact, Stemple knew when he signed the agreement with Weiss that the initial $31,000 S&B was to pay included some work on the Marina Landfill project, as the *original* draft agreement reviewed by Stemple expressly *included* Marina (Ex. 42), and the *final* agreement signed by S&B was for the *same amount* ($31,000) as the draft. Ex. 23A. RT 1186:5-1187:23; 1237:22-1238:2. The signed agreement excluded *future* work by Weiss on Marina, but not *past* work.

[21] Stemple admitted that he had never mentioned any problem regarding billings for work on Marina Landfill to Weiss, to Crawford, or to Glynn, and had never mentioned it at his deposition. RT 1237:2-18.

might have been made, he concluded that Weiss was guilty of dishonesty. RT 1205:20-23; 1211:13-15. When the Court asked Stemple if he would not have signed the agreement had he known that it covered work on Marina, he said he did not know. RT 1208:4-10.

Stemple testified that he had "never disputed" that S&B owed Weiss the $21,135 due on the contract. RT 1222:20-23. He had refused to pay it, however, because Weiss had "sneaked in" another $20,000 which Stemple felt he did not owe. RT 1227:7-14; 1230:1-6. He asserted that he did not have to pay the $21,000 he admitted he owed because Weiss had materially breached the agreement, and this somehow excused Stemple's duty to pay. RT 1228:15-21. He claimed that "this contract to me is clearly voidable", but "I opt to declare it valid". RT 1221:2-10.[22] Later, Stemple appeared to back off from this, stating that he didn't know if he had changed his mind as to the $21,000. RT 1229:12-13.[23] Stemple then said that he owed the $21,000 "minus whatever was put in this charge for the Marina landfill" (about $7,000). RT 1231:3-6. When asked why he did not pay the remaining $14,000 he conceded he owed, he said because Weiss had breached — "That relieved my performance to pay." RT 1231:17-22.

Regarding Olfacto, Stemple testified that he had failed to pay the $45,000 due under its contract because Olfacto had breached by "nondisclosure" and by performing work without Stemple's prior approval. RT 1241:26-1242:15. But he then admitted that he had always believed that he *did* owe Olfacto the $45,000. RT 1244:10-24. Stemple knew of the alleged breach before Olfacto's Dr. Amoore testified in Crazy Horse, but Stemple did not tell Amoore that he was not going to pay him for his testimony. RT 1245:15-24.

Stemple then gave another reason for failing to pay both Weiss and Olfacto. He claimed that Glynn was obligated to pay Weiss and Olfacto, and that Glynn, Crawford, Weiss, and Olfacto had "conspired" to defraud S&B by threatening to withhold expert witness services in Crazy Horse unless S&B agreed to pay Weiss and Olfacto. RT 1252:4-16. He claimed that Vonder Haar was "an instrumentality" of this conspiracy. RT 1252:17-1253:21. Stemple supposedly believed that such a conspiracy existed because before Stemple signed the contracts with Weiss and Olfacto, Glynn had told him that Glynn was not going to pay Weiss and Olfacto, and "unless you pay those bills, I'll let the case go down the toilet" (RT 1263:18-26; 1265:18-26), but after Stemple signed the agreements with Weiss and Olfacto, Glynn told Stemple that Glynn had been willing to sign instead of Stemple. RT 1260:19-1261:8. Stemple testified that because Weiss was in fact willing to accept Glynn's signature, the fact that Weiss and Olfacto accepted S&B's signature showed that they had conspired with Glynn and Crawford to defraud S&B, as they led Stemple to believe that Weiss would not have testified without Stemple's signature. RT 1284:19-1285:18.

---

[22] Upon hearing this, Weiss's counsel stated: "I need a Valium." RT 1221:11.

[23] Prompting the trial court to comment: "You know, this is almost more than I can take." RT 1229:15.

Boyajian also testified. He said that Weiss coerced S&B to sign the contract "just to get Mr. Glynn out of it." RT 2459:26-2460:4. He testified that S&B would owe Weiss the money only if Glynn failed to pay Weiss — even though S&B's contract with Weiss contained no such condition. RT 2581:20-25. He admitted that he paid the initial $10,000 in order to induce Weiss to provide Vonder Haar's testimony, but nevertheless refused to pay the cost of that testimony once it was provided. RT 2660:20-2661:3. He flatly contradicted Ms. Springston's testimony that he had told her that S&B never intended to pay Weiss. RT 2487:2-2488:10; 2556:15-17.

In this Statement of Facts, it is difficult to capture the full extent of the evasiveness and lack of credibility of Boyajian's testimony, which goes on for several hundred pages of transcripts. At one point, he testified that Olfacto's depositions did *not* show that Olfacto had conspired, and less than a minute later, he testified that these depositions showed that Olfacto *had* conspired with Weiss. RT 2778:1-28. At another point, when Boyajian was asked a simple question — why didn't he pay Weiss? — he gave an evasive and spurious answer. *See* RT 2515:11-2523:12. (We suggest that this Court read those eight pages of transcript in order to taste the flavor of Boyajian's testimony.) Boyajian finally testified that he did not pay Weiss because such payment would require him to sue Glynn, and Boyajian wanted "to avoid litigation"! RT 3393:16-3394:4. At a later point, Boyajian's frustrating evasiveness caused the trial court to remark: "I want you to listen to the question and answer the question. I have had it, simply had it with the semantic games that you play, Mr. Boyajian. It is awful." RT 2758:12-16.

In order to confirm S&B's assertion to Crawford that S&B had already spent $100,000 on the case before Crawford agreed to take it over, Boyajian submitted a document which he prepared for trial, itemizing $129,155 in expenses which S&B had allegedly incurred in the Crazy Horse case prior to Crawford's involvement in the case. Ex. 100; RT 2853:27-2855:4. Boyajian testified that Exhibit 100 showed expenses *only* for the Crazy Horse case. RT 2858:4-8. In fact, however, many of the expenses shown in this exhibit did *not* relate to Crazy Horse. For example, Boyajian admitted that this exhibit included expenses which Stemple incurred in renting a hall in Salinas in order to address large groups of asbestos workers — an activity which had nothing to do with Crazy Horse. RT 2874:10-25. Later, he testified that perhaps this hall was rented for Boyajian's wedding! RT 3462:18-26. He then testified that "I don't know" why the hall was rented. RT 3463:2-17. Boyajian claimed that Exhibit 100 listed "only part" of the expenses S&B incurred in Crazy Horse. RT 2907:1-6. Later, he admitted that Exhibit 100 included expenses incurred in unrelated asbestos cases as well as Crazy Horse. RT 3402:5-12. In fact, Exhibit 100 included expenses incurred by Mr. Gamotan for his work on the "Tireworkers Litigation Project"[24] (RT 3677:9-3679:1) and certain other expenses unrelated to Crazy Horse, for travel (RT 3723:23-3724:1), a projector use for a meeting with tire-

---

[24] See footnote 8, *supra*.

workers (RT 3728:10-17, 3821:18-3822:17), telephone (RT 3729:5-18), X-rays used for the Tireworkers (RT 3733:1-19), and a bill from a physician who "may have" performed services for Crazy Horse (RT 3798:8-3799:8).

In view of the deficiencies in Exhibit 100, the court ordered Boyajian to submit correct documentation supporting the expenses in Crazy Horse. Boyajian supposedly instructed his accountant to prepare such a document (RT 3745:4-18), and S&B submitted Exhibit 112, which itemized a new total of $106,360 in expenses allegedly attributable to Crazy Horse. But *this exhibit too* included many expenses which should not have been attributed wholly to Crazy Horse, including an apartment rental (RT 3465:13-19), an office rental (RT 3781:13-24), travel expenses (RT 3468:22-24), telephone bills (RT 3500:2-26), and expenses from an unrelated lawsuit (RT 3496:18-3497:25).

In sum, while S&B presented records purporting to show that they spent $129,000 of their own money on the Crazy Horse case (RT 1932:6-10), it turned out that S&B spent only $16,000 on Crazy Horse. CT 2806-2807. The trial court found Boyajian's testimony on this matter to be "extremely disturbing." CT 2807. As the trial court concluded:

> Stemple and Boyajian were not credible witnesses in almost any respect. They also provided intentionally inaccurate documents to the court concerning their current financial conditions. They did not spare any expense or effort to thwart Olfacto's and Weiss' receipt of their legitimate, well-earned, fair, and long overdue payment. Stemple and Boyajian's conflicting, internally inconsistent, and vacillating testimony regarding their professional obligations to their clients, and to the Crazy Horse creditors, was especially abhorrent because lawyers should be familiar with simple contract law and ethics. [CT 2806.]

On September 6, 1991, Weiss and Olfacto finally obtained judgment against S&B — more than 4 years after they performed their work for S&B. CT 2780. The judgment has not been satisfied, so they still remain unpaid. The plaintiffs in Crazy Horse won a judgment for almost $4 million (CT 342, 658).[25] Though that case is now on appeal, S&B stand to recover attorneys fees of over $1 million. They already received $133,000 in attorneys fees when the City of Salinas settled (RT 1521:12-19). They admitted that the work of Olfacto and Weiss helped make this settlement possible (RT 1913:9-1914:1), but they have not seen fit to pay for that work. Both Olfacto and Weiss had expected timely payment of their bills, and their businesses were damaged by S&B's refusal to pay them. CT 2804, 3352; RT 2057:5-16; 2197:14-2204:7. Stemple admitted that he gave no thought to the effect on Olfacto's business of not receiving the $45,000 S&B owed it. RT 1512:7-24.

---

[25] They were also awarded costs, which included billings submitted by both Weiss and Olfacto. C.T. 679-680.

S&B recklessly cross-complained against Dr. Stephen Vonder Haar, who did work on Crazy Horse for Weiss and also had his own consulting firm. S&B's claims that Vonder Haar had committed fraud and conspiracy caused Vonder Haar's insurance company to cancel his insurance, and prevented him from obtaining other insurance. RT 1144:9-24.

S&B knew that these effects would flow from their refusal to pay, but refused to pay anyway — *even though they had the cash on hand to pay both Weiss and Olfacto.* RT 2493:9-11; CT 2805-2806.

Despite these effects, in 36 volumes of Reporter's Transcript, there is not a single indication of remorse from either Stemple or Boyajian. As the trial court found:

> Stemple and Boyajian have never shown any remorse, concern, or even the slightest embarrassment, for the effects of their calculated decision to defraud Olfacto and Weiss. They would do it all over again to Olfacto and Weiss, and will continue to do it to others in the future, if they believe that they can escape without punishment. [CT 2806.]

The trial court also found that S&B's treatment of Weiss and Olfacto were not aberrations, but were part and parcel of their way of doing business.

> Stemple & Boyajian's wrongful conduct exemplified their calculated and continuous tactics designed to "stiff" many of their creditors. In order to lure people into working for them, Stemple & Boyajian would make false promises that they would pay, while never intending to do so. [CT 2805.]**26**

The trial court summed up its view of Stemple and Boyajian:

> Stemple & Boyajian's wrongful conduct was extremely reprehensible because they used their position and skills as lawyers to abuse and to take advantage of experts who provided important services for the benefit of the defendants and their clients. Stemple and Boyajian engaged in a conscious, deliberate, premeditated pattern and practice of fraud and cheating. Stemple & Boyajian have shown no indication that they intend to change their wrongful manner of doing business. To the contrary they would do it again now, if they thought that they could get away with it. They will not be motivated to change their ways, unless there is a substantial assessment of punitive and exemplary damages against them. Only that will have even the possibility of a remedial effect on them. [CT 2809.]

Regarding Crawford, the trial court found that when Crawford retained Weiss and Olfacto, he intended to deceive them by implicitly representing

---

26 *See also* CT 3202-3206, showing several claims against Boyajian by people who provided services and who were never paid.

that he was able to and intended to pay them, and by failing to tell them that he had no ability to finance the litigation himself, and that he had no intent to pay either of them. CT 2818; RT 5651:4-17; 5715:4-11; 5942:22-26. Crawford admitted that he had no ability to pay Weiss. CT 1058; RT 764:25-765:2, Ex. 34.

Based on the above facts, the trial court entered judgment for Weiss as follows (CT 3354-3359):

> I. Against S&B: (1) for unpaid services, $63,956, plus interest of $25,742 (at the contract rate of 10.5%), for a total of $89,698; (2) for consultant's time spent in this case (as provided by the contract), $50,075; (3) for damages for fraud, $88,473 (consisting of the amount for unpaid services ($63,956) plus interest at the legal rate of 10% ($24,516), "plus $1.00 for nominal damages for unascertainable business harm to Weiss Associates"); and (4) attorneys fees of $133,406.

> II. Against Crawford: (1) for unpaid services, $63,956, plus interest of $25,742 (at the contract rate of 10.5%), for a total of $89,698; (2) for damages for fraud, $88,473 (consisting of the amount for unpaid services ($63,956) plus interest at the legal rate of 10% ($24,516), "plus $1.00 for nominal damages for unascertainable business harm to Weiss Associates"); and (3) attorneys fees of $133,406.

The court also awarded Weiss $4 million punitive damages against S&B (or $2 million each against Stemple and Boyajian). The court explained this award as follows:

> The court has taken very seriously the reprehensible nature of the conduct of these defendants, the broad pattern and practice of this conduct, the continuing nature of this conduct, the absence of any showing of remorse, the absence of any showing that such conduct will be discontinued in the future, the unjust enrichment to these defendants due to this pattern and practice, the net worth of these defendants, and the need to impress on these defendants the fact that this conduct is intolerable and must stop. [CT 2810.]

To ensure that the judgment[27] did not put S&B totally out of business, the court structured payment of the judgment as follows. First, compensatory

---

[27] The court also made the following awards:

Olfacto against S&B: $533,442 in compensatory damages, $131,902 in attorneys fees, and $4 million in punitive damages. CT 2782, 2784.

Olfacto against Crawford: $200,000 compensatory damages. CT 2783.

Crawford on his cross-complaint against S&B: $500,000 compensatory damages and $2 million in punitive damages. CT 2784.

S&B on their cross-complaints against Weiss, Olfacto, Crawford, and Glynn: Nothing. CT 2788.

Declaratory relief as to whether S&B, Crawford, or Glynn are liable to creditors in Crazy Horse litigation: All are liable to creditors for most debts, but Crawford is entitled to indemnification from S&B. CT 2786-2788.

damages shall be paid forthwith. Second, Boyajian shall forthwith pay $2 million of the punitive damages awarded against him to Weiss, Olfacto, and Crawford, pro rata. Third, the remaining $8 million in punitive damages owed by S&B to Weiss, Olfacto, and Crawford shall not be paid forthwith, but shall be paid to them pro rata from 20% of the contingent fees collected by S&B, as those fees come in. (If the parties discover any other assets of S&B which were not disclosed during trial, those may also be executed upon.) CT 3357-3359.

ARGUMENT

I. THE COMPENSATORY DAMAGES AWARD TO WEISS IS SUPPORTED BY SUBSTANTIAL EVIDENCE.

A. The Contract Damages are Supported by Substantial Evidence.

At page 12 of S&B's Opening Brief, they contend that the compensatory damages awarded to Weiss improperly included $6,850 for work Weiss performed for Crawford on the Marina project. But this amount was for work Weiss did for Crawford in the *past*, *before* S&B signed its contract with Weiss promising to pay for Crawford's outstanding debt to Weiss, and it was included in the $31,135.34 that S&B promised to pay Weiss. See Ex. 23A, last page. Ms. Springston testified that the S&B-Weiss contract *included* past work on Marina for which Crawford had not paid Weiss, though it would not cover future work. RT 1056:5-19. She also contradicted Stemple's testimony that he had told her that he would not pay for work on Marina. RT 1060:14-20. S&B points to the final contract, which had removed specific references to Marina which were in the earlier draft, but S&B overlooks the fact that the "outstanding balance" which S&B promised to pay in the final contract was *exactly the same* as the amount in the earlier draft — $31,135.34 — so this obviously included the *past* work on Marina. Compare the last pages of Exhibits 23A and 42.

Even if S&B had not realized that the $31,135.34 included the Marina project, such a mistake would not have been material.44 It is clear that S&B agreed to pay Weiss the $31,135.**28** which Crawford owed Weiss, as this appears as ¶1 of the Special Provisions of the Service Agreement. It is also clear that Weiss had refused to do any further work on any of Crawford's cases unless S&B promised to pay the *entire* $31,135.34, and that the *source* of the $31,135.34 was *irrelevant* to both Weiss and S&B. Weiss wanted Crawford's bill paid in full, period, as S&B well knew, and S&B promised to pay all of Crawford's bill. Their belated claim that they cared about the *source* of the $31,135.34 they promised to pay is simply not credible.

---

28 A mistake "*must affect in some material way* one of the essential elements of the contract, such as the parties, subject matter, offer or acceptance, *so that it clearly appears that the complaining party would not have entered into it* except for his mistaken belief." 1 Witkin, Summary of Calif. Law, *Contracts*, §368. *See also Vickerson v. Frey* (1950) 100 Cal. App. 2d 621, 628.

In any event, as S&B should know, credibility issues are for the trial court, not this Court. S&B must show that no substantial evidence supports the trial court's finding, and this they have not done. The evidence must be viewed in the light most favorable to the judgment (*Nestle v. City of Santa Monica* (1972) 6 Cal. 3d 920), and the testimony of a single witness is sufficient (*Marriage of Mix* (1975) 14 Cal. 3d 604). Here the testimony of Ms. Springston was more than sufficient. The trial court properly found that S&B were liable for the portion of the $31,135.34 which included past work on the Marina project. CT 2816:12-16.

At page 12, S&B also contend that Weiss improperly billed them on September 16, 1987, for $20,097 of work done in August of 1987, which had "not been disclosed" to S&B.[29] But when S&B signed the contract with Weiss on September 14, 1987, S&B *knew* that Weiss was working on Crazy Horse on an ongoing basis. Like most businesses, Weiss billed for its work periodically, not daily, so there must have been some work performed which had not yet been billed. RT 903:4-9. Weiss billed clients for the prior month's work in the middle of the next month. This resulted in sending out the bill for August work on September 16. RT 1095:15-1096:22. S&B knew that Weiss would send out bills only once a month, as ¶9.1 of their contract with Weiss expressly said this. *See* Ex. 23A.

Please note that Weiss sent bills to S&B which *clearly showed* that the $20,097 included work done before the contract was signed (Ex. 30, 40). If S&B truly believed that they had legitimate objections to paying this $20,097, they would have done one of two things: call up Weiss and object to it, or refuse to pay it and pay the remainder of the billings. They did neither. RT 295:18-20; 970:22-25; CT 2814:12-17. S&B accepted that amount as proper, and its belated challenge to that amount is just one more attempt to frustrate Weiss's efforts to obtain payment for its work.

At page 13, S&B argues that Weiss should not have been compensated for the time it spent litigating this matter, even though the contract with S&B expressly provides compensation for such "consultant's time." First, S&B contends that ¶11.2 of the contract (in Ex. 23A) permits such compensation only if the dispute relates to "performance of the services to be provided under this agreement," and this dispute "was over payment, not performance." Not so. In defense to Weiss's claim for payment, S&B's answer expressly alleged that Weiss "performed no services, work or labor of any kind whatsoever for this answering defendant at any time during the period alleged in Plaintiff's complaint, at said defendant's request or otherwise." CT

---

[29] S&B does not deny that the written contract includes this amount. The contract required S&B to pay "Any additional invoices from Weiss Associates" (§2 of the Special Provisions, in Ex. 23A.) Also, note that ¶1 of the Special Provisions says that, "As of August 30, 1987 there is an outstanding balance of $31,135.34 *that has been billed* to Robert K. Crawford & Associates." This shows that there might be other amounts owed by Crawford which had not yet been billed.

80:4-10. S&B's settlement conference statement claimed that Weiss had breached his contract with S&B and had overcharged for its services. CT 397:16-23. These spurious defenses caused Mr. Weiss to spend many hours in preparation and on the witness stand rebutting them. *See* RT 2001 *et. seq.*, 5112 *et. seq.*, 5305 *et. seq.*, and 5942 *et. seq.* His testimony about payment was brief: after the initial $10,000 payment, there was none. But his testimony about his performance under the contract was lengthy indeed. *Id.*[30]

Second, S&B argues that "public policy" invalidates this provision, as it "fosters litigation." Quite the contrary. A defendant faced with a legitimate claim for payment — knowing that he might also have to pay for the consultant's time in court — might prefer to pay up rather than raise spurious excuses which force the consultant to litigate. (Unfortunately, in the instant case, nothing seemed to convince S&B to deal honestly with Weiss.) If S&B's argument were accepted, then contractual provisions for attorneys' fees would also be invalid, as they might also give an attorney an incentive to litigate. But the law upholds such provisions, as they help to "make whole" a party who has been forced to litigate a just claim. The same is true here. The hours Weiss spent in court were taken from hours he could have spent working for his clients, and the compensation for "consultant's time" simply reimbursed him for fees lost for other work he could have been doing.

Third, at page 15, S&B argue that because Weiss's testimony was "clearly not for geological consulting services," Weiss cannot recover for its consultant's time in testifying. The contract clearly contemplates, however, that such consultant's time will occur in litigation *over the contract*, not over geology.

At page 15, S&B claims that Weiss should not be paid for consultant's time incurred after Weiss supposedly rejected a pretrial settlement offer from S&B. But there is no credible evidence of any such settlement offer. S&B cites "RT 2507:13-2508:14," which contains Boyajian's vague, hearsay testimony that Stemple (not Boyajian) had offered Weiss "140 or 150 thousand dollars to settle the case" and that "one of the sticking points we could not agree on" was compensation for consultant's time. The trial court found Boyajian not to be a credible witness. CT 2806. In any event, even if there had been a settlement offer, Weiss would have had no obligation to accept any offer he found inadequate, and there is no evidence that S&B made any formal settlement offer under CCP § 998, which could have cut off rights Weiss might have had to recover for subsequently-incurred expenses.

B. The Finding that S&B Defrauded Weiss is Supported by Clear and Convincing Evidence.

At pages 15-16, S&B claim that "there is no credible evidence to suggest that when Stemple signed the service agreements, either partner lacked

---

[30] Weiss's associates, Mr. Vonder Haar and Ms. Springston, also testified re performance of the contract. *See* RT 878 *et.seq*, 946 *et. seq.*, 1103 *et. seq.*, 5324 *et. seq.*, and 5933 *et. seq.*

intention to pay." They argue that Beth Springston's testimony does not show that S&B had no intent to pay when the contract was signed. In fact, Ms. Springston's testimony could not have been clearer: "[Boyajian] said to me that even when they signed the contract they had never intended to pay it to us." RT 884:1-11; CT 2800; Ex. 38. The trial court found Springston to be "a truthful, careful, and accurate witness" (CT 2800:22-24), and therefore the court "believes Beth Springston's testimony" (CT 2800:25-28015). The court also found that Boyajian's testimony to the contrary was "not credible" (CT 2801:6-8).[31]

S&B also assert that because S&B made the $10,000 initial payment on the Weiss contract, they must have intended to comply with the contract. But S&B *had* to make this payment, because it was due before Weiss was scheduled to testify in Crazy Horse, and S&B knew that Weiss would not testify without this payment. The trial court found that this payment was made to induce Weiss to testify in the Crazy Horse case, and that S&B planned to make no further payments after they got the testimony they wanted. CT 2799:8-12. S&B made the initial payment knowing that they could repay themselves from Glynn's account anyway. CT 2799:13-18.

Boyajian also told Springston that S&B would refuse arbitration (even though the contract provided for arbitration) and that if Weiss sued to collect for his work, S&B would make sure that "it would be in court forever." RT 883:19-24.

In fact, the evidence of fraud, oppression, and malice was overwhelming. *In addition* to Springston's testimony, the evidence showed that S&B *carried out* their threat to "stonewall" Weiss by making frivolous efforts to move the case to an inconvenient forum (in Los Angeles, then in Monterey, still far from Weiss's Bay Area office), raised frivolous defenses that they themselves did not believe in, submitted false documents, and presented false evidence on the witness stand. *See* Statement of Facts, *supra*.

Even during this appeal, S&B *continue* to refuse to take responsibility for what they have done. At the top of page 18, they continue to deny that Boyajian told Springston that S&B had never intended to pay, even though the trial court found that Springston told the truth and Boyajian did not. At footnote 8 on page 11, they *still* claim that they "initially believed the Service Agreements to be invalid because they were executed under duress" and "as a result of conspiracy and fraud," even though the trial court found that "The entire time Stemple & Boyajian asserted these theories, either as affirmative defenses or in their cross-complaint, neither Stemple nor Boyajian believed that any of them was true" (CT 2802:1-3). Perhaps an affirmance and execution of the judgment will finally bring the message home to them.

---

[31] Crawford testified that Boyajian told him too that "he had no intention to pay" Weiss and Olfacto. RT 716:28-717:25, 829:5-9.

C. The Statute of Limitations Does Not Bar The Fraud Judgment Against Stemple and Boyajian As Individuals.

Beth Springston testified that Weiss first discovered S&B's fraud during her phone conversation with Boyajian, on February 23, 1988. RT 882:22-884:16. Weiss's complaint against S&B (the partnership) was filed on October 12, 1988 (CT 45), well within 3 years of the phone conversation.[32] That complaint, however, neglected to name Stemple and Boyajian as individuals. The oversight was corrected on December 19, 1990, when the court allowed Weiss to amend the complaint to add them as individual defendants. RT 2525:23-28; CT 1324.

At pages 18-20 of its brief, S&B contend that allowing the amendment was error, because by that date the Statute of Limitations had run on the fraud claim. They argue that Weiss first discovered the fraud not on February 23, 1988, when Springston spoke to Boyajian, but earlier, on November 17, 1987, when Weiss filed a citizen's complaint against Stemple and Boyajian with the State Bar (Ex. 153).

But Weiss testified that when he said in that complaint that S&B had committed "fraud", all he meant was that Stemple "said he was going to pay and didn't," *not* that Stemple did not intend to pay *when he made the contract.* RT 5309:26-5310:16. Weiss filed his State Bar complaint without any legal assistance (RT 5307:10-5310:18), and he used the word "fraud" as a layman would, believing it to be "fraud" when someone promises to pay and then refuses to do so (RT 5313:12-21). This does not show that he then knew the fraud which was the basis of the judgment below: S&B's signing the contract while not intending to pay. Please note that there was no evidence that, when he filed the State Bar complaint, Weiss had any information indicating that S&B had signed without intending to pay. Weiss testified that he ceased believing that S&B intended to pay only when he heard about the Springston-Boyajian phone conversation of February, 1988. RT 5313:7-11.

The trial court found that Weiss's State Bar complaint did not show that he was then aware that Stemple and Boyajian intended to defraud him by signing the contract without intent to pay. RT, volume 36, at 40:6-22. In its Statement of Decision, the court expressly found that S&B "for the first time" revealed that it never intended to pay Weiss during the Springston-Boyajian phone conversation, and that "before this conversation occurred, neither Olfacto nor Weiss had learned of, nor had any reason to suspect, Stemple & Boyajian's fraud." CT 2800:2-22. The determination of when a plaintiff was or should have been aware of damage is a question of fact for the trial court. *Day v. Rosenthal* (1985) 170 Cal. App. 3d 1125, 1164. We sub-

---

[32] CCP §338(4) requires a fraud complaint to be filed within 3 years of discovery.

mit that Weiss's testimony, described above, provides substantial evidence supporting the trial court.[33]

II. THE PUNITIVE DAMAGE AWARD WAS PROPER.

A. California's Punitive Damage Procedure is Constitutional.

At page 32, S&B challenges the constitutionality of our punitive damage procedure. This argument was rejected in *Wetherbee v. United Insurance Co. of America* (1971) 18 Cal. App. 3d 266, and *Wollersheim v. Church of Scientology* (1992) 4 Cal. App. 4th 1074. (On July 31, 1992, the California Supreme Court agreed to review *Wollersheim*.) We submit that those cases were correctly decided.

B. The Finding that S&B Committed Fraud, Oppression, and Malice is Supported by Clear and Convincing Evidence.

At page 33, S&B argues that "there is no basis" for the findings that S&B committed fraud, oppression, or malice. This astounding claim is refuted by the overwhelming evidence summarized in our Statement of Facts, *supra*, which we will incorporate rather than repeat here. A false promise may be the basis for a fraud action and support an award of punitive damages (*Glendale Fed. Savings & Loan Assn. v. Marina View Heights Dev.* (1977) 66 Cal. App. 3d 101, 135), and that is exactly what happened here.

At page 34, S&B continue to deny that they invented their contract defenses, despite the obvious weakness of those defenses, despite S&B's failure to mention them to Weiss prior to this litigation, and despite the trial court's finding that S&B themselves never believed that their defenses had any merit. CT 2802:1-3.

S&B then argue that the fact that they willfully presented fabricated defenses cannot be considered, because California does not permit recovery for "malicious defense." However, Weiss did not seek recovery for "malicious defense," but for *fraud*. The fraud began well before this action was commenced, and continued right through the lawsuit. S&B lied about their intent to pay Weiss, threatened to manipulate the legal system if Weiss sued, and followed through on that threat by raising spurious defenses. This was one continuous course of conduct constituting fraud, oppression, and malice justifying punitive damages on Weiss's basic action for fraud. Where a party is sued for a pre-litigation tort, that party's litigation tactics

---

[33] Even if Weiss had known of the fraud earlier, the trial court still had discretion to allow the amendment. Where a complaint is properly amended to add new parties on the same general set of facts, the amendment "relates back" to the date of filing of the original complaint, thus defeating any statute of limitations defense. *See Smeltzley v. Nicholson Mfg. Co.* (1977) 18 Cal. 3d 932. It should be noted that neither Stemple nor Boyajian was prejudiced by the fact that the original complaint did not name them as individual defendants, as the trial court found that they had personally managed the case against the partnership anyway. RT 2525:23-2526:3; and volume 32, at 42:21-24.

may shed light on his intent, and may be considered for that purpose. *See, e.g., Oren Royal Oaks Venture v. Greenberg, Bernhard, Weiss & Karma, Inc.* (1986) 42 Cal. 3d 1157; *White v. Western Title Ins. Co.* (1985) 40 Cal. 3d 870. This is what happened here.

Also on page 34, S&B claim that they relied on the advice of counsel before refusing payment. The burden of proving an "advice of counsel" defense is on the party seeking to benefit by it. *Bertero v. National General Corp.* (1974) 13 Cal. 3d 43, 54. S&B did not sustain that burden. They cite only "RT 1249:25-1250-14": Stemple's testimony that "one of my attorneys" (i.e., his own employee), Peter Kunstler, found in Witkin the proposition that one party's breach excuses the other party's duty to perform. Even if this testimony were true,[34] it was insufficient. Stemple did not testify that he told Kunstler any *facts* about Weiss's alleged "breach" or the fact that Boyajian had told Beth Springston that S&B had *never intended* to perform. The "advice of counsel" defense fails "if the initiator acts in bad faith or withholds from counsel facts he knew or should have known would defeat a cause of action otherwise appearing from the information supplied," and it also fails if the advice is not sought in good faith (*id.* at 53-54). S&B failed to prove that Kunstler was told all the relevant facts, and they failed to prove that they sought the advice in good faith.

Sadly, S&B continue to proclaim that their determination not to pay Weiss and Olfacto stemmed from "a misunderstanding of contract law and a misperception of the reasons they were forced to sign the Service Agreements in September of 1987." AOB, pp. 34-35. This was their position throughout the trial, but the evidence showed — and the trial court found — that this was a lie. S&B's refusal to pay their just debts was not based on any misperceptions of law or fact, but on greed. Even now, S&B refuse to acknowledge this and take responsibility for their actions.

C. The Amount of the Punitive Damage Award is Supported by the Evidence.

At page 35, S&B call the amount of punitive damages awarded "ridiculously excessive." But the amount was quite modest, in light of the extreme seriousness of S&B's conduct and their wealth. S&B's continuing lack of remorse and the size of their remaining fortunes suggest that the amount was not high enough.

1. *S&B's Misconduct.*

First and foremost of the factors relevant to punitive damages is the nature of the defendant's misconduct. "[T]he more reprehensible the act, the greater the appropriate punishment." *Neal v. Framers Ins. Exchange* (1978) 21 Cal. 3d 910, 928. As explained in the Statement of Facts, *supra*, here two

---

[34] The trial court found Stemple's testimony not credible "in almost any respect". CT 2806:12-13.

lawyers lied to lay people, exploited their work for the lawyers' own gain, threatened to manipulate the legal system in order to defeat legitimate claims, and then imposed on the taxpayers and the court system by filing frivolous actions, raising defenses they knew to be without merit, and — perhaps worst of all — actually taking the witness stand and lying, not once but many times. In our research, we found no case which involved such a pattern of egregious conduct.

Gordon Stemple and Berj Boyajian are lawyers, with special obligations to deal fairly with the public. In *In re Waleen* (1933) 250 N.W. 798, 799, the Minnesota Supreme Court disciplined a lawyer who had defrauded several non-clients, stating:

> Respondent, as an attorney at law, even in ordinary business transactions, was bound by more rigid rules and was bound to exercise a higher degree of care and diligence than would a layperson engaged in the conduct of his private business affairs.[35]

In California, we follow the same principle. A lawyer may be disciplined for an act of dishonesty "whether the act is committed in the course of his relations as an attorney or otherwise." Bus. & Prof.C.§ 6106.[36] Attorneys have been disciplined for dishonest relations with non-clients. *See, e.g., Rhodes v. State Bar* (1989) 49 Cal. 3d 50, *Marquette v. State Bar* (1988) 44 Cal. 3d 253, and *Lee v. State Bar* (1970) 2 Cal. 3d 927.

The purposes of punitive damages are to punish the defendant and to deter him and others from such conduct in the future. "Because the quintessence of punitive damages is to deter future misconduct by the defendant, the key question before the reviewing court is whether the amount of damages 'exceeds the level necessary to properly punish and deter.'" *Adams v. Murakami* (1991) 54 Cal. 3d 105, 110. Here, the trial court found these purposes can be met only by imposing substantial punitive damages:

> Stemple and Boyajian have shown no indication that they intend to change their wrongful manner of doing business. To the contrary, they would do it again now, if they thought that they could get away with it. They will not be motivated to change their ways, unless there is a substantial assessment of punitive and exemplary

---

[35] Other states agree. *See, e.g., Nebraska State Bar Assn. v. Leonard* (Neb., 1982) 322 N.W.2d 794, 796; *Matter of Franklin* (N.J., 1976) 365 A.2d 1361; *In re Kirtz* (Mo., 1973) 494 S.W.2d 324, 328; *Murphy v. Erie County Bar Assn.* (N.Y., 1972) 328 N.Y.S.2d 949, 951. *See also* Aronson & Weckstein, *Professional Responsibility in a Nutshell*, p. 495 (West, 2d ed., 1991): "Even when a lawyer is playing another role, whether it be real estate dealer, car salesman, or politician, the lawyer is expected to rise above the morals of the marketplace if they are not as high as the standards required of attorneys."

[36] *See also* ABA Model Rules of Professional Conduct, Preamble: "A lawyer's conduct should conform to the requirements of the law, both in professional services to clients and in the lawyer's business and personal affairs." *See also* ABA Standing Committee on Ethics & Prof. Responsibility, Formal Opinion 336 (1974).

damages against them. Only that will have even the possibility of a remedial effect on them. In order to have an appropriate deterrent effect on these defendants in light of their financial condition, the imposition of punitive and exemplary damages in the amount being assessed here is necessary. [CT 2809:18-2810:1]

In *Moore v. American United Life Ins. Co.* (1984) 150 Cal. App. 3d 610, the court held that a punitive damage award of $2.5 million (83 times the compensatory damages) was not excessive, partly because defendant had not changed its wrongful practices, and therefore the award "was necessary in order to get defendant's attention." *Id.* at 638. Here, too, the trial court properly determined that its award was the only way to get S&B's attention.

2. *The Ratio Between Punitive and Compensatory Damages.*

At page 36, S&B contend that the ratio between the compensatory and punitive damages awarded to Weiss was too high. However, as the court held in *Gagnon v. Continental Casualty Co.* (1989) 211 Cal. App. 3d 1598, 1604:

> There is no fixed ratio to determine the reasonableness of the relationship between punitive damages and actual harm done, and a comparison of ratios of exemplary to compensatory damages awarded in other cases does not provide a means of determining a reasonable relation.[37]

Nevertheless, if such a comparison were made, we would find that California cases have affirmed ratios which were *higher* than what we have here. Weiss's compensatory damages were $89,698 for unpaid services plus interest, $50,075 for consultant's time, and $133,406 for attorneys fees — a total of $273,259. CT 3354-3356.[38] The $4 million punitive damage award is about 14.6 times the $273,259. This 14.6 is *lower* than the ratio allowed in *Neal v. Farmers Ins. Exchange* (1978) 21 Cal. 3d 910 (78 to 1); *Downey Sav. & Loan Assn. v. Ohio Casualty Ins. Co.* (1987) 189 Cal. App. 3d 1072 (32 to 1); *Moore v. American United Life Ins. Co.* (1984) 150 Cal. App. 3d 610 (83

---

[37] In *Moore v. American United Life Ins. Co.* (1984) 150 Cal. App. 3d 610, 636-637, the court explained: "If the overriding consideration in an award of punitive damages is whether it bears a reasonable relation to the actual damages suffered, the result may be to thwart completely the purpose of punitive damages. One example of this is the situation where a plaintiff has suffered only minor injury or is only able to prove a small amount of actual damages, yet the conduct of the defendant has been especially wanton or malicious. This would seem the precise situation in which a large award of punitive damages would be necessary to ensure that the defendant does not repeat his act and that others do not imitate him. Application of the reasonable relation rule, however, would limit the punitive damages to an amount not disproportionate to the actual damages suffered. This example illustrates the fact that in its operation the reasonable relation rule can ignore the punitive and deterrent functions of exemplary damages."

[38] In *Commercial Cotton Co. v. United California Bank* (1985) 163 Cal. App. 3d 511, 517-518, in considering the ratio between punitive damages and compensatory damages, the court included in compensatory damages "expenses incurred following the breach to obtain restitution (i.e., costs of litigation)."

to 1); *Vosseler v. Richards Mfg. Co.* (1983) 143 Cal. App. 3d 952 (20 to 1); and *Wetherbee v. United Insurance Co. of America* (1971) 18 Cal. App. 3d 266 (almost 200 to 1).

But this does not tell the whole story. As part of its award for fraud damages, the court awarded Weiss "$1 for nominal damages for unascertainable business harm to Weiss Associates." CT 3356:17-21. This $1 was for real harm which S&B inflicted on Weiss. Because the amount of such harm could not be proved with sufficient certainty, only nominal damages were awarded, but the harm was nevertheless inflicted. The purpose of considering the ratio between compensatory damages and the award of punitive damages is to ensure that the amount of punitives bears some reasonable relationship to the harm inflicted by the defendant, and usually the amount of compensatory damages is a fair measure of that harm. In this case, however, the harm was greater: the $1 indicates harm which was actually inflicted by S&B, but which cannot adequately be expressed in compensatory damages. For this reason, the actual harm caused by S&B was higher than $273,259, and the ratio was in reality lower than 14.6 to 1.

Our case law recognizes that the usual view of ratio should change when nominal damages have been awarded. Witkin says (at 6 Witkin, Summary of Calif. Law, *Torts*, § 1374) that "ordinarily the punitive damages must be in some reasonable proportion to the actual damages suffered." However, he then states in the same section that: "This rule does not, however, preclude a large award of punitive damages based upon substantial actual damages, even though, because of the difficulty of ascertaining the extent of the actual damage, the basic award is only a *nominal* sum," citing *Sterling Drug Co. v. Benatar* (1950) 99 Cal. App. 2d 393, where an award of $1 nominal damages supported a punitive award of $200 (200 to 1), and *Werschkull v. United California Bank* (1978) 85 Cal. App. 3d 981, where $1 nominal damages supported a punitive damage award of $550,000 (550,000 to 1)![39] *See also* § 1328, where Witkin notes that § 908 of the Restatement of Torts 2d, Comment c, states that:

> [P]unitive damages may be awarded even though there is no substantial pecuniary or physical harm; i.e., a tort cause of action must

---

[39] *See also Finney v. Lockhart*, 35 Cal. 2d 161 (allowing actual damages of $1 and $2,000 in punitive damages) and *Commercial Cotton Co. v. United California Bank* (1985) 163 Cal. App. 3d 511, where the jury awarded $4,000 for withholding of funds, $20,000 for intentional infliction of emotional distress (on an individual co-plaintiff, who was principal shareholder of Commercial Cotton Co.), and $100,000 in punitive damages. The appellate court reversed the $20,000 award, but affirmed the punitive damage award:

> Here, the record shows as a matter of law UCB's breach of its covenant of good faith and fair dealing to Commercial Cotton caused it and its principal (Dr. Calvin), *actual damages in an unspecified amount*, including the loss of use of the $4,000 improperly withheld for several years . . . , and derivable income, *and expenses incurred following the breach to obtain restitution (i.e., costs of litigation)*. Accordingly, our reversing the emotional distress damages award does not affect the validity of the exemplary damage verdict. [*Id.* at 517-518, fn. 2; emphasis added.]

be shown, but *an award of nominal damages is enough to support a further award of punitive damages where the tort is committed for an outrageous purpose.* [Emphasis added.]

Finally, the ratio is simply not that important where the conduct of the defendant is especially reprehensible. In *Betts v. Allstate Ins. Co.* (1984) 154 Cal. App. 3d 688, 712, the court stated:

[I]f the defendant's conduct is sufficiently reprehensible, the ratio between compensatory and punitive damages is less important; however, where the ratio of compensatory to punitive damages is extremely high and the conduct is somewhat less reprehensible, this ratio carries more weight. [Citations] The proper consideration is whether the punitive damage award bears a reasonable relationship to its principal purpose of punishment and deterrence.

As we have shown, the term "sufficiently reprehensible" aptly applies to S&B's conduct in this case.

3. *S&B's Wealth.*

The purpose of punitive damages is to punish the defendant . . . and the wealthier the defendant, the larger the award of punitive damages need be in order to accomplish this statutory objective. [*Zhadan v. Downtown Los Angeles Motor Distributors, Inc.* (1980) 100 Cal. App. 3d 821, 835.]

The trial court found that Stemple was worth over $22 million, that Boyajian was worth over $29 million, and S&B was worth $40 million. CT 2808:18-23. At page 37, S&B appear to claim that these findings are not supported by substantial evidence. As these amounts consist partly of S&B's rights to contingent fees in cases they have farmed out to other lawyers, S&B now characterize them as "pure speculation."

But these amounts come from S&B's *own loan applications* to the Bank of America, in which S&B *asked* the Bank to consider these contingent fees as valuable assets. Ex. 171, 173. The Bank *granted* the loans! RT 6544:4-16, 6666:11-16. And now S&B asks this Court to presume that banks loan millions of dollars on "pure speculation"! S&B did not hesitate to sign loan applications listing these contingent fees as assets, but now they claim that the same contingent fees are "pure speculation." As the trial court said at one point, "You know, this is almost more than I can take." RT 1229:15.

S&B contend that the total of the punitive damage awards to Weiss, Olfacto, and Crawford ($10 million) amounts to "17-23% of net worth, a percentage so large that it shocks the conscience." AOB, p. 39. Together, Stemple and Boyajian are worth over $51 million. $51 million minus $10 million leaves them with a combined fortune of over $41 million, a tidy sum for two men. While this result might shock the sensitive consciences of Mr. Stemple and Mr. Boyajian, it did not shock the conscience of the experienced trial judge who heard and saw what they had done. What shocks the pocketbook does not necessarily shock the conscience. "[O]bviously, the function of deterrence . . . will not be served if the wealth of the defendant allows him to absorb the award with little or no discomfort." *Neal v. Farmers Ins. Exchange* (1978) 21 Cal. 3d 910, 928.

Our courts have upheld punitive damage awards which represented a percentage of net worth as high as the award here. See, e.g., *Greenfield v. Spectrum Inv. Co.* (174 Cal. App. 3d 111 (100% of net worth); *Greenup v. Rodman* (1985) 184 Cal. App. 3d 662 (20%); *Devlin v. Kearny Mesa AMC/Jeep/Renault Co.* (1984) 155 Cal. App. 3d 381 (17.5%). In *Devlin*, the court said: "[T]here is a range of reasonableness for punitive damages reflective of the factfinder's human response to the evidence presented". Id. at 391.

At page 39, S&B complain that the award is high relative to their income. We note, however, that most of the cases which examined punitive damages as percentages of income and net worth concerned corporate defendants, not individual defendants. Where punitive damages are assessed against a corporation, they are in reality imposed on the shareholders, who did not actually commit the wrongs and not all of whom are rich — realities which give courts pause in upholding large awards against corporations. In our case, however, the punitive damages were assessed against wealthy parties who actually committed the wrongs: Stemple and Boyajian as individuals, and the partnership which they wholly own.

4. *The Punitive Damages Were Awarded By The Judge, Not A Jury.*

The case at bench is somewhat unusual, in that the punitive damages were awarded by a Superior Court judge, rather than a jury. This is important, because appellate review of punitive damage awards is normally meant to ensure that such awards do not stem from the unrestrained passions of inexperienced jurors. Judges are not as susceptible to such passions, and they have greater experience in measuring degrees of wrongful behavior.

> Judges have more familiarity than do juries with distinguishing "wrong" from "very wrong" behavior (and fixing the appropriate level of punishment therefor) upon a formal social scale, and judges should have in general less rigid preconceptions that may bias the result. [Thompson & Sebert, *Remedies: Damages, Equity and Restitution*, p. 127 (2d ed., 1989).][40]

---

[40] *See also* Wheeler, *The Constitutional Case For Reforming Punitive Damage Procedures*, 69 Va. L. Rev. 269, 302 (1983): "Judges are generally more experienced than juries in making the policy judgments required when balancing conflicting penal purposes. . . Judges are, of course, subject to passion or prejudice. Yet trial judges who have heard the same evidence as the jury frequently remit or vacate jury awards on a finding that the award was based on passion or prejudice. This fact may indicate that judges are less influenced by passion or prejudice."

In Mallor & Roberts, *Punitive Damages: Toward A Principled Approach*, 31 Hastings L.J. 639, 664 (1980), the authors state:

> Although the judge is in no better position to decide whether the defendant's conduct was outrageous, the question of punishment calls for expertise. Delicate issues of economics and social policy are involved in deciding the amount of punishment — issues with which the ordinary juror is likely to have little familiarity. Beyond being more aware of the public policy implications of the award of punitive damages, judges have more experience in meting out punishment. They are less likely to be impressed by the histrionics of counsel and so to be inflamed by passion or prejudice.[41]

This distinction between judge and jury has been recognized in California. In *Devlin v. Kearny Mesa AMC/Jeep/Renault Co.* (1984) 155 Cal. App. 3d 381, 392, the court upheld a punitive damage award which was 27 times compensatory damages and 17.5% of defendant's net worth, stating:

> This is not a case where an unreasonable award was rendered by a runaway jury. Rather, the award was the result of a measured deliberation by a conscientious judge. Deference to the trial court requires appellate restraint.

S&B complain that the punitive damage award was too large. However, an award of punitive damages will be reversed as excessive *only* when the entire record, viewed most favorably to the judgment, indicates that the award was rendered as the result of passion and prejudice. *Devlin v. Kearney Mesa AMC/Jeep/Renault, Inc., supra*, 155 Cal. App. 3d at 388. There is no evidence of such passion or prejudice here. The trial judge was very experienced: she had practiced law for 18 years and served 12 years on the Municipal Court bench and 13 years on the Superior Court: *43 years* at bench and bar. See footnote 1, supra. While annoyed by S&B's conduct — as any judge would be — she nevertheless bent over backwards to be fair to

---

[41] In Owen, *Punitive Damages Products Liability Litigation*, 74 Mich. L. Rev. 1257, 1320-21 (1976), the author recommends having judges rather than juries impose punitive damages: "[I]t would reduce the probability that punitive damages awards might be unduly influenced by emotion, since most judges are presumably more detached in their deliberation, and therefore more likely to render objective damages assessments. * * * * Further, judges would be able to call upon their experience in criminal sentencing, unavailable to jurors, in evaluating the need for punishment and deterrence in particular cases. Finally, trial judges usually have a more sophisticated appreciation than jurors of the often far-reaching effects that punitive damages awards may have on the operations of particular corporate defendants."

Former Attorney Griffen Bell also suggested that judges, not juries, set punitive damages. Bell, *Punitive Damages and the Tort System*, 22 U.Rich.L.Rev. 1, 2 (1987). Some states now provide for this. *See, e.g.*, Kan. Stat. Ann. §60-3702(a); Ohio Rev. Code Ann. §2315.21(c)(2). The Kansas Tort Reform Committee reported that, "The Committee believes the bifurcated trial procedure and the listing of factors considered will help insure that punitive awards are not excessive." *Report on Kansas Legislative Interim Studies to the 1987 Legislature*, p. 591 (1986).

them. She sustained their objections to evidence 144 times,[42] and she chastised *plaintiffs'* counsel several times. *See* RT 2554:2-12, 5648:12-24, 5654:12-18, 5661:19-26, 6604:2026.

The trial judge heard hundreds of hours of testimony and reviewed 174 exhibits. She saw Stemple testify; she saw Boyajian testify. This Court, however, sits as a court of review, not a trial court, and has not had (and cannot now take) the opportunity to examine the evidence as closely as the trial judge did. In these circumstances, the judgment should be reversed or revised only if the appellant *clearly demonstrates* that the award was the product of "passion or prejudice." S&B have made no such demonstration. As the court held in *Devlin, supra,* "Deference to the trial court function requires appellate restraint." 155 Cal. App. 3d at 392. We submit that such deference is most appropriate here.

California cases recognize that deference should be given to the trial judge on punitive damages issues, "for it is in a far better position than an appellate court to determine whether a damages award was influenced by passion or prejudice." *Institute of Veterinary Pathology, Inc. v. Calif. Health Laboratories, Inc.* (1981) 116 Cal. App. 3d 111, 122. In *Moore v. American United Life Ins. Co.* (1984) 150 Cal. App. 3d 610, 642, the court upheld a jury's punitive damage award, noting that the trial judge had denied defendant's motion for new trial:

> Although the trial court's determination is not binding on a reviewing court, it is to be accorded great weight because having been present at the trial, the trial judge was necessarily more familiar with the evidence.

As S&B has presented no sound reason to upset the trial court's award, it should be affirmed.

III. THE STRUCTURE OF THE JUDGMENT WAS PROPER.

At pages 40-42, S&B argues that the structured payment aspect of the judgment was improper. This structure was unusual, because the bulk of S&B's assets are unusual, consisting of contingent fees. Without the structured payment, plaintiffs could immediately execute on the entire judgment, forcing an execution sale of S&B's rights to the contingent fees, no doubt at "distress prices," to the disadvantage of all parties — including

---

[42] *See* RT 1412, 1430, 1572, 1674, 1739, 1754, 1766, 1782, 1868, 1961, 2049, 2056 (twice), 2059, 2061, 2071, 2086, 2154-55, 2205, 2321, 2457, 2480, 2487, 2557, 2584, 2591, 2608-09, 2623, 2628, 2711, 2818, 2834, 2906, 2923, 2932 (twice), 2945, 2977, 2985, 3264, 3274, 3305, 3321-22, 3336, 3338, 3345, 3375, 3431, 3433, 3443, 3447-48, 3457, 3458, 3466, 3522, 3523, 3453, 3454, 3455, 3567, 3618, 3745, 3788 (twice), 3791, 3793, 3796, 3834, 3836, 3869, 3895, 3923, 3928, 3930, 3965, 3989, 3989-90, 3991-92, 4006 (twice), 4029, 4032, 4653, 4655-56, 4737, 4738, 4837-38, 4853, 4873 (twice), 4874, 5152-53, 5194, 5207, 5225, 5239, 5261, 5269, 5273-74, 5278, 5285, 5290, 5386, 5389 (twice), 5395 (twice), 5398, 5401, 5411, 5412-13, 5419, 5435 (twice), 5444, 5550-51 (motion to strike), 5554, 5556, 5556-57 (twice), 5560 (twice), 5562, 5630, 5639-40, 5706 (motion to strike), 5707 (motion to strike), 5709, 5709, 5712, 5739, 5747 (motion to strike), 5792, 5813, 5872, 5904 (twice), 5905, 5907-08, 5909, 5913, 5915, 5954, and 6043.

S&B. The structured payment permits the plaintiffs to recover a portion of the contingent fees only as they are received by S&B. This preserves the value of the contingent fees, apportions them fairly among the plaintiffs (preventing the "fastest" plaintiff from grabbing all of them), and leaves the largest share (80% of each fee) to S&B itself. We submit that this creative solution is fair to all.

At pages 41-42, S&B argues that the judgment avoids procedural safeguards for judgment debtors, but the judgment nowhere says that plaintiffs may execute the judgment in disregard of any proper exemptions which S&B might claim. The judgment nowhere permits plaintiffs to ignore wage garnishment and other statutory exemptions, and it should not be construed to allow this.

IV. THE ATTORNEYS FEE AWARD WAS SUPPORTED BY SUBSTANTIAL EVIDENCE.

At page 43, S&B appears to challenge the attorneys fee award by attacking the trial court's finding that S&B used bad faith tactics. In fact, S&B's tactics were strikingly similar to those described in *National Secretarial Service, Inc. v. Froelich* (1989) 210 Cal. App. 3d 510, 525, fn. 13:

> It is quite apparent to this court that defendants have used the legal system in an attempt to club a legitimate creditor into submission by forcing and extending this litigation when they in fact had no valid defenses. That defendants held a license to practice law and thus had an access to the courts that was more advantageous than that enjoyed by their small business creditor only makes defendants' conduct the more reprehensible. Defendants are fortunate that the trial court was more tolerant of defendants' conduct than we intend to be. National's attempts to obtain sanctions in the trial court under CCP § 128.5 were, in our view, certainly justified.

In any event, the trial court's finding led to no monetary award. CT 2896-2897. Instead, the court awarded attorneys fees under the S&B-Weiss contract, which expressly provided for attorneys fees. *See* Exhibit 23A, ¶11.2.

The court found that 90% of the attorneys fees were incurred as a result of S&B's claim that it was not liable under the contract. S&B challenges this finding, but it is well supported by the evidence. Weiss sued for its fees under the contract, as well as fraud, and S&B's defenses all said the same thing in various ways: "We are not liable under that contract." *See* CT 80:4-10; 397:16-23. Some of the attorneys fees were incurred because Weiss's attorney had to sit in court watching S&B, Crawford, and Glynn blame each other for their failure to pay their experts, but this occurred because S&B chose to file a cross-complaint against Crawford and Glynn and litigate their claims in the same action. CT 59. Weiss's attorney could hardly leave the courtroom and do other work when such testimony was intermittently being presented. These attorneys fees were necessarily incurred as part of Weiss's efforts to collect on his contract.

CONCLUSION

S&B characterize the judgment below as "ridiculous" and "grotesque." We submit that these appellations more aptly apply to the conduct of S&B which led to the judgment. Two members of our profession (and officers of this Court) induced lay persons to perform work for them, with no intention to pay. When payment was requested, the lawyers threatened to manipulate the legal system if suit were filed. When suit was filed, the lawyers carried out that threat. When the fraud was uncovered, they expressed no remorse, but continued to prevaricate on the witness stand. And now that judgment has been entered — leaving the two lawyers with most of their fortunes intact — they *still* refuse to acknowledge that they acted wrongfully, saying that their acts stemmed from no more than "a misunderstanding of contract law and a misperception of the reasons they were forced to sign the Service Agreements in September of 1987." S&B's Opening Brief, at pp. 34-35.

At page 11, S&B quote Dickens. We find the Bard more fitting. While escorting her husband's corpse, Lady Anne encounters Richard, the Duke of Gloucester, who murdered both her husband and her father-in-law.

Gloucester: Say I slew them not.

Anne: Then say they were not slain. But dead they are,
and, devilish slave, by thee.

Gloucester: I did not kill your husband.

Anne: Why, then he is alive.[43]

S&B plead: "Say we defrauded Weiss not." Lady Anne might reply, "Why, then Weiss has been paid!" But unpaid Weiss remains, more than 5 years after payment was due.

The judgment in this case sends three messages. The first message tells Stemple and Boyajian that their conduct was wrong and that they should be punished for it. The second tells the Bar that dishonest conduct and manipulation of the legal system by lawyers will not be tolerated. And the third message tells the public that our courts will not "close ranks" and protect fellow members of the legal profession when they violate the standards of the profession. We urge this Court not to weaken the clarity of those messages.

The judgment should be affirmed.

Respectfully submitted,
Myron Moskovitz
Donald A. Jelinek

Date: April 26, 1993

by: _____
Myron Moskovitz

---

[43] Shakespeare, *King Richard III*, Act I, Scene 2.

EPILOGUE

This book is — I hope — concise and readable. Each section is short, and most sentences are short. I tried to get into my point quickly, state it completely, and get out. Do the same on appeal, both in your brief and your oral argument.

Good luck, and remember: old lawyers never die, they just lose their appeal.